EXECUTION
by HUNGER

EXECUTION
by HUNGER
The Hidden Holocaust

MIRON DOLOT

W · W · Norton & Company · New York · London

Copyright © 1985 by Miron Dolot
All rights reserved.
Published simultaneously in Canada by Stoddart, a subsidiary of
General Publishing Co. Ltd, Don Mills, Ontario.
Printed in the United States of America.

The text of this book is composed in Times Roman, with display
type set in Bauer Topic Medium. Composition and Manufactur-
ing by The Haddon Craftsmen, Inc.
Book design by Nancy Dale Muldoon

First Edition

Library of Congress Cataloging in Publication Data

Dolot, Miron.
    Execution by hunger.

    1. Ukraine—Famines. 2. Collectivization of
agriculture—Ukraine. 3. Soviet Union—Economic
policy—1928–1932. I. Title.
HC337.U5D59 1985 363.8′0947′71 84–16568

ISBN 0-393-01886-5

W. W. Norton & Company, Inc.
500 Fifth Avenue, New York, N. Y. 10110
W. W. Norton & Company Ltd.
37 Great Russell Street, London WC1B 3NU

1 2 3 4 5 6 7 8 9 0

I DEDICATE THIS BOOK
to those Ukrainian farmers who were
deliberately
starved to death
during the Famine of 1932–1933,
my only regret being
that it is impossible for me
to fully describe their sufferings

Introduction

THIS IS one of the rare eyewitness accounts of the Great Famine which struck several regions of the Soviet Union in 1932–33. The author experienced its horror as a young lad in a Ukrainian village, and Ukraine was one of the areas struck most cruelly by the disaster: it is estimated that five to seven million Ukrainians starved during that terrible year. Famine also raged over other parts of the USSR. In the Soviet Asian republic of Kazakhstan, half the native population fell victim to its ravages.* But Ukraine, along with the North Caucasus (also severely stricken), is normally the most fertile area of the vast country, hence all the more paradoxical and poignant the tragedy that overwhelmed the second most populous nation of the Soviet Union.

Famines when caused by natural factors such as drought and crop failure are terrifying phenomena. But what endowed the one of 1932–33 with special horror was that it was both caused and compounded by the policies of the Soviet government or, more specifically, those of Stalin, by that time the absolute dictator and the main author and enforcer of the scheme that caused the deaths of millions of his countrymen, as well as untold sufferings to the entire rural population of the USSR.

The somber tale begins somewhat earlier. Since 1921—the end of the Civil War—the Soviet peasants had been left in relative peace, free to cultivate their own plots in return for the obligation to turn over part of their produce to the government at a price fixed by the latter. This policy led to a remarkable

*Though the Soviet authorities sought to conceal the tragedy for which their policies had been responsible, even the official statistics bear witness to the extent of the holocaust. Four million Kazakhs were listed in the USSR census of 1926, three million in that of 1939, a figure at least 1.5 million short of what the population should have been at the latter date, given normal growth. The bulk of starvation in Kazakhstan occurred during the first wave of collectivization, 1929–31.

recovery of the Soviet countryside from the ravages of the Revolution and the Civil War. The Soviet Union, just as Imperial Russia before 1914, had become a major exporter of the grain. Yet, by the same token, this partial toleration of free enterprise in the countryside stuck in the throat of the more doctrinaire of the Communist rulers. Marxism-Leninism, they argued, taught that the existence of a multitude of small units in agriculture (the landed estates, of course, had been expropriated in the Revolution) was both inefficient and politically dangerous. Inefficient because small-scale production in agriculture was allegedly uneconomic, conducive to low productivity and absorbing too much of the labor force of the country. Dangerous, because unlike in the other branches of the economy, the government did not completely control the producers; if not paid adequate prices, they could withhold their products from the state.

Already in 1926–27, the Communist rulers began to squeeze the peasants and farmers (then constituting some 80 percent of the population): the more prosperous among them were subjected to heavy taxes; the prices for grain were arbitrarily cut by 20 percent; increased pressure and growing persecution of the most efficient producers lowered incentives to the peasantry as a whole to produce and sell grain. Had the government planned to cause a food shortage, it could not have devised a more effective way. And indeed in 1928 deliveries of foodstuffs to the state fell off sharply.

Instead of adopting what would have been the commonsense solution of the problem, i.e., raising the prices paid to the producers, the government embarked on a drastic campaign against the peasantry as a class. The year 1928 marked the beginning of what a Soviet poet writing during the period of de-Stalinization described as (the government's) "war against the nation." The peasants were not to be bargained with through the market forces, or offered incentives to produce more. They were to be coerced and regimented, so that they would become not merely employees, but virtual slaves of the state, just as their ancestors in Imperial Russia before 1861 had been serfs of individual landlords.

The machinery for that transformation was to be the collectivization. The individual holdings of some 25 million peasant households were to be amalgamated into approximately 250 thousand collective and state farms. Land, cattle, farm implements, in some cases even their dwellings, were to be taken from the individuals and transferred, in theory to the peasant community, in fact to the state. In name the collective farm was an agrarian cooperative, in reality, as the "reforms" were being implemented between 1928 and 1930, it was much closer to a penal colony whose inmates' work, cooperation, indeed the entire manner of life was prescribed from above and run by outsiders, often people quite ignorant both of agriculture and the local conditions. Mr.

Dolot portrays vividly the havoc and confusion wrought by forcible collectivization in his native village. His picture must be magnified several thousandfold to obtain an idea of what was happening throughout the Soviet Union in those years.

Since the Communist Party did not trust any peasants, even those completely loyal to the regime, to enforce this servitude upon their fellows, it sent into the countryside 25,000 of its members, mostly young Communists, the "thousanders" of this book. And as the latter shows, most of them were fanatical Communists, indoctrinated to view the peasant as a "petty capitalist" and "class enemy," and utterly without scruples when it came to browbeating the villagers to join the collective farm.

Faced with this challenge to his immemorial ways of life and what he viewed as the robbery of his property, the peasant, whether in Russia, Ukraine, or Central Asia, fought desperately against this spoliation. The government sought to facilitate its task by trying to split its victims and turn them against each other. The only ones who were against collectivization, and hence subject to persecution, the official line went, were the *kulaks,* i.e., the more prosperous stratum of the peasantry. Yet those whom official propaganda presented as such and as exploiters of their fellow villagers were for the most part simply more efficient producers, and as such the benefactors of the countryside and the nation, rather than the "bloodsuckers" and "parasites" of the opprobrious oratory of the Communist propagandists. With official blessing, the village riffraff was incited to acts of violence against the *kulaks,* they and their families were being thrown out from their homes, beaten, men occasionally lynched, and their property plundered.

Yet for all such divisive tactics, collectivization was being resisted by the peasantry as a whole. In their despair the villagers were drawn at times to terrorist acts against their oppressors. As against those incidents, the authorities instituted systematic terror against the entire class. The most active resisters were executed and their families exiled to the barren northern regions. In the course of one year, 1929–30, some five to eight million people were thus repressed. Others were resettled outside of their native regions, forced to clear swamps and eroded areas. The secret police and even army units were sent into the recalcitrant villages.

Unable to counter force with force, the peasants turned to passive resistance. One, and from the government's point of view the most dangerous, manifestation of it was the villagers slaughtering their livestock rather than surrendering it to the *kolkhoz*. In 1928, the USSR had 32 million horses; by 1934 the figure stood at 15.5 million. In January and February 1930 alone, 14 million head of cattle were destroyed. Confronted with this disaster, the government called a halt to its war. In what was surely a masterpiece of hypocrisy, Stalin in March 1930 announced that the local officials had *erred* in compelling villagers to join the collectives and in forgetting that his and the Party's instructions insisted that membership in them had to be through *voluntary* accession. As he wrote, "Who would wish for such abuses, for that bureaucratic ordering of the collectivization movement, for those unworthy threats against the peasant?" And graciously he allowed those peasants who wished to do so to leave the collectives. How voluntary the process had been is best illustrated by the following figures: before Stalin's pronouncement, on March 1 the number of collectivized households stood at 57.6 percent for the whole country. Two months later the figure was 23.6 percent. One can imagine the chaos and the damage done to agriculture in that one terrible year.

But the peasant had won not a victory but a reprieve. By the end of 1930 the government resumed its drive to regiment the rural population into the collective farms. Force was this time combined with slight concessions to the peasant's longing for something he could call his own. He was now allowed to retain the so-called garden plot—about half an acre per household, and sometimes a single cow. By September 1931, 60 percent of rural households were again within the collectives. But the damage already done to the rural economy was soon to contribute to a disaster surpassing even that of 1929–30.

The collectivization drive was synchronized with the Soviet government's first Five Year Plan, which was designed to industrialize in a hurry the hitherto predominantly rural country. An essential ingredient in the plan was the acquisition of foreign machines, patents, and experts. How were those imports to be paid for? At the time the only way for the Soviet Union to earn large quantities of foreign currency for the sinews of industrialization was through the exports of raw materials. Hence the increasing pressure on the already devastated and impoverished countryside to extract from it grain not only for the Soviet Union's growing urban population, but also for export. In 1930, with the harvest of 83.5 million tons, the regime extracted from the peasants 22 million and exported 5.5. In the next year the country, largely for the reasons already adduced, produced 14 million tons less, but the regime squeezed out of the terrorized peasantry 22.8 million and exported 4.5. It did not take an agronomist to see that this was a path to disaster, yet the regime went on raising its quotas for compulsory deliveries. In 1932 there were portents of serious crop failures in large areas, including Ukraine, as early as the spring, and yet the state procurement plan was fixed at the highest amount yet, 29.5 million tons. By the end of the year people were already starving— the USSR exported 1.5 million tons of grain, an ample amount to feed the six to eight million people estimated to have perished from hunger in the course of 1932–33.

Such then is the background of the events described in Mr. Dolot's book.

When it became clear in the course of 1932 that the quota for state grain procurement could not physically be met, Stalin in his fury ordered all the available stocks to be seized, no matter what the consequences for the local population. It is not an anti-Communist refugee, but a Soviet author during the Khrushchev era when one could allude to such things, who wrote the following about the results of a visit by a lieutenant of Stalin's to one of the afflicted areas: "All the grain without exception was requisitioned for the fulfillment of the Plan, including that set aside for sowing, fodder, and even that previously issued to the *kolkhozniki* as payment for their work." And another Soviet source: "Many *kolkhozy* experienced great difficulties with provisionments. There were mass cases of people swelling up from hunger and dying." These two sentences appear in the middle of a lengthy technical article which, in general, takes a very positive view of collectivization, even though, as it was the fashion under Khrushchev, it reprimands Stalin and his henchmen for their "errors." Today, of course, in line with the partial rehabilitation of Stalin, it is unlikely that a Soviet author would be permitted to be so indiscreet about what really happened during those terrible years.

Was Stalin's policy motivated by the need to extract all the available grain for feeding the cities and export, the goal against which the preservation of a few million peasants' lives was deemed unimportant, or was it also, as our author implies, a deliberate attempt to stamp out Ukrainian nationalism and thus solidify the *Russian* domination of the Soviet Union? This is a hypothesis strongly argued by several other writers, not all of them, by any means, Ukrainian. And to be sure, already by 1930 Stalin sought to make *Russian* nationalism the main psychological bulwark of the Soviet regime and his own personal power. Anything even remotely resembling nationalism or demands for autonomy for other of the numerous nationalities of the USSR was being stamped out by him and his henchmen even before 1930. And in the great purges of 1936–39, those officials and intellectuals suspected of even the slightest sympathy with Ukrainian national aspirations were ruthlessly repressed. In a previous great famine that struck many parts of the USSR, including Ukraine, that of 1921–22, the Soviet government did not seek to prevent its victims from fleeing the stricken areas in search of food, and it called upon the capitalist nations to help and succour the suffering millions. In 1932–33, the Kremlin sought to keep the news of mass starvation from spreading even within the USSR, so that the inhabitants of other regions remained ignorant of what was happening in Ukraine and North Caucasus. Far from outside help being sought, the government banned the import of food into these stricken areas. The militia and GPU (political police) detachments barred starving people from leaving their villages, and trying to save their own and their families' lives. Some news of course trickled out. In a poem which when discovered by the authorities was to cost him his life, the Russian poet Mandelstam wrote of Stalin: "Ten paces away and our voices cannot be heard. The only one heard is the Kremlin mountaineer, the destroyer of life and the slayer of peasants." In the West, there were just some very sparse and muted echoes of the manmade disaster. And so all the more valuable and heartrending is this testimony of the death of the once peaceful and self-reliant Ukrainian village.

Adam Ulam
Director/Russian Research Center
Harvard University

Author's Note

THE POLICY of compulsory collectivization introduced at the end of 1929, called for all farms to be collectivized, and the farmers to be firmly bound to the collectives just as they used to be bound as serfs to the feudal estates some seventy years before. The farms were collectivized, but not without struggle. The farmers fiercely resisted the collectivization efforts. They clung to their plots of land and their possessions for dear life, and the struggle became one for life or death. But unarmed, disorganized, and leaderless, the farmers were no match for government forces. They were crushed mercilessly. Their villages were ruined and depopulated. Millions died. Many were sent to concentration camps, or banished from their villages to God-forsaken northern regions, and still others simply disappeared mysteriously, without a trace. Those who survived swallowed their pride and finally joined the collective farms in order to save themselves and their families. Thus the battle came to an end: the farmers lost and the Communists triumphed. Within only a few years—four in all!—the traditional patterns of village life were destroyed.

Famines broke out throughout the Soviet Union, in Kazakhstan (Soviet Central Asia), in the Kuban (North Caucasus) area, and in the Don River area, but here I deal exclusively with the famine of 1932–33 in Ukraine.

It is generally believed by some that the famine of 1932–33 in Ukraine was the result of the collectivization. Others believe that it was an artificial famine, forcibly induced upon farmers for the purpose of herding them into collective farms. And finally, still others feel that it was a genocidal famine, the outcome of a deliberate and premeditated plan, undertaken as a means of destroying the Ukrainian people as a nation.

It is outside the scope of this book to analyze the causes of the famine. That must be left to historians and economists. However, I feel beyond any doubt that this famine had political and nationalistic, or rather, antinationalistic overtones. I believe there was a direct connection between this famine and the policies toward nationalism, especially in the Ukrainian Republic.

Along its collectivization policy, Moscow had in 1929 initiated a full-scale campaign against anything that could identify Ukraine as a separate nation, starting with the destruction of Ukrainian scientific and cultural organizations and institutions, and ending with the arrest, execution, or banishment to concentration camps of all those who dared to raise their voices in defense of Ukrainian self-determination.

But the most brutal campaign was carried out against the Ukrainian farmers. Moscow realized that the Ukrainian farmers were the mainstay of the national movement, as they were the ones who most obstinately clung to their national identity and opposed both Russian colonial rule and the Soviet regime. Stalin himself wrote that the farmers constitute the driving power of the national movement. He emphasized that the nationalist question was actually the farmers' question.

Before going any further, I must explain two terms which I consider essential for the reader to understand: farmer/peasant; and *kurkul/kulak.*

The English translation of Ukrainian word *selianyn* as "peasant" is not only imprecise but even misleading. According to available reference sources, "peasant" is a person engaged in agricultural labor, a farm hand, as the Ukrainian *batrak* had been in the past. However, the Ukrainian *selianyn* always cultivated his land. No matter how small his landholding, he was his own farmer. In contrast to the Russian *krestianin,* who as a serf was the property of his landlord, to be bought and sold, the Ukrainian *selianyn* was a free Cossack-farmer before the Russian occupation of Ukraine. For this historical reason Ukrainian farmers had a much stronger sense of private ownership and deeper feeling of freedom and independence. Therefore I strongly feel that the word *selianyn* is most properly translated by the word "farmer," and I am using it throughout my book instead of the word "peasant," which I use only in references to organizations, concepts, or quotations.

The word *kurkul* in Ukrainian, or *kulak* in Russian, was officially defined in the Soviet Union as a village usurer, or rich farmer. This definition found ready recognition in the West and consequently we often hear here that *kulak* means a rich or well-to-do farmer.

Such a translation or interpretation of this epithet is wrong and misleading because the person labeled a *kulak* by the Communists was often a pauper in comparison to an American tenant farmer.

The label *kulak* was widely used during the collectivization of agriculture, and it became a term of abuse for all farmers whom the state wanted to destroy.

This book has a long history. The first 24 chapters were written before

1953, the twentieth anniversary of the famine. Thirty years later, approaching my seventieth year, wiser and more critical, I decided to complete it and place it in the hands of readers. During this long span of time, I was constantly engrossed by these great human tragedies, still not fully comprehended by many. I am now confident that I have fully appraised the events under consideration and have come to my own unequivocal conclusion.

History has not recorded another such crime as the famine perpetrated against an entire nation, nor one ever carried out in such a cold-blooded manner. I have researched famines, looking to history for an occurrence comparable to the Ukrainian famine. There have been many cases, such as the Irish potato famine in the middle of the nineteenth century and famines in China and India that occurred periodically and killed millions of humans. Yet, all these calamities had natural causes that were at the time humanly impossible to prevent. They were the results of crop failures due to weather or to ravages by insects and vermin. The Irish potato famine was due to the failure of the potato crop, a staple of Irish diet, and the famines in China and India were brought about by drought and overpopulation.

But the famine of 1932–33 in Ukraine was a political famine. In the words of Malcolm Muggeridge, who personally witnessed the famine, "it was the deliberate creation of a bureaucratic mind." Indeed it was a genocidal famine, the one that was employed by Stalin and his followers as a means of subduing the Ukrainian farmers.

The famine of 1932–33 in the Soviet Union has been an entirely ignored, neglected, misinterpreted, and distorted event. To this day even though Soviet dignitaries themselves matter-of-factly discuss it, some "experts" on the Soviet Union ("Sovietologists") here in the United States persistently adhere to the original Soviet denial of its existence. This probably explains why no thorough study of this famine has ever been made in the USA. Americans have had difficulty in accepting a story so unbelievably inhuman.

In this book, I have described what happened in my village during those four years, between 1929 and 1933. It is a reconstruction of what I saw and experienced personally. Everything recorded actually happened; only authenticated facts are presented. Although conversations and speeches are not reproduced verbatim, they accurately convey what was said at specific times. I based them on living memories.

Some of my readers will wonder how I could reconstruct so many events, in such detail, after so many years. Actually, there is no mystery involved. First of all, one does not forget the trauma and tragedy of one's life, no matter how hard one tries. Secondly, one cannot forget the details of one's struggle to survive. This was the time when all people, in all of Ukraine, lived from one campaign to another, from one leader's speech to another, from one Party resolution to another, from one government decree to another, and finally from one village or factory meeting to another. I cannot forget these things. Details and dates of the events described within this book have been verified through Soviet periodicals of that time which can be found in major American libraries. This book gives an accurate portrayal of events in my village during the collectivization.

There is one other detail that must be pointed out to my readers: Miron Dolot is my pen name, under which I have published articles and brochures about the famine in the USA, Germany, and Switzerland.

CHAPTER 1

I GREW UP in a typical Ukrainian village, in the county of Cherkasy, some hundred miles south of Kiev, the capital city of Ukraine. My village stood on the north bank of the Tiasmyn River, one of the many tributaries of the Dnipro (Dnieper) River, and it was beautiful. Green hills rose in the south behind the river, and the rich tar-black soil of the plains stretched to the north. The plains were divided into strips of fields. Every spring and summer these strips would disappear beneath miles of wheat. Waves of rich grain, green in spring and golden in summer, gently rolled in the summer breeze. After the harvest, the fields again bared their soil as if in mourning for their lost beauty. Near the end of the year, the new cycle of color—winter's white—blended with the horizon of the plains into the gray-blue frosty sky.

It was a large village, with some eight hundred households comprising a population of nearly four thousand people. In the center stood the communal buildings—the church, school, store, local government building, post office, and the house where the doctor lived and worked. A square in the center served as the playground, meeting place, and market.

As was customary in all Ukrainian villages, the farmers' houses were grouped together. The unpaved streets were nameless, although each house was numbered. Through the village ran a road, also unpaved, connecting us with the outside world.

Our houses were of simple design and construction. They were rudely beamed, plastered with clay, and usually thatched with straw. A tin roof was considered a sign of prosperity, and I recall few such roofs in the village. Most of the houses had only one room which was used for all purposes, including cooking and sleeping. Wooden floors were also rare; like the walls, the floors were made of clay. But no matter how plainly they were constructed, and how primitive our living conditions, the houses were clean and neat.

Each home had its plot for flowers and a few fruit trees, and chickens, geese, and ducks were kept in the backyards. Barns housed a horse, one or two cows, and a few pigs. A dog would usually be lounging on the porch or at the gate.

In our poor and overpopulated village only a few farmers owned more than fifty acres of land. But though destitute, the villagers were neither hopeless nor forlorn. After a hard day's work in the spring and summer, the young people gathered in neighborhoods at the crossroads and danced, sang, and played long into the night. Families visited relatives and friends, or enjoyed plays, dances, parties, and other kinds of entertainment, all accompanied by much eating and drinking. Though it was prohibited, the villagers usually found a way to distill their own brandy.

Our village was a close-knit community. It was customary for neighbors to help one another with their labors or in emergencies, and after the work was done they would join in a party. An accordion player and a fiddler, hired for the occasion, provided music for dancing, and food and drinks were always served. Such a party would often last until dawn.

We were completely free in our movements. We took pleasure trips and traveled freely looking for jobs. We went to big cities and neighboring towns to attend weddings, church bazaars, and funerals. No one asked us for documents or questioned us about our destinations. We were free individuals.

Hospitality was a matter of honor. Anyone who happened to visit us was welcomed into our homes. We might not have had enough to eat ourselves, but we always offered our visitors the best we could.

Even though we were in continual want for various necessities of life, we were completely free from fear. We never locked our houses during the daytime. Old and young could come and go freely in and out of our village without fear of molestation.

The coming of winter was greeted with joy by us all, and it seemed to me the more severe the winter, the greater the excitement, especially among us young people. There was no end to ice-skating, skiing, and sledding. The cold heavy frost, deep snow, and blizzards made winter a time of leisure for the farmers, provided there had been a good harvest. Throughout the short winter days and long nights, we spent most of the time in our homes. No one complained of the cold, for firewood was plentiful. After caring for the domestic animals and completing other daily chores, we were content in our homes—reading, writing, telling stories, playing, singing, and dancing.

In 1929, we began to hear rumors that the Communist Party and the Soviet government had decreed the collectivization of all farmers. Collectives in the form of a TSOZ (or SOZ), *artil*, commune, or radhosp (Russian, *sovkhoz*) had, in fact, been in existence for a long time. Actually, except for the radhosp and commune, these collectives or the agricultural cooperatives, as they were known, were not communist innovations, for they existed in prerevolutionary times. They were organized as a free cooperation of farmers. Security of the market, state credits, and mutual help with farming implements and seeds, were the main incentives for their organization. In Ukraine two types of such agricultural cooperatives were known: the TSOZ and artil. TSOZ stood for the Association for the Joint Cultivation of Land. Only labor and land, or part of them, and heavy agricultural implements were collectivized. Livestock, dwellings, and even some land could be owned and operated privately. This was a rather loosely organized association, and the membership could easily be dissolved.

Artil (*artel* in Russian) meant "team," or a group of people belonging to the same kind of vocation, organized in a production cooperative. Agricultural artils were associations of farmers who pooled together all their land and other means of production, as well as their labor and draft animals. They were paid for their labor in kind and money according to the amount of work put in. Members of an artil could keep their main dwelling, a cow, and such animals as sheep, goats, swine, as well as poultry. During the total collectivization in the Soviet Union, the artil was accepted as the basic form for what is known today as the collective farm.

Agricultural communes which, according to Communist theory, were supposed to be the highest form of rural organizational life and labor, were established during the period of War Communism (the Civil War of 1918–1921). Usually they were set up on estates of former local landlords. Agricultural communes were based not only on collective farming, but also on communal living in communal

3

houses, with communal kitchens, nurseries, and so forth. The members of such communes were deprived of private possessions, except for their personal belongings. These communes received great support from the Communist Party and its government, but nevertheless, they proved to be a failure, and consequently were either dissolved or, in most cases, turned into state farms.

Radhosp is the Ukrainian term for *sovkhoz,* an acronym for Soviet farm. In reality, it was a state-run agricultural enterprise with hired farm laborers who were paid regular wages. The agricultural laborers working on such farms were not farmers at all, in the full meaning of the word; they had no voice in distribution of the profits, nor in management.

All these collectives were organized on a voluntary basis and thus seemed to present no threat to independent farming. Moreover, the farmers had often witnessed the collapse of these types of collective farms, and therefore laughed at the rumors of collectivization. Why would any government wish to repeat its mistakes? But they laughed too soon.

Sometime toward the end of December 1929, when the rumors of compulsory collectivization were becoming a reality, strangers came to our village. Soon we learned that they were the official representatives of the Communist Party and the Soviet government. They had been assigned to the village to organize a collective farm.

The head of the group of about ten men was known as the "Twenty-Five Thousander." His collaborators were called propagandists. Such titles were strange to our ears, but it did not take long for us to learn their meanings.

To carry out compulsory collectivization, the Central Committee of the Communist Party had mobilized twenty-five thousand of its most active and loyal Party members throughout the country. Consequently, the members of this elite group of Communists became known as the Twenty-Five Thousanders. We called them simply Thousanders. After a brief period of instructions in the methods of collectivization, these Thousanders were sent to various localities. To make their mission more effective, they were given practically unlimited power. They were responsible directly to the Central Committee of the Communist Party of Ukraine.

Each Thousander was accompanied by an entourage of propagandists. They were selected from among those in each county *(raion)*

4

who were Communists or members of the Komsomol, the Young Communist League.

The Thousander and his propagandists were people who had always lived in cities—professors, teachers, and factory workers. When these strangers appeared in our village, some of them tried to make contact by attempting to strike up conversations with passers-by. Others simply walked around, curiously looking at everything and everybody, as if they had never seen anything like the countryside and country folk before.

Their personal appearance amused us. Their pale faces and their clothes were totally out of place in our village surroundings. Walking carefully to avoid getting snow on their polished shoes, they were an alien presence among us.

Although they exhibited curiosity and enthusiasm about their new environment, they could not hide their ignorance of country ways. The villagers laughed at their citified behavior, and within a few days the strangers had become the butt of many funny stories.

The name of our Thousander was Zeitlin—Comrade Zeitlin, to be exact. This was the only name by which we knew him, although he stayed in our village for a few months. Comrade Zeitlin was to us more the embodiment of the regime he represented than a person. We did learn that he had come from Kiev, and that he had been a member of the Communist Party even before the revolution. Although none of us knew his previous occupation, it was obvious that he knew little about country life. Nor could anyone determine his nationality. He spoke some Ukrainian, but he certainly was not a native.

Comrade Zeitlin was rather short with a huge head resting on his narrow shoulders. We never saw him smile; he always seemed to be preoccupied with some problem. He spoke rarely, and when he did, it was only about official matters in a language of Party slogans and trite phrases. Only occasionally would he greet a villager, and then in a disrespectful manner.

All Party and government representatives who came to our village wore some kind of weapon, usually carried discreetly. But Comrade Zeitlin was probably unsure of his popularity in our village because he always prominently displayed a revolver on his person. He assumed authority without delay. On the day of his arrival, he began going from house to house. Many stories originated from these visits. One anecdote about Zeitlin was especially popular: It was said that

5

while he was visiting a farmer's stable, a mare happened to twitch her tail in his face, depositing some dung on him.

"Woo," he growled angrily, "that damn cow!" and he kicked the mare's hoof. The mare responded in kind, and the farmer had to help the flustered Comrade Zeitlin to his feet.

The mare's blow failed to deter him from his inspection. In the cattle pen, he reversed his error. Perhaps to convince the farmer that he still was not afraid of animals, he approached a calf.

"What a fine colt!" he exclaimed.

The farmer was a polite man, and hesitated to correct his visitor after the first mistake, but after the second, he gently remarked:

"This is not a colt. It is a calf; the offspring of a cow. The colt is the offspring of a mare."

"Colt or calf," Comrade Zeitlin retorted, "it does not matter. The world proletarian revolution won't suffer because of that."

The latter phrase was his favorite expression, although at that time we villagers did not understand its meaning. But we were amused by a representative of the Party and government not knowing the difference between horses and cows and their young.

Comrade Zeitlin did know his job, however. He also knew the Party's instructions as to how it was to be done. While the villagers were entertaining and diverting themselves with stories about Comrade Zeitlin's ignorance, the center of the village was alive with activity. Messengers called designated villagers to the center, thereby instilling both curiosity and fear in us. Other strangers, often high-ranking army officers, appeared in our village almost daily. Often we would see the Thousander with both village officials and strangers inspecting houses.

One day, a team of telephone workmen arrived and quickly laid a telephone line between our village and the county center. Only a few villagers knew what a telephone was, but even they probably could not have guessed the real reason for bringing the telephone into our village. The officials did not neglect to point to it as a symbol of the great progress the village was making under the Communist regime.

CHAPTER 2

WE DID NOT have to wait too long for Comrade Zeitlin's strategy to reveal itself. The first incident occurred very early on a cold January morning in 1930 while people in our village were still asleep. Fifteen villagers were arrested, and someone said that the Chekists[2] had arrived in the village at midnight, and with the cooperation of the village officials, had forced their prisoners into their van and disappeared before the villagers awakened.

The most prominent villagers were among those arrested: a school teacher, who had been working in our village since prerevolutionary times; the clerk of the village soviet (council), an influential and popular figure who gave advice in legal matters; and a store owner. The remainder were ordinary farmers of good reputation. None of us knew for what offense they had been arrested, nor where they had been taken.

This was frightening. Our official leadership had been taken away in one night. The farmers, mostly illiterate and ignorant, were thereby left much more defenseless.

Almost immediately the families of the arrested farmers were evicted from their homes. I witnessed what happened to one such family. We lived not far from one of those arrested, Timish Zaporoz-

---

[2]A Chekist was a member of the original Soviet secret police, the Cheka, which is an acronym for Extraordinary Commission, or more precisely, All-Russian Extraordinary Commission for Fighting Counterrevolution and Sabotage (1917–1922). It was succeeded by the GPU. The old title, Chekist, is still in use. Even today's members of KGB are often referred to as Chekists. Communist propaganda eulogizes them as national heroes.

hets, whom we children called Uncle Timish. Sometime around noon, a group of the village officials arrived at his house. The official in charge, facing Uncle Timish's wife, announced that inasmuch as her husband had been arrested as an "enemy of the people," all his possessions were to be immediately confiscated and declared state property. The woman, confused and upset, tried to argue with the officials. She asked them what treason her husband had committed against the people that he should be proclaimed their enemy. But the officials were in no mood to discuss such a matter. The order to leave the house was repeated. She was also told that she might remove from the house only her own and her children's personal possessions, such as clothing. Everything else had to be left behind.

By now, she realized that the officials meant business. With tears in her eyes, she begged them to let her stay in the house at least overnight so that she could collect her things. But she pleaded in vain. The order was again repeated; then she fainted and fell to the floor. Her children started to cry. The man in charge ordered her to be picked up and taken out to the sleigh which was standing ready in front of the house. She came to herself at that moment, and sobbingly told the officials that she did not have any place to go. This had been her home for many years. She, with her husband and children, had built the home.

Neither tears nor pleas helped. The officials only urged her to hurry. The man in charge took her by the shoulders. Screaming, she tore herself away from him. The one in charge ordered her to be evicted bodily from her house. When they grabbed her, she struggled and pulled their hair. She was finally dragged out of the house and thrown onto the sleigh. While two men held her, the children were brought out. A few of their possessions were thrown onto the sleigh and it moved off. Still restrained by the two officials, Uncle Timish's wife and his children, wailing and shouting, disappeared in the winter haze.

We later found out that they were taken to the railroad station and herded into a special freight train headed north. The same fate also befell all the families of the other arrested men. We never heard of them again.

A few days after the arrest of those fifteen villagers and the eviction of their families, we were summoned to a meeting by a messenger. It took place in the former house of the same Timish Zaporozhets. The interior of the house had already been completely changed. The inner walls had been removed, and what had been a three-room house had become a type of hall, furnished with crude benches. Now it became clear to all of us that Timish had been a victim of his own house. The officials had arrested him because they needed a large building.

At this meeting we were told that a new administration was about to be established in our village. This at first did not arouse any suspicion in us. Our village was simply to be divided into units and subunits called Hundreds, Tens, and Fives.

I was only a youth at that time and I certainly was not concerned with the consequences of such a division. But later I realized what an inescapable trap that new system of "Cut your own throat"[3] administration was. Through these divisions and subdivisions, the Thousander, with his group of Party functionaries, was able to establish undisputed control over the villagers. Moreover, he was able to detect and destroy any opposition to Party policy and thereby rapidly collectivize the entire village.

Our village comprised about 800 households and 4,000 inhabitants. It was divided into 8 Hundreds, 80 Tens, and 160 Fives, or a total of 248 units. Since each unit had an individual in charge assigned to it by the village soviet (council), our village had 248 subdivisional functionaries or officials. Besides that, a special propagandist[4] was assigned to each Hundred, and one agitator[5] to each Ten and to each Five. This doubled the number of functionaries to 496. In addition, a so-called Bread Procurement Commission was appointed to each Hundred.

These commissions were set up in all villages throughout Ukraine.

---

[3]"Cut your own throat" is an expression I use here to describe the new village administration, established at the onset of collectivization in which the farmers were forced to take active part and which eventually destroyed them. In other words, the farmers were put in a situation where they destroyed themselves through their own actions, i.e., they cut their own throats.

[4]Propagandist was the official Communist title of a person whose duty it was to spread and disseminate Communist ideas and ideology. During the collectivization of farmers, the propagandists served as the eyes and ears of the Communist Party. They were the ones who introduced the Party's policy of collectivization to the population at "grassroots" level. They were usually appointed from among the Party and Komsomol members.

[5]Agitators differed from propagandists in that they were supposed to stir up and mobilize the people for support of a certain course of action. But, in reality, there was not such a difference between them. Anyone with a mouth tuned to the Party line was qualified to be appointed an agitator. Even children were given this title and sent from house to house with propaganda materials in their hands and prefabricated phrases in their mouths.

At first there was one commission for the entire village. Now, at the beginning of collectivization, such a commission was attached to each village subunit, as for example, to each Hundred. Controlled by the Communist Party, these commissions and brigades were organized with the single purpose of securing the collection of grain quotas. Later, when total collectivization and the policy of "liquidation of the kurkuls[6] as a social class" was announced, these commissions became the major force in organizing collective farms and in expropriating kurkuls. In fact, they became the arbitrary rulers of the countryside.

This new bread commission consisted of ten or more members, increasing the number of village subdivisional functionaries by eighty to 576. Finally, there were three permanent *vykonavtsi,* locally appointed militia deputies, for each Hundred, or twenty-four in all. The permanent *vykonavtsi* were important officials because they actually performed the function of the local militia, the Soviet police. They could make arrests without any legal formalities. This made 600 subdivisional functionaries, or 75 functionaries for each Hundred. Thus, each unit of a hundred households was controlled by 75 persons. This number could be increased if one included the 35 members of the village soviet and the 17 kolhosp[7] officials. Actually, there were

[6]The Ukrainian word kurkul (Russian kulak) was the official definition of a village usurer in the Soviet Union. Any farmer who employed hired labor, who possessed heavy machinery, or hired out such machinery, or contracted to work on other farms, who leased land for commercial purposes, etc., was branded kurkul. This definition found ready recognition in the West, and consequently we hear here that kurkul means a rich or well-to-do farmer. Such translation or interpretation of this epithet can be misleading because the Communists applied this label indiscriminately to all farmers, even to genuine paupers.

During the collectivization this label was widely used, and it became an epithet of abuse for all those farmers who refused to join the collective farm. The policy of "liquidation of kurkuls as a social class," introduced by the Communist Party in 1929, resulted in the disappearance of millions of farmers labeled as kurkuls. Many of them were simply murdered; others were starved to death during the famine of 1932–1933 in Ukraine; and still others were deported to the "corrective labor camps" or to the concentration camps. The label kurkul was attached to anyone, even to nonfarmers, who showed the slightest sign of disagreement with or opposition to Communist agricultural policy during that time. The possession of a one-room house, a cow, and a few chickens, or the possession of a house with a tin roof or board floor was enough to be labeled as a kurkul.

[7]Kolhosp is the Ukrainian acronym for collective economy or collective farm (*kolkhoz* in Russian). According to the statutes, a kolhosp was supposed to be a voluntary cooperative undertaking of a group of farmers who collectivized their land and agricultural implements and were paid in kind and money according to their labor days. But in reality, the kilhosp was forcibly imposed upon the farmers and came under complete

652 active functionaries for the entire village. In other words, there was one functionary for every six villagers.

The majority of appointees to these subdivisional positions were selected from among the ordinary farmers, and as such, they found themselves in a precarious situation. There was nothing they hated as much as collective farming, yet they became the instrument for its implementation. They were appointed to tasks as soldiers are. There was no choice but to do as they were ordered. The individuals with any function in such organizations or institutions were looked upon as officials, no matter whether they were government employees or not. This title of "official" meant a great deal, for it secured almost unlimited power for those who bore it. Indeed, a representative of an administrative organ or organization was given unlimited rights to command and to demand. Thus, anything with the slightest ring of officialdom became dreaded by the ordinary villager, while the attainment of it gave this same person a tremendous advantage.

An ordinary farmer would become an official as soon as he was assigned to a commission, committee, or some type of brigade or group established for an official purpose.

According to the Communist concept, to be a Soviet official was an honor. Refusal to accept this honor would mean disloyalty to the Soviet regime—an intolerable offense. Anyone who refused to accept an official appointment, or who opposed an official's activity, incurred a severe penalty as a suspected enemy of the people. This policy had been carried out with such rigidity that few dared to refuse an appointment or to show opposition.

In order to be able to demand of his charges the fulfillment of certain obligations to the state, an official had to meet them himself and set an example. Failure would lead to an accusation of refusal to obey Party and government. Since the task of these officials was collectivizing and gathering foodstuffs, they thus had to collectivize themselves and deliver their quotas.

Previously, there had been one authority in the village, the Village Soviet, elected at the village general meeting, which chose the executive committee with its chairman and clerk. At that time, political

---

control of the Communist Party and the government. It became nothing less than a state agricultural enterprise. The members of the kolhosp had no say in farm policy or in the distribution of income.

organizations such as the Communist Party and the Komsomol did not yet play any important roles within the village administrative system, for membership in these organizations was a rarity in our village.

This kind of self-government was, however, abolished with the start of total collectivization. Both the village general meeting and the village soviet lost their power to the Communist Party, the membership of which was increasing rapidly among our villagers. The Communist Party organization, while replacing the village soviet in all its initiative functions, became master of the village by dictating its will to the village general meeting. As a result, the general meeting became merely a puppet for the Communist Party. So it was with the village soviet. Only Party or Komsomol members or persons of unquestionable loyalty to the Party and the government could be elected or appointed to its executive offices.

About the time of the Thousander's arrival, two institutions were introduced into our village: the Special Section and the Workers and Peasants Inspection. Both became horrors in our lives.

The Special Section was a branch of the GPU,[8] the political secret police. Officially, the Special Section was represented by only one man who occupied an office in the building of the village soviet, and always wore a full dress GPU uniform. The recruiting that went on behind his doors, and the identity of his secret agents, remained a mystery.

[8]GPU is the abbreviation for Gosudarstvennoe politicheskoe upravlenie, or State Political Administration. It is the name of the Soviet secret police which replaced the Cheka in February 1922. See also Chekist (note 2). In 1923, the GPU was renamed OGPU, which meant United State Political Administration. But the acronym GPU continued to be used popularly even after 1923. OGPU remained a separate institution until 1934 when it was absorbed into the NKVD, the People's Commissariat for Internal Affairs. In 1941, the People's Commissariat for State Security (in Russian, Narodnyi kommissariat gosudarstvennoi bezopasnosti) was created, known under the acronym NKGB. Thus state security was divorced from the NKVD, but not for long. With the beginning of the war with Germany in June 1941, state security was returned to the NKVD until 1943. It existed as a separate agency until 1946. When the people's commissariats were redesignated as ministries, the People's Commissariat of Internal Affairs became the Ministry of Internal Affairs (Ministerstvo vnutrennikh del, or MVD as its abbreviation). The People's Commissariat for State Security became the Ministry of State Security (Ministerstvo gosudarstvennoi bezopasnosti, or MGB). Thus the NKVD and NKGB became the MVD and MGB. During the power struggle that followed Stalin's death, the MVD absorbed the MGB, but then the security service was once more divorced from the MVD. In March 1954, the state security agency emerged as the KGB, which is an acronym for Komitet gosudarstvennoi bezopasnosti, meaning the Committee for State Security.

However, it was generally believed that one agent was planted in each Hundred to inform the GPU of the activities of each villager in that particular Hundred.

The Workers and Peasants Inspection was a local branch of a commissariat[9] of the same name. Today it is known as the Commission of State Control. It was in charge of checking practices of the government agencies, and the loyalty and efficiency of officials. With the decree of total collectivization, the Party and government delegated the commissariat to control the fulfillment of this policy.

The Workers and Peasants Inspection was also represented in our village by one man. He was an outsider, of course. A commission of five local people was appointed to assist him. He also maintained his own secret agents who spied on the local officials. When he found "discrepancies," he assumed the role of both arbiter and judge. His decisions were final.

To implement the policy of collectivization, the Party and government mobilized all their central and local forces; namely, the entire Party propaganda machinery, the armed forces, the secret and civil police force, and actually, all institutions and organizations. Such political organizations as the Komsomol, the Pioneers, and Komnezams were the most active and effective forces in the hands of the local communists.

Komsomol is an acronym for the Young Communist League, established in 1918. Young people between fourteen and twenty-six years of age may be members of this organization, which is considered to be the future of the Communist Party, and thus is accorded second place in the Soviet political hierarchy. Directed by the Communists, these youths proved to be most vigorous and effective in our village. Their responsibilities and positions were second only to the Communists themselves. The leader of the Komsomol organization was a Party candidate sent to the village by the county center.

The Pioneers was a political organization for school children between the ages of eight and fourteen. Members of this children's organization served in double capacity as messengers and agents. The well-known case of Pavlik Morozov serves as an example of how the

[9]Commissariat was the name given to central government departments, corresponding to ministries, during 1917–1946. In 1946, these People's Commissariats were renamed ministries.

13

Communist Party and the government used children in their scheme. The son of a poor farmer, Pavlik lived in a village somewhere beyond the Urals in Siberia. This fourteen-year-old schoolboy became the most celebrated individual in the Soviet Union overnight by denouncing his father and some of his neighbors for hiding food from the state. The accused and his father, were arrested and disappeared without a trace. Pavlik was killed by the enraged villagers, including his uncle. The entire Soviet propaganda machine eulogized him. He became a national hero; his name was given to a multitude of villages, organizations, streets, and military units and his story was prominent in encyclopedias and dictionaries.

Thus, the Party encouraged children, especially those who belonged to the Pioneer organization, to spy on their parents and to denounce them, and anybody else, for that matter, who defied the Party. Such denunciation was considered a heroic deed, the best expression of Soviet patriotism.

Komnezam is an acronym for the Ukrainian *Komitet nezamozhnych selian* (Committee of Poor Peasants). Such committees were first set up in Russia in the summer of 1918 by the local Party organizations from agricultural laborers and poor farmers, and there they were known by the Russian acronym Kombedy. In Ukraine, on the other hand, these committees, the Komnezams, were introduced in May 1920, when the Communists invaded the Ukraine for the third time. Whereas in Russia the Kombedy were soon dissolved (in November 1918, by the decision of the Fourth All-Russian Congress of Soviets, November 6–9, 1918), in Ukraine, these Committees of Poor Peasants lasted until 1933 and became the most effective instruments of aggressive Communist policy in the Ukrainian countryside. The Komnezam was an important feature of every Ukrainian village. Its purpose was twofold: to introduce the Revolution into the village, and to assist in the enforcement of food deliveries to the state. In Ukraine, the Communists used these committees also as instruments in the collectivization of agriculture. In general, they became known as organs of proletarian dictatorship in the Ukrainian countryside.

Thus this monstrous machine of collectivization was set in motion. It ground, it pulled, it pushed, and it kicked. It was run by human beings, and it worked on human beings. It was merciless and insatiable. Once it was started, it could not be stopped, and it consumed

14

more and more victims. The Hundreds, Tens, and Fives with their commissions, propagandists, agitators, and executors: the Komsomol, Pioneer, and Komnezam organizations; and the village general meeting, the village soviet, and the village executive committee became cogwheels in an ugly machine, and the Party its skillful operator.

CHAPTER 3

WE FELT the effects of this new administrative machine at the very first meeting of our Hundred. After explaining how the new village administration would work, and praising the Party for introducing such a "flexible and effective" village government, the meeting chairman introduced the speaker, a propagandist assigned to our Hundred. The chairman called him Comrade Professor. As a schoolboy at that time, I had great admiration for men of learning. However, what he said was no different from what we had heard previously; he was repeating phrases from official speeches we had already learned by heart.

At first, Comrade Professor described the injustices that the farmers had suffered at the hands of the rich. The time had come, he said, when the villagers could redress their wrongs. He called on the poor farmers to have no mercy on the kurkuls (kulaks), and, what struck us most, he called on us to destroy them. Killing the rich, he declared, was the only way for poor farmers to attain a better and more prosperous life.

We sat silently, letting the words flow over us. But we could not be completely indifferent to what he was saying. A foreboding of coming disaster overcame us. We had previously heard about collectivization, about dekurkulization, and even about the annihilation of kurkuls as a "social class." But so far we had not heard about the arbitrary killing of kurkuls. He now talked about killing them as a matter of honor and merit.

After a pause, Comrade Professor began to talk about collectivization. He offered a simple and attractive explanation. The Party and government, he said, wanted to make the life of each farmer easier and more secure. Work on the collective farm would be less arduous and more profitable. There the farmers would be protected from exploitation by the rich farmers, the kurkuls. And, finally, after looking at his notes, he made it clear that the Party and government had decided to collectivize us and there was nothing we could do about it. He added, matter-of-factly, that we should be thankful for it, for what was good for the Party and government was also good for us farmers. He then put his notes in his pocket, drank some water, took a cigarette out of a fine case, and sat down. We remained silent.

Following the propagandist, the chairman of the Hundred rose and declared his wish to join the collective farm. He said that the propagandist's speech was so clear and so convincing that there was no doubt left in his mind about what was the best future for the farmers, and that he was the happiest man in the world to be among the first to join the collective farm. Then he asked who would follow his example. To our surprise and consternation, there were some who did follow him. A member of the Bread Procurement Commission got up, approached the chairman's table, and declared his willingness to join the collective farm. Then he threw down the challenge of "socialist competition," calling on a fellow member of the commission to do likewise. We were still more surprised when the latter approached the table and accepted the challenge and challenged another member; that member in turn challenged another, and so on down the line. After the commission members came the functionaries of Tens and Fives. This was something we had not expected. In a few minutes, more than fifteen households of our Hundred had become members of the hated collective farm.

When the functionaries were enrolled, an ordinary farmer unexpectedly approached the table. He too declared his desire to join the collective farm, and he also called upon his neighbor, Shevchenko, to follow him. But this time the officials were unlucky. Shevchenko hesitated. He mentioned many excuses for not joining the collective farm at that moment: he had to think it over; his wife was ill, and besides, he liked to be completely independent. He insisted he couldn't do it now, maybe later. The officials pressed him to do it right away and he struggled desperately. Time dragged on. No one was permitted to leave the meeting room.

Suddenly a voice called from the back: "Join it! We don't want to stay here all night long!" That was a good chance for Shevchenko to get off the hook.

"If you are that eager, come here and sign it yourself!" he shouted back and quickly went to his place, disregarding the chairman's order to stay where he was.

The chairman at first insisted that Shevchenko return to the official table. Then he angrily urged all who were present at the meeting to come up and sign for the collective farm. But we remained adamant. No one moved.

The officials were not discouraged by our silent opposition. They seemed to have been well instructed in what to do in such a case. As the farmers continued to keep their silence, and the situation was becoming embarrassing, Comrade Professor offered a suggestion. He thought it would be appropriate to celebrate such a "highly patriotic and happy occasion" by sending telegrams to the Central Committee of the Communist Party, to the Soviet government, and to Comrade Stalin. And, without waiting for our consent, Comrade Professor produced a piece of paper out of his pocket and started to read. This was a telegram which stated that, after having attentively listened to the "highly patriotic and educational" speech of the district representative,[10] and after having realized what advantages a socialist agricultural system had over that of an individual one, the farmers of the First Hundred (it was our good fortune to belong to the First Hundred, and we were often called upon by officials to prove ourselves worthy of being Number One) solemnly promised to achieve one hundred percent collectivization by the first of May.

This was a ridiculous promise, as far as we were concerned, but none of us dared to criticize the telegram. It was adopted unanimously.

The chairman then returned to his previous business. He tried to smile this time.

"Well, since we agreed upon, and promised to achieve, a hundred percent collectivization," he said casually, "there is no point in wasting time, eh?"

He waved his pencil and paper over his head.

[10]A Party representative was the one who represented the Communist Party. But this designation does not express the true meaning of this title. It should be understood as "Party Extraordinary and Plenipotentiary Representative," one with unlimited and arbitrary power to command, control, and demand.

"Come and sign up, eh?"

We all stayed in our places.

"Come on! It's late," he urged us. "The sooner you sign in, the sooner you go home."

No one moved. All sat silently. The chairman, bewildered and nervous, whispered something in the propagandist's ear. The latter got up briskly and reminded us, as if we were kindergarten children, that it was not nice to break a promise, especially one given to Comrade Stalin. Since we had promised to join the collective farm, we had to do it now. But his fatherly admonishment did not move us. We kept our silence. This irritated the officials, especially the chairman. A moment after the propagandist finished his admonishment, the chairman rushed from behind the table, grabbed the first man before him, and shook him hard.

"You . . . you, enemy of the people!" he shouted, his voice choking with rage. "What are you waiting for? Maybe Petliura?" Petliura had been a Ukrainian leader during the war for independence a decade before. All his followers were later persecuted in one way or another, and now the label "Petliura" meant death. But the farmer remained calm.

"Take it easy," the farmer said composedly. "The telegram says that we must join the collective farm by May first, doesn't it? It's February now, isn't it? Why hurry?"

This seemed to have disarmed the chairman completely. He had not expected this turn of events, nor had any of us. Probably every farmer in the house was trying to find some way out of the trap set by the telegram, and here was the solution. We still had plenty of time!

The chairman hesitated for a second or two, then he took his hands from the man's shoulders, and went back to the table. There he conferred with the propagandist. As we watched them talking, we saw the propagandist take a paper out of his pocket and correct something on it. It was obvious that they were preparing some other trick.

"Before this meeting adjourns," started the propagandist, "it is only appropriate that we adopt a resolution." Then he started reading from the paper he held in his hand. The resolution was quite similar to the telegram, but with one difference: the word "May" was replaced by the word "immediately."

"Those who are against this resolution, raise your hands," announced the chairman. The officials knew that not many would vote for it. On the other hand, they were sure that no one would dare vote against it. As expected, no hand rose against it. Then, the chairman announced that the resolution had been accepted by all members of the First Hundred. Immediately he raised his pencil and paper again.

"Who's next?" he asked, pushing the pencil and paper to the opposite edge of the table.

Silence. The farmers stared ahead, unmoving. The chairman, drumming on the table with his fingers, looked down. Two militiamen stood at the doorway, barring the way out.

The silence was interrupted by Comrade Professor. He got up and glowered at the audience.

"What does this mean?" he hissed. "Is this a silent rebellion?" And then, after a deliberate pause, he told us that the Communist Party had given us an opportunity to join the collective farm voluntarily, but we, ignorant farmers, had misused this chance and had stubbornly defied the Party's policy. We had to join the collective farm now! If we did not, we would be considered "enemies of the people" who would be exterminated as a "social class." Having said this, he sat down.

It made no sense to us, for the words "voluntarily" and "must" did not mesh. We knew he meant what he said, however. Still, no one responded to his threats.

Both of them, propagandist and chairman, seemed exhausted. They looked at us in silence. We were silent also.

This state of affairs could not last for long. With so many people packed in a small room, something was bound to happen, and soon it did. A man asked to leave the room. The chairman said no, he could not leave the room as long as he refused to join the collective farm. For that matter, no one could leave the room. Only those individuals who had already joined the collective farm could go out. The propagandist whispered something in the chairman's ear, then announced:

"Yes, all those comrades who have already joined the collective farm must go home!"

We noticed that he said: "must go," not "may go." All the functionaries, except for the progandist and the chairman, started to leave the room. Some of them did it reluctantly, for as we knew, they did not want to be different from the rest of us.

The man who had asked to go outside still stood like a schoolboy before the teacher.

"But I must go!" he insisted. It was obvious he had to go to relieve his bladder.

"Take him outside, and bring him back immediately!" the chairman ordered one of the two militiamen.

So the man left the room under escort, like a prisoner, leaving us behind with the embarrassing thought that he would have to do his business under the watchful eyes of a Party man. Then, like mischievous schoolboys, other farmers asked to go outside. We were curious to see how the chairman would solve this problem with just one militiaman left.

"Nobody is going outside!" he shouted. "And that's that!" Some brave souls tried to insist on their right to answer the call of nature without official interference, but the chairman said those wanting to go outside were "enemies of the people" who wanted to undermine the meeting.

Having overcome this "toilet rebellion," the chairman and propagandist again conferred with one another.

"Whoever is for the Soviet regime and collectivization, raise your hands," the chairman ordered.

The farmers hesitated.

"You mean you are against the Soviet regime?" the propagandist hissed. "Isn't that an open rebellion? You mean, you would dare to do that?"

Then he repeated the question and changed his order: those who were for the Soviet regime had to move to the left, and those who were against it, to the right.

For a moment, no one moved. Then slowly, one, and then another, and another, got up and moved to the left. The propagandist took a pencil and started to write a list of those who still stood in their places, loudly asking their names. This did the trick. Soon all attempted to move to the left side. This was impossible in the small room, so the propagandist ordered everyone to sit down in their places.

The chairman waved his pencil and paper over his head, saying: "Now, let's get it over with! Who's first?"

No one stirred. The chairman looked angrily at us, and the propagandist stared helplessly. Then a voice from behind filled the vacuum. It was that of an old man, maybe seventy years of age.

"Why such a hurry, comrade-sir?" he shouted. All heads turned towards him, as to a savior. The chairman ordered him to step forward.

"Why such a hurry, comrade-sir?" the old man repeated, after he had reached the official table.

"I am not 'sir,' " the propagandist interrupted him. "I am 'comrade.' "

The old man became thoughtful.

"How come? I've never seen you in my life! How can you be my comrade?"

Whether the old man was baiting the propagandist or not was not important to us. What bothered us was the question he raised: why did the officials want to destroy, in one evening, a way of life the farmers had so long known?

The chairman and the propagandist answered the old man, using official Party slogans, and ready-made phrases. They replied that we had to join the collective farm immediately because that was what the Party demanded of us.

It was already well past midnight and we were all tired, especially my mother. Probably realizing the futility of continuing the meeting, the officials permitted us to go home, but this was only after the chairman ordered us to come to a meeting the following night.

Thus the new administration was set in motion.

There was still a great deal of mystery about collectivization. Perhaps the collective farms would mean a new kind of serfdom. So far, the only thing clear to us was that we would have to give up our land, which meant life itself to us.

One decade separated us from the Revolution and the Civil War. Most of our villagers had been affected by those events: many had lost their relatives or parents; others had returned home from the fighting crippled. But at least they had all received land. We asked ourselves if the Party really wanted us to give up our land, go to a collective farm, and work like city proletarians. Wasn't the Revolution for us, the poor farmers? Could it be possible that the Party had decided to return to the large estates? There still was at least one hope; the propagandist had told us that collectivization was voluntary. We were happy on our little farms, and we wanted nothing else but to be left alone. We wouldn't join the collective farm for any price.

We wondered why the members of the commission and the rest of the officials had joined the collective farm in such a hurry. It turned out that the day before the meeting, our Thousander, Comrade Zeitlin, had called all the functionaries of the village to a secret meeting. Giving them instructions about collectivization, he ordered them to declare their willingness to join the collective farm at the Hundred meeting with no hesitation. As the overwhelming majority of those functionaries were farmers, there was strong opposition to the Thousander's order. Comrade Zeitlin had a solution to this problem. He proposed a pretended joining of the collective farm by the functionaries. Those who were still not ready to join the collective farm would be registered on a special list which later would be destroyed. This was to set an example for the rest of the villagers. Whether they agreed with this plan gladly or not, we did not know. After that meeting at which we had seen the functionaries accepted as collective farm members Comrade Zeitlin refused to admit that he had suggested a fake registration. On the next day, the collective farmers visited their houses and took away horses, cows, and whatever else could be taken to the collective farm. In one night, Comrade Zeitlin collectivized almost twenty percent of our villagers, and also turned some of those farmer-functionaries into ferocious executors of the Party policy in the village. Having lost their own farms, they could only cling to what they had left, their official position, and so they exercised their newfound power whenever possible.

CHAPTER 4

ONE FEBRUARY morning in 1930, we heard an artillery barrage. Soon the crash of all kinds of weapon fire reverberated through the air. The sound was coming from the fields.

By noon, our village was overrun by regular army units. First, a cavalry detachment bolted through at full gallop. Then a brass band struck up a march on the village square, and the troops poured in.

As the companies marched, one after another, dogs howled and our anxiety increased. Soon we realized that we had become involuntary hosts. Without asking permission, fully armed soldiers entered our homes.

The soldiers were armed with propaganda materials and Party and government instructions for conducting a collectivization campaign. As soon as they were settled, the propaganda activities began but nothing new was said, since the instructions were the same as those presented by the civilian propagandists. The key difference was that the soldiers were more persistent.

The next day, as if in support of the propaganda, the army continued the exercises. But now they were different. Cannon had been placed in the fields within range of our village. Farmers and their families were still sleeping when the big guns began to roar. The whistling shells whipped over our village and exploded in the river on the other side.

Shooting and shouting began within the village. The cavalry again galloped through the streets. Confined to our homes, we were forced to remain spectators.

In the evening, arms were again exchanged for leaflets, and the villagers had to read and listen. And so it was every day: firing over our heads during the day, propaganda reading at night.

This military spectacle lasting about a week. Then, accompanied by band music and shell bursts, the army left in the direction of a neighboring village.

The shooting had not yet faded away when we all became the targets of another bombardment, this time by a so-called propaganda brigade. A few hundred people from neighboring cities marched in orderly columns, like soldiers. The brigade included ordinary industrial workers, students, office clerks, and others who had been taken from their jobs, given instructions concerning the nature of their task, and ordered to join the propaganda brigade.

Just as the entry of the army was intended to show the strength of the government, this brigade had its political purpose. It was supposed to demonstrate unanimity between the village and the city. This was in keeping with the Soviet attempt to do away with differences between city and rural people. Its main purpose, however, was to show the farmers that the policy of collectivization and the confiscation of grain had the support of the industrial populace. Thus, the farmers were to be convinced that their resistance to collectivization would be overcome by the unity of the entire country.

The propagandists, like the soldiers, were assigned to the homes of the farmers without their consent.

Some aspects of this propaganda brigade resembled an annual fair or market or a circus. The brigade started its activities the very moment it arrived in our village—on a Saturday afternoon. A terrible unceasing noise was its trademark.

In the evening, propaganda films were shown in the school buildings and also outdoors. In an improvised theater, a group of dancers twirled on stage, as did a merry-go-round brought by the brigade.

In spite of all these attractions, the villagers were in no hurry to meet the brigade members. Most of them stayed at home. To be sure, the children, the young boys and girls, the members of Komsomol and the Komnezam went to the square, but that was not what the county Party and government officials had in mind. They were interested in the adult farmers; those whom they had orders to collectivize.

Even though the officials might have been disappointed, they were not discouraged. They had to go ahead with their plan no matter how the villagers reacted. And so, within a few hours after their arrival in the village square, the propagandists were knocking at the doors of our homes. Some didn't bother to knock—they just walked in. Armed with all kinds of propaganda materials, they intruded into our houses and told us that individual farming was evil; that the way to paradise was through collective farms. The villagers listened to this new propaganda barrage, but the ready-made quotations, speeches, and explanations failed to convince them. Nothing could yet move them.

The propagandists also had orders to bring the farmers to the square the next Sunday morning. At least one family member had to go. Since there was no choice, many villagers obediently appeared in the square. I went there, too, perhaps more from curiosity than anything else.

When I arrived, there were already many people around. The villagers—men, women, and children—could not hide their anxiety. They were nervous, tired, and gloomy. The fast-talking city dwellers, the propagandists, tried to mingle with the villagers. With smiles and airs of simplicity, they approached us and even tried to joke with us. However, there was no response from us and our passivity only increased their hostility.

The atmosphere in the square then became tense. Suddenly, we heard the heavy din of a machine. The din almost immediately subsided into a smooth clanking, and soon we saw its source.

"A tractor!" somebody shouted. "Look over there! A tractor is coming!" Everyone turned toward the store, and there we saw it for the first time. It moved slowly from behind the village store in our direction. A tractor was a thing unknown in our village, although we recognized it from pictures we had seen. It was quite an impressive show, and the officials knew it.

The machine moved ahead. A big red flag was flying on its front. The driver, holding the steering wheel with both hands, looked straight ahead. He became an instant hero to the young boys and girls watching him.

On arriving at an apparently previously prescribed place, the tractor stopped, and became silent. Village and county officials appeared as if from nowhere, gathered around the tractor, and the county Party commissar[11] took his place on it. A hush came over the villagers as he began speaking.

What the commissar said was again repetitious. He declared that the governments of the capitalist countries did not care for poor farmers; farmers all over the world in the capitalist countries were being ruthlessly exploited; the farmers in those countries were working with primitive implements. Only in the Soviet Union were farmers taken care of: they were happy; they were embarking on the socialist way of production (he said this as if it were an accepted fact); and they were supplied with the best agricultural machinery.

"Look here," he said, pointing with both hands at the tractor. "Where else, but in the Soviet Union, do poor farmers like you have tractors of their own? Nowhere! Only you have this advantage!"

I was standing close to the tractor and, bored with the speech, I began to examine it as well as I could from my place. On the tractor's exhaust pipe, I noticed the trademark "International," cast in Latin characters.

[11]Commissar was the designation for high-ranking government officials in the USSR. The most important of these were the people's commissars, who in 1946 were renamed ministers. The title "commissar" was also widely used by high-ranking county officials.

CHAPTER 5

"**O**NLY YOU, in our beloved country, have tractors, the mighty machines that will work for you. . . . But the enemies of the people are conspiring against our beloved Party and people's government," the commissar shouted. He raised his hands. And, as if on cue, the church bells began to ring. The bells pealed more and more loudly. The crowd grew silent. All looked at the church.

No one knew who gave the signal or order, but when the Comrade Commissar raised his hands to point at the church, saying that the ringing of the bells was purposely instigated by the enemies of the people in order to sabotage his speech, the propagandists broke loose. The entire assemblage stirred with agitation. A voice near the tractor shouted:

"Down with the church!"

Another voice seconded this, and then it was repeated from one end of the square to the other.

"Down with the church! Down with the church! Down with the church!"

Suddenly posters appeared around the square, painted in white on red cloth. The posters read: "Down with the Church!" "Long live the Collective Farms!" "Long live the Communist Party!"

"Let's go!" a voice roared.

"Let's go!" some other voice seconded.

Shouting "hurrah," like soldiers before hand-to-hand combat, the crowd ran toward the church in a stampede. Arriving there, they threw stones, bottles, and sticks, smashing windows and doors.

Long ladders appeared at the church wall, and dozens of propagandists quickly reached the cupolas. Then long ropes were tied around the crosses. And, amid shouting, laughter, and cursing, the propagandists yanked on the ropes until the crosses fell, smashing the roof. Then the bells were taken down, and the cupolas destroyed.

While this was happening on the roof, another group of propagandists was working inside the church. The interior was demolished. What had been a beautiful church, the pride of our village for many years, was reduced to ruins within a few minutes.

The villagers were unable to defend their place of worship. When the stampede started, some of them went home, but the majority of them stood silent, with bared heads lowered, and prayed.

We realized that this political orgy actually had been carefully planned and executed. The tractor was the focal point, and the Party Commissar, no doubt, was in command of the entire operation. We were sure that the pealing of the bells during the commissar's speech was a part of the plan, for a propagandist rang them. We realized that the slogans had been carefully composed, and the posters painted long before being brought to our village.

The church, or what was left of it, was converted into a village theater. That very evening the propagandists danced on the place where the altar had stood.

No one knew where our priest had been during the attack on the church. It was Sunday morning, and he should have been there, but he wasn't. Later we learned that he had actually been a collaborator of the propaganda brigade. His name was Ivan Bondar.

Bondar possessed that talent of assessing situations and using them to his advantage. Only the previous year, he had served in the church as deacon. He was tall and handsome, with a powerful voice. He could read and write, and was considered an educated man. Many of the villagers thought he would be a good priest. No doubt he himself had hopes of becoming a priest some day, for he even started to grow his hair long, a privilege reserved for Orthodox clergy. Then came collectivization, and the government stepped up the campaign against the church. Bondar suddenly disappeared from the village.

There was speculation about his disappearance. Some thought that he had been abducted by the secret police. Others thought that he had sensed the coming danger and had disappeared to some faraway region, leaving his family in the village. But shortly before the coming of the Propaganda Brigade, he reappeared in our village with long hair and pretensions of being a holy man.

One Sunday morning, when the time came to start the liturgy, none other than Bondar appeared at the altar. Without the slightest hesitation, he announced that he was our rightful priest. As if trying to avoid questions and protestations, he immediately started singing some verses in his powerful bass voice. We never received any explanation.

Later that day we learned that our old priest was gone. We never found out what happened to him; we could only guess that he had been taken away by the secret police during the night.

This all happened before the church was destroyed. There was an attempt by the church elders to find out what was going on, but all in vain. Bondar kept silent, and so did the village officials. Soon, some church elders and other active villagers began to disappear. Then the villagers started to pass the news to each other that, in confession, the new priest was very much interested in the political opinions of the penitents. It suddenly struck us that the new priest was a secret police stooge and provocateur. Bondar's survival of the Propaganda Brigade's assault on the church strengthened our suspicions. As we recalled, no one could find him on that fateful day. We had no doubt in our minds that he had received instructions and a warning from his bosses in advance.

After the Propaganda Brigade left the village and the ruined church behind, Bondar's disguise was dropped. He openly associated with the Party and government officials and with their political line. This explained why he neither protested the destruction of our church, nor tried to reopen it or provide for religious services in some other way. He started to appear wherever Comrade Zeitlin and other Party officials were. He spoke at every political rally like one of their officials. Interestingly, he continued growing his beautiful beard and long hair. Indeed, he still looked like a priest.

We soon learned that Comrade Zeitlin and other officials called him Saint—Comrade Saint. The villagers, on the other hand, had their own name for him. They called him Judas—Comrade Judas.

The brigade stayed with us almost one week. We had not been allowed to leave the village all this time except for working in the fields. In the evenings, we had to stay at home, listening to the propagandists.

On Friday, the brigade left in the direction of a neighboring village, where cannon rumbling could be heard.

But we were not relieved. The army, and later the Propaganda Brigade, had now shown us the nature of Party policy. The message was clear: the Party and government had ordered compulsory collectivization, and that was what would be done.

So the trap had snapped shut, and we realized that there was no way out. Hastily introduced measures were now pulling the villagers deeper into the new system.

When the last columns of the Propaganda Brigade had left the village square, we thought we would be left alone for a while. We were tired, and confused, and deafened by the noise. We were all greatly concerned about the collectivization of our farms. Without his own land, a farmer could have neither material security nor freedom. In the course of just a few weeks so many incomprehensible and frightening events had passed. Multitudes of people had tramped through our yards and had eaten our food without asking, and our beloved church had been destroyed. We were terrified. We felt that something horrible was approaching, and we saw no escape.

The next Saturday, the last Saturday in February, less than a week after the departure of the Propaganda Brigade, more strangers arrived in our village. These were GPU men, a small detachment of security troops, and many militiamen. Patrols walked everywhere, even in the most remote corners of our village. The greatest shock came when we saw a heavy machine gun set up in the ruins of the church, manned by three soldiers. A few other machine guns were posted around the square.

We discovered that we were being carefully guarded. A sentry was posted on every main road which led out of the village. His duty was to keep track of everyone leaving or entering the village. Those sentries checked not only peoples' identities, but also their belongings. Everyone had to give detailed information concerning his destination and reason for leaving the village.

We took the cruelty and lawlessness in stride. We were prepared to be arrested without a warrant, or to be deprived of our property. We were used to unjust taxes and extortions under various pretexts. But we did not expect such a measure of control over our everyday routines.

On that same Saturday afternoon, the village was alerted by messengers who ran from house to house, summoning the farmers to a meeting which was to take place the next day. All heads of households were ordered to appear on the village square. There was no choice.

In the middle of the square was the raised platform on which the propagandists had danced a week ago. This was the place for the speakers and officials. Portraits of the Party and government dignitaries were displayed on the platform. Party slogans hung below the pictures.

Around the platform stood armed sentries. From the ruins of the church, the machine gun faced us. Heavily armed soldiers walked around the square. And in the middle of the square, the farmers stood, huddled together, silent but restless, for it was very cold.

At the appointed time, the officials appeared on the platform. The schoolchildren started to sing the anthem. The teacher conducting them urged the farmers to join in the singing, but they remained silent.

As soon as the last words of the anthem faded away, the chairman of the village soviet opened the meeting and introduced the officials from the county government.

Three commissars stood on the platform. They were the commissar of GPU, the commissar of the county Party organization (whom we had met when he commanded the Propaganda Brigade), and the commissar of the MTS.[12] The village functionaries also stood on the tribune. The Thousander, Comrade Zeitlin, the chairman of the village soviet, and the leaders of the Komnezam and the Komsomol stood close behind the county commissars.

After the introductions, the chairman of the village soviet announced that the Party commissar was to make a speech.

Comrade Commissar started his speech with all the pomp of a typical Communist orator. He took a place at the front of the tribune, coughed into his fist, drank some water from the glass handed to him by Comrade Zeitlin, glanced indifferently at the gathered farmers, and started.

It was the typical speech we had come to expect from a Communist official. He quoted all the fathers of Communism, and spoke about

[12]MTS is an abbreviation for Machine and Tractor Stations, a state enterprise which, until 1958, supplied all machine works for collective farms. For their services, MTS received payments in kind. Since January 1933, when the political sections were established, MTS became the main force behind the expropriation of agricultural products from farmers.

every revolution that had occurred since Adam and Eve. He described the miserable life the farmers in foreign countries led, and how savagely they were exploited by the "imperialistic sharks."

Then he changed his tone of voice, and spoke of the happy life in the Soviet Union. Paradise existed in the Soviet Union; a paradise on earth.

"Could a meeting such as this take place somewhere else, in the capitalist countries?" he asked plaintively. "No," he hurriedly answered his own question. "No! There is no freedom there, and the farmers like you," he pointed to us with both his hands, "the farmers like you don't have this privilege. They don't have their own meetings. . . ."

His rhetorical hysteria continued. Several times he repeated himself. Only after naming all the parts of the world, and after using all his profanity to describe "the imperialistic sharks," did he finish his speech, calling on the farmers to join the collective farms, and warning that there were many kurkuls among us.

"Kurkuls are our enemy," he shouted, "and we must exterminate them as a social class. There should be no place for the sharks among the harmless fish," he added. Then he described the kurkuls as an evil tool of capitalists who were preparing an attack on the Soviet Union.

"Damn them all!" he shouted, finishing his propaganda harangue. "Damn every single kurkul! Damn every member of their families!"

After he had cried out these slogans, the officials on the tribune, the soldiers, the militiamen, and the children responded to his speech with long and loud applause.

But the farmers just glanced at each other and did not applaud. Clapping of the hands as an expression of excitement and satisfaction was a novel city custom, but we were farmers so we refrained from this show of enthusiasm.

Seeing this indifference, the officials seemed to be confused, but the situation was saved by the commissar of the GPU. As soon as the applause was over, he took the speaker's place. He spoke in short, clear sentences.

"Comrades," he started, sending his cold look out upon the farmers. "Comrades, it was a great pleasure to hear such a beautiful and truthful speech from our dear Comrade Commissar. But it is a horrible thing to see that these highly patriotic words of our beloved commissar are ignored and boycotted by the enemies of the people."

The farmers glanced at each other with apprehension. The commissar, after a deliberate pause, continued:

"What has happened now is the best proof of the presence of the enemy of the people among us. Comrade Commissar spoke in behalf of our beloved Communist Party and our people's government. He spoke in behalf of our great leader, Comrade—"

An explosion of applause interrupted him. He stopped. The applause grew louder. The farmers also applauded more energetically this time. They understood him very well. As soon as it was quiet again, the commissar continued:

"Comrades, the words of the commissar were the words of the Party—" Somebody started to applaud again, but the commissar ignored it, and went on: "But, comrades, you met those words with silence, and thus, with opposition." He paused for a moment.

"To me, as your GPU commissar, it means that among you are those who act like the enemy of the people—kurkuls—that capitalist element to whom those words are not sympathetic and who would be willing to strangle Comrade Commissar rather than greet him with joyous applause."

Checking the effect of his words on his listeners, he stopped for a few minutes, looking at the audience. Then, speaking through his teeth, he gave a warning:

"We'll have to take the bull by the horns," he said angrily. "I am forced to warn you that even the smallest attempt to oppose the measures of our beloved Communist Party and the people's government will be suppressed ruthlessly. We'll crush you like detestable vermin!"

With those words, he finished his speech. Loud applause echoed through the square. The farmers, looking shamefully around, beat their hands more quickly, and then all became abruptly quiet.

The farmers gazed straight at the platform. In front of them, on the church ruins, they saw the machine gun. The service men stood watchfully around the square.

The silence was interrupted by the chairman of the village soviet as he called for other speakers. One after another, all the officials on the platform spoke. Even a few farmers took the stand, most of them well-known members of the Komnezam and active supporters of the Communist regime in our village.

But we did not listen any more. We clapped our hands after every

34

speech, though our minds were elsewhere. The officials had made it clear that the villagers had to join the collective farm or be banished to Siberia or other cold Russian regions. They talked about destroying kurkuls as if they were speaking of destroying some agricultural vermin or animal pest. We too were to participate in destroying them, they told us. We were not instructed how, but we were given to understand that any way or means would be justified.

Although I was still a young boy at that time, many questions plagued me after those speeches. Who were those kurkuls? Who could be labeled a kurkul? I asked myself: is my neighbor a kurkul also? And what about my family and relatives? Are we all kurkuls?

Someone shouted, "What does kurkul mean?"

The Party Commissar answered: "Kurkuls are exploiters of the poor; they are the remnants of the old regime, and they must be liquidated as such. Also those who oppose the policy of the Party and Government will be considered kurkuls. They will also be liquidated." This explanation suggested that anyone could be labeled a kurkul.

As the winter sun set behind the ruins of the church, Comrade Zeitlin proposed that the villagers send a telegram to the Central Committee of the Communist Party and to the Soviet government, expressing thanks for the prosperous and happy life of the Soviet villagers, and particularly for the introduction of the collective farms. As at the Hundred meeting, there was only one question: "Who is against it?" Since no one dared object, the telegram was approved by acclamation.

When the applause ended, the chairman of the meeting read the inevitable resolution. It stated that the farmers were happy to join the collective farms, and that they had promised the Party and government to complete the collectivization of the village by the first of May. Again, since not a single voice was raised against it, the resolution was adopted, and the meeting adjourned.

CHAPTER 6

THE CHAIRMAN of the First Hundred's Bread Procurement Commission was Ivan Khizhniak. He had once been our neighbor. Comrade Khizhniak was about forty, short and heavy, and semiliterate. His face was lined with deep wrinkles, and his thick dirty-blond hair and cold, dull-green eyes half-covered with wrinkled eyelids and bristly eyelashes gave him a porcine look.

This was the man who was in charge of the Bread Procurement Commission in our Hundred. His physical ugliness seemed to shape his mind and his morality. He was cruel, rough, and embittered. His manner of speaking was sarcastic and vulgar, or limited to pat, official phrases. Sometimes he would try to speak in an urbane manner which he had picked up somewhere during his absence from our village, but even then he would insert the foulest profanity into his language.

Comrade Khizhniak was the only known Communist in our village when the October Revolution began. During the Revolution, as chairman of the Committee of Poor Peasants (the Komnezam), he was one of the most eager and active organizers of the local revolutionary government. After the Revolution, he remained a loyal executor of the Communist policy in the village. Indeed, he became a powerful village politician, and as such, he caused the death of many prominent villagers.

Shortly after the Revolution, when one of the frequent Communist policy shifts had gone into effect, he disappeared from the village, leaving a tangle of loose ends behind. No one knew where he had gone or what he was doing. The villagers began to forget about him, but when the collectivization started, Khizhniak reappeared.

In organizing the Hundred's Bread Procurement Commission, Comrade Zeitlin and his Party and government assistants seemed to have drawn mainly on the degenerate elements of our village for their workers. Khizhniak's commission serves as a vivid example of this. True, there were honest and industrious villagers whom we knew and respected among the members of the commission, but its core was composed of individuals with sadistic impulses. Besides Comrade Khizhniak, one of the other members that I knew was the vicious Vasil Khomenko, a man whose sadism made him infamous in our village.

The other commission members were not so notorious as Khizhniak or Khomenko; nevertheless, they still belonged to that troublesome group that made the villagers' lives insecure and miserable.

Ivan Bondar, or "Comrade Judas," was another member. He came to our Hundred a few days after the church was destroyed. As our Hundred happened to bear the number "One," the village officials wanted to make it a model for the other Hundreds. Therefore, they staffed it with the most trusted individuals. Comrade Judas soon found perfect accord with Comrades Khizhniak and Khomenko.

Almost absolute power was given to these Party and government functionaries. Their abilities were measured by the amount of foodstuff they could extract from the farmers and by the number of farmers they could collectivize in the shortest amount of time. They used whatever methods were effective in accomplishing their task. The Communist dictums that the end justifies the means, and that the winner is always right, were the credos of the day.

There is a Ukrainian proverb that says that a master is not as cruel as a servant would be in his place. Comrade Khizhniak and his lieutenants, all farmers themselves, promoted to official positions, became drunk with power; they used their officialdom to exert a ruthlessness and cruelty unheard of in our village. There seemed no limitation to their arbitrariness and vanity. The activity of the commission was carefully planned and coordinated. Comrade Khizhniak, the propagandist, and a few other members of the commission presided at the court in the Hundred's headquarters. They would summon those farmers who had shown themselves to be stubborn or suspicious and would "work" on them individually. Comrades Khomenko and Judas, with the rest of the Hundred's functionaries, worked through the Tens and Fives, also individually. However, they concentrated their efforts on conducting meetings of members of those units. We had to attend one meeting or another practically every day, Sundays included. The Sunday meetings would usually start early in the morning and last all day long.

The commission functionaries of our Hundred, as well as those of all the others, used strictly prescribed methods in dealing with us. One method, unsophisticated but effective, was "path treading," as the functionaries termed it. A farmer would be called to his Hundred and the usual interrogation would follow. Why had he not joined the collective farm? This same question would be asked repeatedly. The Hundred's officials would tell him that only an "enemy of the people" opposed the Communist policy of collectivization. Since there was no place for an "enemy of the people" in the Soviet Union, there would be no choice for him: he either had to join the collective farm, or be eliminated. Finally, they would give him a pencil to sign the application and thus avoid all trouble. Some did sign, but the majority refused, using various excuses and pretexts.

At this point, the "path-treading" method would be used. The official would tell the farmer to take some message to the neighboring Hundred, say to the Second Hundred. Since no one could refuse to accept an official assignment, the man would take the message, whatever it was, and start his trip through the village. When he had arrived at the Hundred to which he had been assigned, he found that they had been expecting him there. Immediately, the farmer was subjected to another interrogation. Again he had to explain why he was not yet a member of the collective farm; again he would be told to join immediately. If he still refused to join, he was sent to the next Hundred, and from there to the next, and so on. After the last Hundred, he would be sent to the village soviet office where Comrade Zeitlin was in charge. Here again he went through the same long, complicated interrogation.

It was winter and the cold was severe. The paths and the roads of the village were snowbound. The victim had to walk through the night across the village, leaving behind a trail in the deep snow; hence, the name "path treading." This method was used by the officials in accordance with an obviously prearranged schedule. About five farmers of our Hundred had to go on this "path-treading" walk every night; and as many as forty or more farmers from other Hundreds visited our Hundred. A panorama of our village on one of these nights would have shown about forty wretched farmers, shivering from cold and exhaustion, slowly moving through the darkness and waist-deep snow.

At dawn, the path treader would return home from his night-long walk, only to find a new summons from the Hundred for the next night. The program for the next night was somewhat different. First, he would be kept waiting for a few hours, and then be subjected to the usual interrogation. Had he changed his mind? Was he going to join the collective farm now? Some said yes, but the majority repeated their "no!" As before, the farmers tried to find some excuses, but now the officials refused to listen to them; they had no time. Would the farmer wait for a while? Of course, he had to wait, but not in the house; it was overcrowded. The shed was empty—well, almost! There were only five or six other farmers there, and so the victim would suddenly find himself in a cold shed that was locked from the outside as soon as he entered.

This kind of persuasion became known as the "cooling off" method. Cold, humiliated, and exhausted from lack of sleep and from harassment, the farmers would wait for hours. In the cold darkness of the shed, some would begin to realize the hopelessness of their resistance.

A few hours would pass, and the functionaries would bring the farmers, one by one, into the office and tell them to sign the application. The majority still refused. So, singly—they could not go in a group—they would again be sent "path treading." This would be repeated the next day, and the day after that until the men, exhausted physically and broken in spirit, would submit to the officials' demand. Every victim's place in the shed and on the "path treading" would then be taken by another villager.

The inhabitants in some other Hundreds experienced still another method of persuasion. One day we heard a story about events taking place in the Second Hundred. The Party functionaries of that Hundred had entered into "socialist competition" with Hundred Seven for the speedy fulfillment of the collectivization quota. During a meeting at which the farmers still stubbornly opposed the collective farm, the chairman of the Hundred ordered a fire to be lit in the building's stove. Then he ordered the stove damper closed. He posted a guard at the door and left the hall. After a while, a few farmers dropped to the floor semiconscious. Finally, someone broke the window.

Whether that chairman finally met his quota is unknown. But the man who broke the window was later tried in the People's Court for "interfering with an official's duty," and for "inflicting damage upon socialist property." He was sentenced to a hard labor camp for ten years and was not heard from again.

Evening and Sunday meetings were extremely humiliating and torturous experiences in our lives. They had undoubtedly been designed not only for the purpose of political and ideological brainwashing, but also as a means of breaking the farmers' spirit of independence. The meetings were to be channels through which the Party could direct farmers towards collaboration with the Party officials in fulfilling the task of collectivization. Party propaganda termed these meetings "mass participation in socialist government."

These meetings played a crucial role in driving the farmers into the collective farms. The meeting would usually start with a long speech about the methods of collectivization. There would follow short speeches, after which some time was allotted to questions and answers. The meeting chairman would then announce that a debate would follow. Of course, these debates were nothing more than small speeches by functionaries and other activists, for no villager would take part in them. We had no choice but to listen until we became stupefied.

Finally, the chairman would announce the next point on the meeting's agenda. This was the summary of the "socialist competition" during the previous week. Every adult was forced to take part in the competition for speedy fulfillment of the collectivization quota.

Our village as a whole competed with a neighboring village. Our Hundred competed with Hundred Eight and also with its own counterpart in the neighboring village. All functionaries competed among themselves as officials and as individuals, and all villagers were also supposed to compete among themselves.

The chairman of the meeting on competition would tell his audience the village's standing in the competition. And no matter what progress was achieved, the officials were never satisfied; so, consequently, we were blamed, scolded, and threatened. Only one hundred percent participation would satisfy them.

Then the chairman would call upon the head of the Hundred to make a report about his Hundred's standing in comparison with its rival and the other village Hundreds. If our Hundred happened to be among the leading ones, then we could hope to go home sooner. But when our Hundred was behind, we would prepare ourselves for another lecture about the importance of the "socialist competition."

The result of the competition within and among the Tens and Fives was also carefully analyzed. The winner subunits, that is to say, the Tens and Fives that collectivized the most farmers during the last week, would ceremoniously be presented the Red Banner and their functionaries would be proclaimed Shock Workers, and officially commended for their good work. The loser subunits together with their functionaries, would be listed on the *chorna doshka,* literally, "black board," which was supposed to be a great disgrace. The least successful subunits could expect to see their names written on pictures of a turtle or a crocodile. The turtle represented slowness, and the crocodile viciousness. The "crocodiles" had the worst part of the whole affair. They were treated as enemies of the Communist regime or, worse still, as saboteurs. Usually these individuals were transferred to other subunits either within or outside of their Hundred with the warning that repeated failure would be followed by arrest or banishment.

The report of the subunits over, the meeting would continue with the report about individual competition. First, the functionaries competed among themselves for larger numbers of collectivized farmers. All of them were forced to take commitments upon themselves in the following manner: a functionary would announce in a stereotyped sentence that, realizing the advantage of the collective system, he solemnly promised the "dear Party and government" to collectivize so many farmers by the next Sunday meeting. Then he also challenged Comrade So-and-so to surpass that goal. The challenged one had no choice but to accept the challenge, and so a chain reaction would start.

Among the villagers, the nature of the competition was a little different. During the week prior to Sunday, the officials would take care to "prepare" some farmers. At the Sunday meeting, these farmers would duly rise and utter memorized phrases about how happy they were to join the collective farm; they would then challenge Comrade So-and-So (a farmer) to do the same.

At the Sunday meetings, the challengers and the ones challenged had to give accounts of their various competitions. A functionary had to report how many farmers he had collectivized since the last meeting. The lucky ones were praised; the losers were reprimanded. They were then warned to do a better job by next Sunday, or else bear the consequences.

Then the farmers would give their accounts. The challenger was left alone, but the one challenged had to either accept or refuse the challenge to the "socialist competition." If not, why? If yes, why was he still not on the list of the loyal Soviet citizens, i.e., the members of the collective farm? This was a painful moment for the honest villager for he could not afford the luxury of flatly refusing and telling all the officials to go to hell, which, no doubt, he gladly would have done. On the other hand, he could not find any acceptable excuse. All the villagers could do was to mumble: "I'm not ready yet." Of course, such a statement would trigger new threats and admonishments.

With the reports on the competition over, the meeting proceeded with the next point on the agenda: personal reporting. Every member of our Hundred had to appear before the assembly and answer the questions of why he had not yet joined the collective farm, and when he intended to do so.

These meetings usually lasted all night, and on Sundays, all day. Hungry and terrorized, the villagers quietly listened and obligingly answered the multitude of questions, but stubbornly stood their ground. Nothing could move them. At least that is what they thought.

But the Communist officials were not ready to give up their ground either. They were waging a war, and they knew that where one tactic did not work, another might. And this was precisely what happened.

At the end of February and the beginning of March 1930, the officials appraised the situation, regrouped their forces, devised new tactics for the offensive, and then delivered a smashing blow.

One Sunday, we learned that, except for Khizhniak, Khomenko, and Comrade Judas, all the Hundred's functionaries, including those of the Tens, Fives, and all the other subunits throughout the village had been reassigned. Some of those whose subunits were not among the first in meeting the collectivization quotas, were assigned to the neighboring villages. At about the same time, some functionaries from neighboring villages and towns arrived in our village. In strange surroundings, these farmer functionaries became more aggressive.

About this time, the village Party strategists introduced a new tactic that we called "dog eat dog." Those farmers who were previously considered kurkuls and those who had been persecuted in one way or another and were still living in the village were reinstated in

42

the good graces of the Communist officials and engaged in active work for the Party and the government. These tactics worked even better than the officials had expected. The farmers were told that they deserved to be shot, but they were being given a chance to prove themselves worthy of living. What they had to do was to help the Party and the Government to collectivize the farmers. Of course, if they proved themselves worthy, they would be accepted into the collective farm also. And so these so-called kurkuls became staunch activists, for the desire to prove themselves "worthy" drove them to become merciless executors of Party policy.

Moreover, since they were farmers, they knew the psychology of their fellow villagers, and therefore were the most capable in devising new ways and means of forcing their fellows to comply with Communist policies and demands.

CHAPTER 7

I DO NOT remember very much about my father, for I was only three when he died in 1919. But I clearly remember his funeral. A Red Guard stood at his deathbed. He wore a red cap, and in his hands he held a huge rifle with a bayonet fixed to its muzzle. He stood motionless and silent, like a granite statue gazing ahead into empty space. Later I was told that only when someone moved closer to the deathbed, or showed an intention of uncovering the dead body would he move, raising his rifle and uttering strange words. My brother thought that he and all the other strangers in uniform did not speak our language.

There were many people out of doors that day, people I had never seen before. I remember that they wore red caps, were dressed in uniforms, and had come on horseback.

My father's body was laid under the icons on a bench which stood in the east corner of the living room. I remember that we, his children —my six-year-old brother, my baby brother, and myself—were brought trembling to the bedside to bid our farewells. Although I could not see my father because he was in a sealed coffin, I was told to say good-bye and kiss him anyway. Someone lifted me, and I remember pressing my lips on the spot where father's head was sup- posed to be. I also remember that my mother and all the other people —relatives and neighbors—lamented and sobbed. But I did not cry. Those strangers with the red caps, guns, uniforms, and horses held my interest more than my deceased father.

As time went by, and I grew older, this scene often flashed through my mind, arousing my curiosity. I wanted to know what had actually happened on that day, and yet mother always managed to avoid my questions. She told me that he died; but she never said how he died.

It was not until one evening, when we returned from one of the village meetings at which the kurkuls had been denounced as the "enemies of the people," that my mother decided to tell us the truth.

My father's farm was hardly big enough to support his growing family and to satisfy the state's demand for ever-increasing taxes. He had only about fifteen acres of arable land; never more than one horse, a cow, a few pigs, and the usual flock of domestic fowl. He never had hired hands, for he would have had no use for them. He did everything himself and enjoyed it; he even would often work for other farmers, or in the towns during the autumn and winter.

Nevertheless, he was a success in his own realm. Raised in the changeless traditions of the country people, he was an industrious and untiring individual. His small farm became a model for many other farmers in our neighborhood. He transformed it into what might have been called a market garden. He managed it so well that he always had some sort of fresh fruits or vegetables to sell in neighboring towns.

After working hard during the week, on Sundays he would load his one-horse wagon with various agricultrual products and go to the market. In this way—by sacrifice and sheer industry—he managed to accumulate enough money to build a house and the necessary auxiliary buildings, a clear indication of his limited prosperity. With this his social status changed. He became one of the most respected individuals in the village, and consequently, was elected head of the village shortly before the Communist Revolution. This position was an honorary one, for he received no payment from the government, but it brought about his death.

One day in 1919, a few days after the Communists had reoccupied Ukraine, my father was arrested, taken to the county seat, and put into prison. He was labeled "a servant of the old regime," "an exploiter of the poor," and "bourgeois-nationalist," for he advocated independence for Ukraine.

This happened so quickly and so unexpectedly that mother was more confused at first than frightened. She was confident that the arrest was a mistake. She knew that no one would harm her husband, a fine man, deeply religious and honest, who worked hard and was always ready to offer his help to anyone. My mother was sure that the jailers would soon realize what kind of man he was and set him free.

But this never happened. The next day, when she went to visit him, she was told that he was dead. Despite her intense grief, her first thought was how to get her husband's body out of the prison, and how to properly bury him. She managed to do both. For some unknown reason, my father's jailers permitted her to take his body home, but only under the strict condition that he be buried without public participation, and his coffin never be uncovered.

My mother had no choice but to accept these conditions. The body was taken from the prison to our home by a small Red Guard detachment.

While telling us this, my mother was calm and composed, as she had always been. She was a most remarkable individual; I seldom saw her cry. In those troubled and lonely years that followed my father's death, she worked in the field, ploughed the land, and harvested the crops. She cared for our domestic animals, kept the entire household wisely, and affectionately cared for us. Through all those years, we heard few complaints from her lips. On the contrary, she appeared to be happy and witty. She encouraged us to be good, and to study hard in school. She laughed and prayed with us, but alone, she was sad and melancholy.

From the time of my father's death, fear dogged my mother's every step. She was afraid that at any moment she would be denounced as the wife of an "eliminated enemy of the people," a charge that would have been fatal to the four of us.

For eleven long years, she labored under that fear, always having to be very careful in her speech. During those years, she had to appease many people in order to avoid quarrels or other frictions which might have resulted in denunciation. Indeed, she lived in a lonely and dangerous world.

Mother would have preferred not to tell this story at all, for she did not want us to grow up embittered by the murder of our father. She was convinced that he had been tortured and murdered in the prison. Her reticence disappeared only after that particular meeting during which the extermination of the kurkuls, as the "enemies of the people" had been declared. She felt the coming of the end and believed we were now old enough to know the truth.

After we had recovered from the shock of hearing the story of our father's death, we remained at the table and talked about the recent events in our village. We finally went to bed after midnight. As soon as we had put out the lights, we heard an energetic pounding at the front door. The knock was repeated, and a stranger's voice demanded that we open the door.

"The Bread Procurement Commission," a voice announced from outside.

We already had heard about the notorious deeds of this commission, and we rushed to comply with their demand. But before we could, there was a crash—the strangers burst into our house.

It was dark, and my mother went to light the petroleum lamp.

"Surprise is my weakness! Ha, ha, ha," said the voice that had commanded us to open the door. "I am just delighted to see you! But where are you? Ha, ha, ha . . ."

It was Comrade Khizhniak.

When Mother lit the lamp, we saw that four men, two women, and one boy, the messenger, were standing in front of her. One of the men held a rifle as if he were expecting a rabbit to hop out from under the bed. We knew all of them personally.

Comrade Khizhniak was drunk, and his lips and jaws moved slowly in a stutter. He could not stand up straight. We were frightened, and instinctively my older brother and I moved closer to our mother.

"How do you do, comrades?" Mother said in a trembling voice.

Comrade Khizhniak stepped closer to her.

"A lot of water has passed under the bridge since we last met each other," he blurted out. "Isn't it sweet to get an unexpected night visit, eh?"

"Glad to see you, comrades," Mother continued, regaining her strength and confidence. "What can I do for you? Please sit down."

The lamp hung in the east corner of the living room. In the farmers' tradition, this corner was a sacred place. Icons hung there on the walls. From the ceiling hung an icon lamp with its ever-burning oil as a symbol of light. A piece of blessed bread lay on one of the icons as a symbol of God's generosity. We faced Comrade Khizhniak and his commission from this corner. My brother Serhiy stood at my mother's left side, and I stood at her right.

Comrade Khizhniak seemed not to have heard what Mother said; he stretched out his hands with the intention of embracing her. She stepped back, and he grabbed her in a shameless way. She slapped his face with all her might. "Swine, get away from me," she cried.

47

Quickly, Comrade Khizhniak grabbed for his gun. I quickly jumped in front of Mother, and Serhiy grabbed Khizhniak. A shot was fired. The bullet hit the icon, and the glass splintered.

The shot was so unexpected that all seemed paralyzed. A woman member of the commission, gazing at the broken icon, started to cry. My younger brother screamed at the top of his voice. I tried to comfort my Mother as Serhiy wrestled with Comrade Khizhniak, who was trying to shoot again. Comrade Judas, probably drunk also, fell on his knees in jest, and mumbled something as if he were praying.

Then an old farmer member of the commission shouted, "Quiet! We came here on official business!"

Comrade Khizhniak stopped wrestling with my brother and put his gun back into its holster. He then turned to the old farmer:

"You will leave the thinking to the horses; they have bigger heads," he sneered in a low voice. "Just whose business are you talking about?"

Then he approached the old man and looked at him contemptuously.

"I'm the business here!" he suddenly roared. "Do you hear me? I'm the business here! No one else! Keep that in your stupid, dirty, lousy old head!"

The old man hesitated; he wanted to say something but it was all in vain. Comrade Khizhniak continued, this time speaking through clenched teeth.

"Look at him," he continued, as he turned to the commission's members, pointing at the old farmer with his finger. "He came here on official business. . . . Isn't that interesting?" Then he again raised his voice. "I repeat; this is my business! I'm the representative of our beloved and dear Party and government here! I am—"

"I only wanted to—" the old man started to say something.

"Shut up!" Comrade Khizhniak interrupted him. Then after a moment of silence, he gave the warning:

"I'll get even with you sooner or later."

Comrade Khizhniak was a member of the Communist Party and the chairman of the Hundred's commission. He had complete power within that Hundred. To oppose him was to oppose the Party and the government. No one, except his superiors, might interfere in his activities. Shouting louder and louder, he warned that he would shoot down anyone who opposed the will of the Communist Party and that of the government.

After a while he turned to my brother Serhiy.

"You are a strong lad, eh! You are a very strong lad, indeed," he said. "Our beloved fatherland needs strong fellows like you. Isn't it a great fortune to have such a strong young generation?"

He then turned to the man with the rifle, signaling him to step closer. Then he turned to my brother again.

"Well, well," he continued in the same manner. "Our socialist fatherland needs strong people. . . ." Then, taking a dignified pose, and in a haughty military manner, he pronounced:

"In the name of our beloved Communist Party and our people's government, I declare you under arrest for physical assault on an official representative of the Party and government while he was performing his official duty." He then ordered the man with the rifle to take my brother into his custody.

My mother could not hide her despair. Crying, she attempted to hold on to Serhiy with both hands, but being too weak to struggle against four men, she fainted. When she regained consciousness, Serhiy was gone.

A few minutes later, after mother came to, Khizhniak continued his "business" as though nothing had happened. "Well," he began, "as you already know, we came here on a serious business matter. On official business, as our comrade has said," he smilingly nodded to the old farmer. "And, indeed, it is very serious."

Mother rose to her feet and brushed back her hair.

"Before you start your official business, whatever it is, I demand a warrant for the arrest of my son," she said in a clear voice. We were all amazed.

"I'm only a helpless widow," she continued. "You can do what you want with me, for I do not have any strength to defend myself. But as long as I am alive, I protest against your intrusion into my house."

Such a protestation was unheard of. The punishment for saying such things was a sentence of life imprisonment or death. No one would even think of demanding permission for arrest or search from an official.

Mother's demand touched off hysterical laughter from Comrade Khizhniak and his lieutenants. Then he moved closer to us.

"Look, sister, don't try to scare me. No one can scare me. I've been in tight spots before . . ."

When Mother tried to say something, he interrupted her. He hinted that he knew what had happened to her husband, and that it would be no trouble to do the same thing to her.

"I know what you mean," Mother said, without changing the tone of her voice. "Nevertheless, as a citizen, I demand justice and my rights."

"Now," he pointed the gun at us: "Now, most loyal and patriotic citizen, you are under arrest. You, too!" He pointed at me with the gun, laughing. We were ordered to turn toward the wall and stand there.

The commission started its official business of searching for something. Comrade Khizhniak, still playing with his gun, seemed to like his business very much. He even looked inside the stove.

After they finished their search in the storage room, Comrade Khizhniak went into the room where Mother kept her clothing and relics in a locked trunk. We soon heard a shot.

Mother and I ran into the room. Comrade Khizhniak was opening the trunk. Not bothering to ask for the key, he destroyed the lock. Mykola, my younger brother, was crying in the corner behind the bed. As Mother and I appeared on the threshold of the room, Khizhniak raised his gun and fired it over our heads. "Stay in your place," he ordered. We left, and he closed the door behind us.

After a while, Comrade Khizhniak came out. In one hand he held a book, in the other, jewels—if this is the right word for the keepsakes of a farm woman. They were mementos of my mother's girlhood.

"Well, Comrade Citizen, will you kindly explain to me what these mean?"

Mother answered; "The book is the Bible and those things are just what you see."

"From whom were you hiding them?" He pointed to his findings. "How did you come by these things?"

"You know those things are mine!" Mother answered angrily.

In vain she tried to explain to him that the Bible had not been hidden; that she had had the jewelry for a long time, from before the revolution, and that in her own house she did not have to hide her own belongings.

"The Bible," Khizhniak said, "had been hidden with the purpose of propagating religion, and the jewels did not belong to you, but to your in-laws. A kurkul will always be a kurkul," he proclaimed meaningfully.

Then he explained that all three of my uncles had been declared kurkuls and arrested. Tomorrow they would be banished from the village and their property expropriated. The commission's "business" in our house was to find anything that my uncles might have hidden in our home. After a thorough search, the commission left.

Confused and frightened, our only thoughts were of Serhiy and our three uncles.

CHAPTER 8

THE NEWS of the arrest of my uncles was a powerful blow. Since the death of my father, they had been our benefactors and protectors. They had helped support us materially, and had taken a keen interest in our welfare. Now we heard that they might be banished from the village, and sent to a distant region. We couldn't understand why such industrious, generous, and upright members of our village would be so treated.

All three of them were farmers. They tilled their fields of fifteen to twenty acres, and managed their households as well as conditions permitted. Only one, Havrylo, seemed to be more prosperous than many other villagers. His house was roofed with tin, a sign of prosperity; he also owned several small auxiliary buildings, and a well-cultivated orchard. These gave the impression that he was a rich man. Yet, he had little more land than the other villagers: skillful management and industry accounted for his prosperity. Following the annual harvest, he worked on the railroad or at highway construction to help support his family.

My other two uncles were also ordinary small farmers. Their thatched-roofed houses and several domestic animals were their only worldly possessions. They and their children went barefoot; their diet consisted of bread and potatoes; and they could not always afford kerosene for their lamps. They did not have the means nor the need to hire workers.

Notwithstanding such evidence of poverty, my three uncles were officially labeled kurkuls and were to be banished from the village. For this reason the commission officials had rummaged through our house, examining every little thing from scraps of paper to pots in the oven. They had been looking for my uncles' valuable. While doing this, they had amused themselves as if they had been performing some heroic deed.

After the commission left, we were allowed to remain at home and were no longer under arrest. However, we could not stay at home, not knowing what had happened to Serhiy and to our three uncles. We assumed Serhiy was in jail. But then he could have been killed on the way or sent immediately to the county center.

Thus it was with our uncles also. We were told that they were about to be banished from the village. But what actually had happened to them, we did not know. We could not help them, but we also could not give up trying.

When Mother and I left the house, the day had already begun to dawn. A dull light appeared on the gray horizon.

Since Uncle Arsin lived closest to us, we decided to visit him first. But when we reached his house, it was already too late; the house was locked and sealed. An armed guard stood at the gate. He informed us that our uncle, his wife, two daughters and son, had been arrested and taken away to the village soviet. They had been allowed to take only the clothing they were wearing.

We decided to follow them, but as we turned back toward the center of the village, a sudden cry—"Help! Help!"—broke the morning stillness. The cry came from the house of an old man, our distant relative, Aleka. Leaving Mother behind, I turned from the road and dashed to his house.

Aleka was a poor farmer who lived alone. Once he had owned a few acres of land and a couple of domestic animals. His wife had died long ago, and his children were married and lived in other villages. But he differed from other villagers because once he had operated a little retail store from his house. His business was only bartering, and we knew that his income was quite meager.

Recently he had sold his store and joined the collective farm. We thought that his age had led him to give up his business, but the officials claimed that he was now trying to cover his past "capitalist activity" and avoid expropriation of his property. They also suspected that he had hoarded a huge sum of money.

When I reached his house, I was not surprised to meet the commission that had left us so recently. The door was open and a few members of the commission were huddled in the entrance hall. The door to the living room was also open.

On the floor lay Aleka, half-naked, vigorously defending himself. A few members of the commission, swearing and shouting, were subduing him. One man pressed his head to the floor; two held his hands; and two struggled with his feet; while another attempted to pull off his boots. There was no doubt that they were after his money. The old man, with surprising strength, fought like a stag against a pack of hounds.

The chairman of the commission, Comrade Khizhniak, meanwhile stood aside, calmly watching the struggle. As the advantage seemed to be on the side of the old man, he lost his patience and temper and elbowed his way to the victim. Then, with the air of practiced experience, he shoved aside the man grappling with Aleka's right leg and jumped on the old man's abdomen with all his weight. Then he kicked his heavy boots into his chin several times. As our relative lost consciousness, Comrade Khizhniak calmly returned to his former position.

The rest of their "business" was done quickly. The boots were removed, and the triumphant officials had found their booty—a few rolls of money wrapped around the unconscious man's ankles. The commission then left. When they were out of sight, Mother and I went to Aleka's aid. He regained consciousness, but he didn't live for long: by evening when we returned, he had died. He was lying in the same place and in the same position as we had left him; there was no one with him. The look of suffering and helplessness on Aleka's face still haunts me.

The morning gray of the east had now spread all over the sky with its warning of snowstorm. It was already light outside, and we still had to go to the homes of my other uncles.

By the time we arrived at Uncle Yakiv's house we were again too late. A guard stood in front of the house. Our uncle's entire family was in the center of the village, the guardsman informed us.

Our Uncle Havrylo's house was in the middle of the village, a few hundred yards from the village government. A guard who stood at his gate told us that we should look for our uncle in the village square. We were again barred from entering the backyard, but we noticed that office furniture was being moved into the building. We were later told that the chairman and the secretary of the village soviet had begun moving into my uncle's house the moment he and his family were arrested.

As we approached the village square, two GPU men barred our way. They ordered us back from where we had come. Mother's pleas to be allowed to look for her son were in vain. Their duty was to keep everyone from the square. But as the soldiers continued their rounds, Mother and I slipped to the side and ran through gardens and orchards toward the square. Soon we reached a fence from which we could see everything that was happening.

It was a sad picture. All the county and local officials who had attended the meeting the day before were gathered around the platform. The county Party commissar sat behind a table covered with bright red cloth, speaking into a specially installed telephone. Flanking him were Thousander Zeitlin and Comrade Pashchenko, the new chairman of the village soviet. On the platform stood GPU and MTS Commissars, facing the square.

Several hundred farmers, women, and children, were milling around in small groups. Screams and laments rose from the crowd; children cried; men loudly protested; the sick and weak ones groaned and called for help.

But no one listened to them, and there was no way out. The square was carefully guarded. Closer examination showed us that it was surrounded by GPU soldiers.

All the arrested villagers were divided into small groups, each assigned to certain spots. Special gunmen, chosen from among komnezam and Komsomol members, watched the groups dutifully.

The military truck that had brought the GPU soldiers stood at a considerable distance from the crowd. Horses were hitched to the sleighs and were ready to be set in motion at any moment.

We quickly sighted our relatives; the three families were gathered together. All of them were standing except for old Uncle Havrylo, who sat on the snow. His wife was sobbing beside him.

A cold wind blew snow on the unfortunates, who were not properly dressed, for they had not been allowed to take warm clothing with them. We wanted to help somehow, and since we could assume that they would be banished to Siberia, we had to get them some heavy clothing.

As I was about to leave for home to gather these things, the noise in the square began to grow louder. The ones who had been sitting stood erect, and the protesting ones raised their voices. The various small groups combined in a spontaneous reaction.

The crowd converged on a line of officials. The guardsmen in front of the officials opened fire once or twice, but the line broke, and the officials disappeared in the mass. Another moment and the square would have been empty. Then, at someone's signal, a machine gun opened fire. Bullets crisscrossed over and through the square. *Vykonavtsi* and GPU soldiers fired their shotguns and rifles; the screams, shouts, and protests mingled with the bursts of firearms.

The crowd gave way, and order was restored. A few dead lay scattered in the square. We learned later that three villagers died there.

After a while, we saw the cause of the outburst. Under careful supervision of soldiers, a score of sleighs moved into the square. They were to take the arrested farmers out of the village. Loading of six to eight persons to a sleigh started immediately, controlled through the use of a list. Kinship, age, sex, and health were not taken into consideration. As a result, husbands were separated from their wives, and children from their parents. The old and sick had to share sleighs with strangers.

As one sleigh moved to join a column, a young man sprang from it and raced toward another sleigh in which his helpless and weeping wife and children were riding. The father obviously wanted to be with his family, but he did not reach them. Comrade Pashchenko, the chairman of the village soviet who was supervising the whole action, raised his revolver and calmly fired. The young father dropped dead into the snow, and the sleigh carrying his widow and orphans moved on.

The loading took about half an hour. Some fifty sleighs lined up one after another, with the leading one pointed toward the district seat. Military wagons armed with the machine guns were placed at the front, in the middle, and at the end of the sleigh train. One civilian gunman was assigned to every two or three sleighs. Some militiamen and GPU men followed the train on horseback.

The commissars and the village officials happily chatted among themselves as this parade passed the speakers' platform. The dead still lay in the road, frightening the horses.

As soon as the last wagon left the square, we went to the Village Soviet hoping to find Serhiy, but we could not see him. We were only told that his case would soon come up for trial in the kolhosp court.[13]

The news of the fate of my uncles and their fellow prisoners returned with the empty sleighs. A freight train had been waiting for them at the railroad station. There they were herded into the box cars. We did not learn what happened to them after that until much later.

[13]Kolhosp court was one of the irregular courts set up in Ukrainian villages during the collectivization. At first they acted as comradely courts, and their jurisdiction never exceeded petty offenses. The kolhosp court was supervised by the village soviet. But during the peak of collectivization, the kolhosp courts acted as regular courts of law with the reservation that cases of political nature, or serious crimes, were referred to higher courts of law or to the security organs. Often, if not all the time, the entire kolhosp court proceeding was conducted by the secretary of the village Party organization.

CHAPTER 9

A FEW DAYS after the arrest of Serhiy, Mother was summoned to appear before the kolhosp court as a witness. The official summons stated that the trial was to take place the following Sunday, at the very beginning of March, and that the name of the defendant was Serhiy.

This was terrifying news. The officials had enlisted Mother's aid in the trial of her own son. As a witness, she would have to tell the story of the struggle between Serhiy and Comrade Khizhniak. We knew the true reason for the struggle would be ignored during the trial, since any resistance to Communist officials was considered an act of treason, even if it was an act of self-defense.

The following Sunday, we left the house to start for what had been until recently a church. It was snowing and bitterly cold.

The theater was already crowded to capacity, and the court was in session. A *vykonavets* was waiting for Mother. She could not stay inside while the court was in session, he told her, shoving her back to the door. As a witness for the court, she had to wait elsewhere until she was called. I wanted to stay with her, but she had to stay alone.

As I stayed inside, what struck me first was the silence. Indeed, it was still like being in church. The people sat solemnly, looking straight ahead without any emotion. All heads were bared as they always had been during church services in the past.

The next thing that attracted my attention was the extensive interior decoration, if this is the correct description. A kerosene lamp glimmered in the center of the ceiling where once had hung a crystal chandelier. On walls, once adorned with icons and religious art, portraits of Party and government leaders now hung. Above the former altar, in place of the painting of the Last Supper, hung a huge red-inked placard: "RELIGION IS THE OPIATE OF THE MASSES." The sanctuary had been transformed into a sort of stage and the platform was liberally decorated with red cloth.

I had never watched a trial before. In fact, we had never had one in our village. We knew that there was a so-called People's Court with its seat in the county center, but we never had close contact with it. Our village community had managed to solve its own problems without enlisting the help of outsiders.

It was midnight when my brother's case was announced. Two militiamen brought him into the theater. He had changed dramatically in those few days. He looked dirty and exhausted, and all could see that he had been beaten. He had black eyes and on his lips and over his face traces of blood were visible. His hands were tied behind his back. Walking toward the bench reserved for the defendants, Serhiy looked around, probably searching for Mother and me. Then he was ordered to take his place.

The kolhosp court, according to the official line, was the supreme expression of the people's will and justice. We saw the Party representative, Thousander Zeitlin, commanding the court ruthlessly, as if he were a judge. When my brother's case was announced, Comrade Zeitlin rose to speak first. The strangers who were supposed to have been the kolhosp court kept silent. Always in the past, Comrade Zeitlin's talk was utterly divorced from reality, and, specifically, from the matter at hand. We braced ourselves for a long speech. But, to our surprise he quickly announced the nature of Serhiy's offense. As we expected, Serhiy was accused of physical assault on Comrade Knizhniak, the chairman of our Hundred. But we learned from Comrade Zeitlin that he was also accused of assault on the militiamen. His "crime" had multiplied since we saw him last. These were, we knew, serious accusations, for attached to them was Comrade Zeitlin's statement that the assaults on the officials "took place while the latter were performing their official duties." The circumstances surrounding these events were not mentioned.

Having pronounced the indictment, Comrade Zeitlin immediately started the interrogation.

"What right did you have to prevent the action of the Party and government representative?" was his first question to my brother.

Serhiy tried to explain that he had not assaulted anyone; he had only grasped the arm of Comrade Khizhniak to prevent the shooting of his mother, a natural instinct, and a moral duty of a son. But this made no impression on either Comrade Zeitlin or the strangers.

"Don't pull the wool over my eyes," Comrade Zeitlin sneered. "Now, give an answer, yes or no: did you grasp the arm of Comrade Khizhniak?"

"Yes and no; it depends on how you look at it," said Serhiy.

"Yes or no?" persisted Comrade Zeitlin.

"No," answered Serhiy. He once again related what had taken place in our home.

But the interrogator was concerned only with the fact that officials had been physically deterred from doing their duty. The interrogation continued, and as it progressed, we heard Serhiy reluctantly repeating "Yes."

During the interrogation, we learned the cause of the black eyes of Serhiy and his alleged assault on the militiaman. My brother had happened to have a pocketwatch with him in the village jail. It had belonged to our late father, and Serhiy treasured it most dearly. This pocketwatch had attracted the attention one of the militiamen who was on duty in the jail. He offered favorable treatment to Serhiy in exchange for the watch. My brother said no. Next, the militiaman offered him food. Serhiy again refused. Then he was called out of his cell in the night and ordered to give up the watch. When he refused, a fight started between him and the militiaman. Both were thoroughly bruised before the colleagues of the latter helped subdue Serhiy. The blackened eyes and swollen nose were damning evidence in court. No one mentioned the whereabouts of the watch.

Comrade Zeitlin now addressed the militiaman who had been guarding Serhiy. "Comrade Militiaman, turn around and face the audience!"

The man did so, and the audience noticed the bruises below his eyes. Comrade Zeitlin then stood up and addressed the court:

"What you see now on the face of Comrade Militiaman is the second assault on a Party and government official, also perpetrated while the assaulted was performing his official duty. The assailant is here, before the People's Court, comrades. I assure you, comrades, this enemy of the people won't escape the people's justice."

This was all he said, but we understood that my brother's fate was sealed. Serhiy knew that too, and he was visibly nervous. He looked frantically around as if trying to find some sort of help.

Next came the witness to the first alleged assault. This was something new, for in all previous cases there had been no witnesses. Comrade Khizhniak was called first. He too, had to answer just "Yes" or "No."

"Did the accused struggle with you, Comrade Khizhniak?"

"Yes."

"Did the accused grasp your arm as you were performing your official duty?"

"Yes."

"Did the accused know that you were an official representative of the Party and government?"

"Yes."

"Did the accused obey your order when you ordered him to leave you alone?"

"No."

"Did you feel physical pain inflicted by the accused?"

There were many other questions put to Comrade Khizhniak. All of them were answered by "Yes" or "No."

Comrade Khizhniak was followed as a witness by the woman who had been present that night as a member of the commission.

"Did the accused struggle with your chairman, Comrade Khizhniak?"

"Yes."

"Did the accused know that your chairman and all the members of the commission, yourself included, were the official representatives of the Party and government?"

"Yes."

The militiaman was then called on the second account. He was ordered by Comrade Zeitlin to face the audience.

"Who inflicted those injuries on you?" was the first question.

"The defendant."

"Did the accused cause you physical pain?"

"Yes."

"Did he know you were a government official?"

"Yes."

"Did he strike you?"

"Many times."

A second militiaman was called to the witness stand. He also was to answer "Yes" or "No."

"Did you see the accused striking the militiaman?"

"Yes."

When my Mother was called as a witness, she appeared calm and determined. Comrade Zeitlin warned her that false testimony would be severely punished under the law, and that only "Yes" and "No" answers would be acceptable.

"Before I answer any question, I would like to know whether I am at a Party conference or in a court?" Mother asked.

This was quite unexpected, especially so for Comrade Zeitlin. Such a question was unheard of. No one could dare to question the merit or wisdom of a Party leader whether he might be small or big. Mother, of course, did not realize then that by daring to ask such questions she worsened Serhiy's plight.

"In a court," quickly answered Comrade Zeitlin.

"If so, then why should I, or anybody else for that matter, answer you, a Party official, and not a judge?" she asked him bluntly.

A murmur rushed through the audience.

Comrade Zeitlin did not let us wait long for a response, and the answer was much less of a surprise than the question.

"Inasmuch as I am a representative of the Party and government here, I am also a representative of the law as well," he briefly stated, then turned to the judge and ordered him to proceed.

But my mother stood her ground again, this time protesting against the unjust treatment of her son. All this time, Serhiy sat with his hands still bound behind his back, obviously in severe pain.

These remarks made in Serhiy's behalf only touched off laughter on the part of Comrade Zeitlin. He then limited her to "Yes" and "No" answers.

"Was the chairman of your Hundred in your house?"

"Yes."

"Did your son, Serhiy, grasp the arm of Comrade Khizhniak, who was performing his official duty in your house?"

"But . . ."

"Yes or no?" demanded Comrade Zeitlin, angrily looking at her.

"He grasped it, but . . ." But Mother could not say what she wanted. Comrade Zeitlin turned toward the judge and said something to him.

Mother then sensed what was happening, rose, and shouted that her son was only protecting her life.

But it was too late. The judge announced that the court had collected enough evidence to show the guilt of the defendant. He then ordered Mother to leave the stand. She broke into tears and rushed to embrace Serhiy, but the officials ordered the militiamen to remove her forcibly from the theater-courtroom.

The court then proceeded to broaden the accusations against Serhiy. Comrade Zeitlin called him a counterrevolutionary, an enemy of the people, and demanded that his case be submitted to the higher court and to the security agencies. Everything was done as Comrade Zeitlin ordered.

Serhiy was escorted from court by two militiamen. It was the last time we saw him. All the convicted were taken away from the village the following morning. None returned.

After two years had passed, we received an anonymous letter. The unknown writer informed us that Serhiy had died from torture and exhaustion while digging the Baltic Sea–White Sea Canal.[14]

---

[14]Baltic Sea–White Sea Canal is a canal connecting the White Sea with the Baltic. It was built in 1931–1933, mainly by Ukrainian farmers who were branded kurkuls and banished to the forced labor camps situated along the building sites of the canal. The majority of those farmers died from exposure, starvation, and hard labor.

CHAPTER 10

AFTER THE ARREST of my brother and my three uncles and their families, our lives became harsh and grim. We felt lonelier and more afraid than ever before. Previously, we knew we would have the advice and support of our uncles. And there was Serhiy, strong and intelligent, the man of the house. We were now alone, without any relatives.

But we were never left alone by the village officials. We felt their constant presence like a heavy weight. Evening or morning, day or night, they were always with us.

We continually had to visit Hundreds, Tens, and Fives, and listen to long speeches about the merits of collective farms. We had to undergo strenuous interrogations about why we hadn't joined the collective farm, and about our possessions.

There was no end to the officials' visits to our home. The Bread Procurement Commission would come almost every day. The propagandist and the agitator would drop in to tell us repeatedly how wonderful life would be on a collective farm. They would also have a word to say about the merit of delivering foodstuff to the state. The official of the Ten would come to plead with us to join the collective farm, for otherwise he would be considered a saboteur. The latter had scarcely left the house, when the Five's official would visit us with the same plea. With tears in his eyes, he would tell us that if we would not join the collective farm, he might be banished from the village.

Then a group of Pioneers would visit our house. They also had been given the assignment of collectivizing a certain number of households. The Pioneers would be followed by a group of members of the Komsomol, and the latter by a group from the Komnezam. Sometimes a group of teachers or farmers from the neighboring villages would come. And so on without end. All of them had the same task—to collectivize us and take our food away.

One afternoon at the beginning of March 1930, my mother was called to our Hundred. Comrade Khizhniak was there, sitting at the table alone and playing with his gun. He did not greet us or ask us to take a seat.

While we stood in front of him, he slowly and carefully took his gun apart. When this was done, he started cleaning it, wiping it with a piece of cloth. Still we remained standing, not knowing what to do.

After a while, he started to reassemble his gun. Having inserted the last bullet, he finally lifted his head, and smiling, raised the gun and aimed it at my mother.

"Ha, ha, ha," he laughed, "glad to see you!"

"What is it that you want today?" Mother asked him, ignoring his gun and his laugh. Strangely, she was not alarmed. Neither was I.

Now he became serious. His wrinkled face contorted into an ugly knot. He seemed to be shocked at this question. Slowly he laid his gun on the table.

"My wish is the wish of the Communist Party and the Soviet government! Is that clear?" he shouted.

"Yes, I have never doubted it," Mother answered.

"Now, my most loyal Soviet citizen," he continued sarcastically, "I have heard that you haven't yet joined the collective farm. I just can't believe that."

He stopped for a moment, but as soon as Mother started to say something, he went on in a serious tone:

"You aren't going to wage war against us, are you?"

Then he picked up his gun and again started to play with it. First he looked into its barrel. Then he took out the ejector rod and started to poke it in his ears. After a while, he put it back, and then looked at us.

"We have this kind of thing," he waved with his gun. "Do you?"

And then he started to laugh again.

"It's funny—ha, ha, ha," he laughed. "She wants to fight! Ha, ha, ha!"

Abruptly he became sullen. He gazed at the gun motionlessly. Then he was laughing again. He laughed louder and louder. Then he jumped from his chair and, as if playing Russian roulette, he spun the drum, and put the muzzle to his temple. We watched.

"Ha, ha, ha," he laughed happily. "Would you like to see me pull the trigger?"

We kept silent—which probably irritated him, for suddenly he stopped laughing.

"If you do not join the collective farm immediately," he shouted like a madman, "I will kill you with my own gun!"

"With who else's?" Mother retorted calmly.

This remark enraged him. Keeping his gun in a firing position, he ran out from behind the table and, breathing heavily, stopped in front of us.

"I'll kill you," he raved. As if to prove that he meant what he said, he started shooting into the ceiling.

This was quite a show. But somehow we were not afraid. Mother, composed as ever, stood quietly. Comrade Khizhniak was apparently surprised by her calmness and self-control. After firing at the ceiling, he seemed not to know what to do next. At first, he started to pack his gun with new bullets, then he put the gun into the holster. Then he took it out again and laid it on the table. Afterwards he took it off the table, spun the drum, and then counted the bullets. Finally, he put the gun into his holster, and ran out of the room.

We continued standing for a while. Mother finally yielded to my persistent requests to sit down and took a place on the bench. However, as soon as she did so, a stranger entered the room as if he had been waiting for that moment.

No doubt he was a city dweller, and he definitely was not a Ukrainian for he could hardly speak a word of Ukrainian. We did not need to be told that he was a new propagandist. He was tall and well fed, with a pale face.

"Are you comfortable?" he asked my mother almost politely. I started to think that we finally had met a pleasant official.

"You seem to enjoy sitting there . . ." he said, looking down at Mother, who remained seated. Then, without waiting for Mother's reply, he suddenly shouted:

"Get up, you dirty *muzhichka!*[15] I'll teach you how to meet a representative of the Communist Party and government!"

[15]*Muzhichka* is a derogatory Russian word meaning a poor, ignorant peasant woman.

Mother might have been expecting the outburst, because I saw no traces of surprise on her face. Slowly she got up. But in the corners of her eyes, I noticed tears. She had been insulted.

The propagandist sat down at Comrade Khizhniak's place and crossed his legs. He let us stand. Slowly and deliberately, he lit an expensive cigarette which he took out of his case and stared at us coldly. Then he pulled his revolver out of his holster and put it on the table.

"All right," he said, looking at us contemptuously. "What do you want?"

This was an unexpected question. We certainly didn't want anything from him.

"This is what I want to ask you," Mother said. "You called me here, and I suppose you will tell me what you want from me."

He jumped to his feet.

"Don't you know why you were called here?" he shouted.

"How should I know?" was Mother's answer.

His anger grew into rage. With all his might, he struck the table with his fists. His gun flew into the air from the impact and landed on the floor. He quickly grabbed it, checked it for damage, and then pointed it at Mother.

"I'll kill you!" he raved like a lunatic.

But we were somehow neither impressed nor scared, probably because in the last few months we had endured so many terrifying experiences that we had grown indifferent to new threats.

For a moment, the propagandist seemed not to know what to do with the gun aimed at Mother. Then he lowered it and fired into the floor. This seemed to calm him down. Without saying a word, he went behind the table and took his previous place. For a moment he was silent. Then he lit another cigarette, and started again the same kind of interrogation as before.

Suddenly the door flew open and my younger brother burst in. He breathlessly told us that the Bread Procurement Commission had entered our house by force and had taken away whatever solid food they could find. Ignoring the propagandist who, of course, tried to stop us, we ran home as fast as we could, but it was too late. When we arrived, the members of the commission were loading the cart with the grain and other food we had had in reserve. It was not much, but it would have been enough for the three of us to survive on until the new harvest. Comrade Khizhniak stood near the door, playing with his gun and smiling. His smile told us that he had outwitted us.

So we were left without food, except for some potatoes and beets buried in the ground, and we would have to wait three more months for the new crop. There was no other source from which we could obtain the necessary food.

A few hours after the commission left us, following the cart containing our grain and other food, the Ten's official visited us. He said that if we had joined the collective farm earlier, this would never have happened to us. After all, we were not kurkuls. We still would have had our bread.

"Oh, that reminds me," he said casually, on leaving our house. "The members of the collective farm receive payment for their labor in food." Saying this, he looked down at his feet, as if he were ashamed of what he was saying. "Therefore, you still have a chance to survive if you join the collective farm." He was right; there was no other alternative for us.

We did not talk much that evening. As if knowing our decision, the commission woke us up in the middle of the night. The propagandist who had interrogated us the day before was in charge. Without any formalities, he asked Mother whether she wanted to join the collective farm. She said: "Yes." He then sat down at the table under our icons and wrote the petition for her. As I recall, it said:

Whereas the collective farm has advantages over individual farming; and whereas it is the only way to secure a prosperous and happy life, I voluntarily request the collective farm's management to accept me as a member of your collective farm.

Signature.

That was all. Mother silently signed it. The propagandist was all smiles while the members of the commission stood huddled in the corner as if they were at a funeral.

The next day, some people arrived in our backyard. Without any explanation, they entered the stable and barn and took away our horse, cow, wagon, plough, and other agricultural implements. Only after the loaded wagon departed, drawn by our own horse and followed by our cow, did a man enter our house. He informed us that we were now registered under the number 168, and that in the future, we should identify ourselves by this number.

Thus we became a mere number—number 168.

CHAPTER 11

A VILLAGE messenger, walking from house to house, informed us that we had to attend the village general meeting on the following Sunday afternoon. Another messenger summoned us to the Hundred meeting which was to take place on the same Sunday evening.

Two meetings in one day could only mean that something extraordinary was in the offing. We had no idea what it could be, but at this point we could anticipate nothing but arrests, banishments, and even executions. When that Sunday came and the two meetings were over, our worst fears had become a reality for many. The victims, however, were not the ordinary villagers, but the village officials.

The general meeting took place in the village theater, formerly our church. Most of the officials on the stage were people we had never seen before. All of them were solemn, even grim. Comrade Zeitlin opened the meeting and introduced the strangers to us. The regional Party representative was first. The rest of them were the highest Party and government county functionaries: the Party county commissar, the commissar of the MTS, the commissar of GPU, and the chairman of the county Soviet executive committee. We had already heard about this quintet, for rumors had spread among the villagers that these men traveled throughout the county arresting people for no apparent reason.

Comrade Representative spoke first. The gist of his speech is as follows: a stray ant is of no account; it can become lost in its search for food; it may be mercilessly crushed by someone, as a nuisance, or destroyed by other means. Who cares about a stray, single ant? What really counts is the anthill, for in it the ant's life is protected and perpetuated. The ants manage to survive only because they live in a close-knit and well-organized ant society. An ant is inconceivable without that society. So it is with human beings: alone, they are helpless; they can be exploited, persecuted, forgotten, or destroyed. Only in the Communist society can an individual find happiness, prosperity, and freedom. The collective farm is everything; the individual is nothing! The collective farm is the first step toward this Communist society; therefore, we all must join it! The Party so orders, and the Party knows what is best for farmers. There is no choice.

After speaking for about an hour, he finished by shouting a widely used Communist slogan: "He who is not with us is against us." Loud applause followed as he went back to his chair.

The county Party commissar then came forward. He told us that our village had fallen behind in meeting its quotas of collectivization and grain delivery. This happened only because the enemies of the people (whom he called "hyenas") had gotten the upper hand in the village. The entire country was joyfully building the socialist society, industrializing and collectivizing, delivering grain and subscribing to state bonds, and competing for speedier fulfillment of quotas. Meanwhile, our village was permitting certain enemies of the people to take a dominating position and sabotage the Party's policy. The Party had uncovered these heinous deeds and would punish these degenerates. We sat silent and stunned. Our breaths were caught in our throats as we waited for these enemies of the people to be identified.

The commissar of the GPU came to the rostrum. He started to look over some papers he held in his hands. Then, taking them in his left hand, he placed his right hand on the holster of his revolver, fixed his eyes upon us, and began to speak.

"I haven't come here to make a speech. I came here to do my job. You have heard Comrade County Commissar of the Party. He told you that your village is in the hands of the enemies of the people. I came here to help you root out these enemies and make this village a socialist community."

He paused and again started checking the papers. Then he cleared his throat and declared:

"According to our reliable sources, your village is in the hands of the most undesirable elements. . . ." At this point, he raised his head, assumed a military bearing, and shouted in a loud voice: "The Chairman of the Eighth Hundred step forward!"

A bearded man, wearing an overcoat of homespun cloth, stood up and approached the stage.

"In the name of the workers and peasants and in the name of Soviet justice, I am arresting you for sabotaging the fulfillment of collectivization in your Hundred," the GPU commissar declared solemnly.

The man looked around in bewilderment and started to say something, but was ignored. Comrade Commissar went on, ordering the chairman of the Second Hundred to come forward. This was Stepan Koshmak, who was despised for his brutal handling of his fellow farmers. We now learned that in spite of his efforts, the Hundred had fallen behind in meeting the state's collectivization and grain delivery quotas.

Comrade Koshmak also tried to say something, but he was overruled. The commissar then called upon and arrested two other victims: the chairmen of the Third and Fifth Hundreds.

To our great surprise, he also arrested the chairman of the village soviet, Comrade Pashchenko. I already mentioned that he was a member of the Communist Party and had been appointed to his post in our village by the Party Organization and government of our county. Now this same Pashchenko was being arrested for failure to collectivize our village! The commissar maintained that Pashchenko (the commissar did not address him as comrade anymore), used his official position to sabotage Party and government policy in the village.

We were even more surprised when the Commissar mentioned the name of Comrade Ryabokin, the chairman of the collective farm and member of the Party.

"As Commissar of the GPU," he announced, "I arrest you for failing to prove the advantage of collective farming over that of individual farming; for letting many horses starve to death; for letting the implements rust; and for failing to prepare for spring planting."

After that, Comrade Commissar turned and left the stage. Two GPU soldiers entered from the side door of the stage. They quickly approached the arrested men and led them out without any resistance. Thereupon, Comrade Zeitlin closed the meeting. It was snowing outside and very cold.

A few hours later, at about seven o'clock in the evening, we arrived at yet another meeting—that of our Hundred. The officials came late.

Among them was the Party regional representative. We were "honored" by such a distinguished visitor because we served as a model Hundred which Comrade Zeitlin loved to show to official visitors.

The meeting started as soon as the officials arrived. Comrade Khizhniak, bursting with pride, called the meeting to order and announced that Comrade Zeitlin would speak. Comrade Zeitlin then introduced the representative to us. He pointed out to us that his presence among us should be an incentive. It should be reciprocated by greater participation in socialist competition for the speedy fulfillment of the collectivization and grain delivery quotas.

To our surprise, the representative repeated the same speech he had made a few hours ago at the previous meeting we had attended, almost word for word. Then Comrade Zeitlin arose and announced that Comrade Khizhniak had the podium. Instinctively, we knew that the time for some of us had run out. Comrade Khizhniak appeared elated by the attention his superiors were paying him in allowing him to conduct the meeting.

Usually drunk and cynical, but now sober and outwardly composed, he was trying hard to be at his best. A rumor was circulating among the villagers that during one of his drinking bouts, he had challenged Comrade Judas to a bet: he would become commissar of the county Party organization sooner than Comrade Judas would become a commissar of the GPU. This was probably the reason why he now was trying so hard to impress his superiors by behaving not as a farmer, but as an urbanite.

However, no matter how much he showed off in front of the representative, he did not succeed in his objective. First, he was paying too much attention to the representative. This was a fatal miscalculation on his part. Comrade Zeitlin considered his behavior an affront to himself. After all, as a Thousander, he was a representative of the Central Committee of the Communist Party of Ukraine. Then, as soon as he opened his mouth to start his speech, Khizhniak made his second error: he became more like a politician. He addressed the women first! To be sure he addressed them as "comrade women," but he put them ahead of the representative, whom he addressed as second in line, and ahead of Comrade Zeitlin who was placed third.

Comrade Zeitlin jumped to his feet and interrupted Khizhniak:

"Comrades," he said in a surly voice, "as a representative of the Central Committee, it is my duty to correct Comrade Khizhniak." He disdainfully pointed out that addressing women first was considered by the Party to be a remnant of the past and a sign of decadence. The Communist Revolution made women free and equal with men, thus no preference should be given to them. Comrade Zeitlin ended his interruption by expressing the hope that Comrade Khizhniak would apologize for his error, and with that he sat down.

The representative just sat there, blowing smoke rings, seemingly unperturbed by all these proceedings. Comrade Khizhniak looked at Comrade Zeitlin as if pleading for mercy. The latter nodded condescendingly. Khizhniak thereupon turned to the audience and mumbled his apology. He was sorry that he let his Communist vigilance relax. He assured all of us that he would never again repeat that decadent capitalist custom of addressing women first. Then he raised his paper and started reading his speech.

To our complete amazement, Comrade Khizhniak actually repeated the entire speech of the representative, including his anthill theory, and the slogan "He who is not with us is against us!" Finally came the subject we were expecting: there were enemies of the people among us; they took over some Tens and Fives, and while in their official positions, they kept sabotaging the brilliant Party policy in our Hundred and in the entire village.

At the end of his speech, Khizhniak took a paper from the table, glanced at it, and then shouted:

"Leader of the First Ten, step forward!" While the poor wretch made his way to the table, he announced:

"In the name of the Soviet People, I have the honor of arresting you for sabotaging the fulfillment of the collectivization and grain delivery quotas in your Ten."

In like manner, he arrested six more people, among them four leaders of Tens and two of Fives. The leader of our Five, who so eagerly wanted us to join the collective farm, was among them.

As the last man was called, the door was flung open, and a GPU soldier appeared on the threshold with a rifle over his shoulder. As soon as Comrade Khizhniak finished reading from the list, the *vykonavets* stepped toward the arrested leaders and pointed at the door. They were still filing by the official table when Comrade Representative finished his cigarette and stood up. Comrade Zeitlin followed him, leaving the task of closing the meeting to Comrade Khizhniak, which the latter hurriedly did.

As we came outside, two sleighs were disappearing into the darkness of the winter night. One was loaded with the arrested leaders; the other with the officials. The next morning we found out that similar arrests had taken place throughout the village. From five to seven individuals were arrested in each Hundred. Since there were eight Hundreds altogether, more than fifty people had been taken away from the village in a single night.

We didn't feel any sympathy for most of the arrested officials, but we didn't feel jubilant either. Those people were purged as scapegoats. That much was clear. But did this mean the end of all purges? Who would be next on the list?

What actually happened next was totally unforeseen. More than two weeks passed without a single meeting. As one meetingless day followed another, conflicting rumors started circulating. Some said that the Party and government had abandoned the policy of collectivization, and would leave the farmers alone. It was also rumored that Comrade Zeitlin had left for the capital city for new instructions. Others alleged that the officials wanted to leave us alone until new jails and concentration camps were prepared for those who still refused to join the collective farms.

The most dedicated Communist activists and officials had disappeared from the village scene. Comrade Zeitlin, we also found out, had actually been summoned to the county center, but we did not know what had happened to Comrade Khizhniak, Khomenko, and others of their kind. No one had seen them in the village since the last meeting. To us it was becoming obvious that something important was soon to take place.

It was said that Stalin had recently written and spoken in defense of farmers. In his article entitled "Dizziness From Success," he attacked local Party functionaries and activists for their overzealousness in implementing collectivization. It was rumored that he had ordered a slowdown of collectivization, and that he would even permit farmers to leave collective farms if they chose to do so. Such a rumor was hard to believe, though, for just recently we had been told at our meetings that Stalin had decided to carry through a program of compulsory collectivization by the first of May, no matter what the cost in human and material sacrifices would be. We were also informed that Stalin had announced a policy of elimination of the kurkuls as a social class.

In compliance with this, the government passed a law which made it legal to banish the kurkuls from their villages and send them into exile. Could it really be possible that he had changed his mind in such a short time?

Many of our villagers did not believe these rumors, and expected the worst. However, the general hatred of collectivization and of the Party henchmen was so great that many indulged in wishful thinking and accepted these rumors as truth. All this uncorroborated information made the villagers fearful and angry.

"Where are those cutthroats?" was a question one could often hear muttered, or exhortations like, "Let's get those damned cutthroats!" "Let's get our horses and cows back from that cursed collective farm!"

No one would have dared to utter such words before; now they could be heard everywhere. The villagers were ready to fight and even kill if necessary. Indeed, a few days later, we saw two fires a distance away at the other end of the village. Later we learned that the headquarters of the Seventh Hundred had burned to the ground. Then the news spread that the villagers were storming the homes of the activists and village officials. We also heard that somebody had attempted to burn down the building of the village soviet; that windows had been smashed in the village club (the propaganda center); and that the telephone connection with the county center had been cut off. More than a kilometer of telephone wire was missing.

Then one night, the first murder occurred. Somebody ambushed Comrade Judas and beat him to death. Curious, as teenagers are, I ran to the place where his body had been discovered. It was still there. He was lying in a shallow gutter at the village main road. His priestly beard was singed, and his face was badly burned. The chasuble he always used to wear was missing. On a piece of newspaper attached to his chest, scrawled in slanting capitals, were the words: "A CUR'S DEATH FOR A CUR!" Finally, at the end of March 1930, we received summons to a Hundred meeting. The meeting hall was decorated in the usual way. The red banner hung on the front wall. From the ceiling was suspended a red streamer with the slogan: "Death to the enemies of the people!" The rostrum beneath it and the official table were draped in red cloth.

At the appointed time, a stranger appeared at the door with one of the members of the village soviet. The talking and the noise subsided. The village soviet member took a piece of paper from his breast pocket, walked up to the improvised speakers' rostrum, and called for silence.

"Before we proceed with the agenda," he read slowly, "I want to introduce to you our Party representative, Comrade Rymarenko."

The audience showed its contempt. A man burst out laughing. Some women began to giggle. But the disruptions didn't last long, and the audience soon quieted down.

The representative was shocked by such a greeting and visibly irritated. He stared around as if seeking assistance. Then he made a gesture of resignation with his arms.

"This is how you welcome your Party representative?" he asked in a low voice. He paused for a short time, looking down at his boots, as if trying to figure out what to do with the offenders. Then he pulled himself together and gave us a warning in a cold and brittle voice:

"As a Party representative, I will not have the Communist Party held up to ridicule." He stopped for a moment, holding the audience's attention with his hypnotic stare. "Laughter and giggling," he continued, "are among the well-known ways the enemies of the people disrupt constructive meetings of Soviet patriots. . . ."

These were familiar words, but we were not ready for them at that particular evening gathering. We had come to the meeting determined to stand up for our rights; to witness the defeat of the local Party functionaries; and to hear the proclamation of a new policy—anything but collectivization! Instead, we met a completely unknown individual—a stranger who bullied us even before we found out who he was. That was too much for us. Spontaneously, pandemonium broke out: everybody began talking and shouting at the top of their voices; I also heard heavy stomping of feet somewhere behind me.

But the representative seemed caught off guard only for a moment by this outburst. He just stood behind the table, playing nervously with his pencil. After staring at the table for a moment, he raised his head and his commanding voice cut through the hubbub.

"I've had enough of you!" he bellowed. His nervous tension had disappeared, and his voice rang out with self-assurance: "I'm acting here on the direct orders of the county Party organization. Anyone who opposes this meeting is against the Party policy. Anyone who insults me insults the Party, for I'm the Party's representative here, whether you like it or not!" His words were as sharp as a razor.

We got the message. A breathless and oppressive quiet fell over the audience. It was a terrifying moment for all of us. Our hope for change was quashed.

To end the embarrassing situation, the member of the village soviet hurriedly proceeded with the formal aspects of the meeting. He asked the audience to elect the chairman and secretary of the meeting, as was general practice. However, no one seemed to be anxious for this honor. All kept silent, as if conspiring to do so, and no one named any candidate to chair and conduct the meeting. This was an unforeseen and tense state of affairs.

The representative stood in front of the audience and continued toying with his pencil. From time to time he would glance indignantly at the member of the village soviet as if reproaching him for his inability to control the people. Seeing that the situation was becoming more critical, he stepped forward. As before, he threw his hands up into the air (this gesture seemed to be his trademark), then he fixed his piercing eyes upon us and remarked casually in a low voice: "People who are against me always regret it sooner or later." He paused, viewing the audience to see what impression his words were making, and then he continued "That applies to you, too, just in case you wish to disregard the fact that I am a representative of the Communist Party." Then he added in the same low tone of voice, but emphasizing each word: "Anyone, I repeat, anyone who opposes the Party deserves to be eliminated!"

His words had the desired effect. The stillness was awesome. No one laughed or spoke. Everyone was mute, unable and afraid to utter any protest.

"These people of yours," he then addressed his companion loudly so that everyone would be able to hear him, "these people are not able, or simply don't want to take advantage of the democracy which is being given to them by the Communist Party."

He paused, expecting a response to his remark, but none came. All were sitting meekly like children in front of a dictatorial father, their attention riveted on him.

Comrade Representative cleared his throat.

"Comrade, proceed with the agenda without any formalities," he ordered his companion who now had to conduct the meeting himself, without an elected chairman and secretary. This he did. After a moment of hesitation, he announced that Comrade Representative was to make a speech. The latter was already heading toward the rostrum.

As mentioned previously, Comrade Representative was a stranger in the village. We did not know who he was or what his occupation was. But we could tell that he wasn't one of us and that he wasn't a laborer—he was a city dweller, like all other newcomers to our village. He was clean, well fed, and dressed in good taste, as far as I could judge. One could easily sense that he resented us, as if we were to blame that he found himself stuck in our village. As he approached the rostrum and raised his head to address us, I had a chance to better scrutinize his physical appearance, noticing that he had a huge nose, and a mouth with thin lips which he was constantly moving as if finishing a tasty meal.

Judging from his previous bullying tactics, we didn't expect to hear anything pleasant from Comrade Representative's speech. But then, as he began, we just couldn't believe our ears! Was this the same man who had spoken to us just a few minutes before? It was unbelievable! He had changed completely, like a chameleon. His tone had become smooth and warm; his manner modest; and he even smiled from time to time.

At first he talked in very general terms so that sometimes it was difficult for us to understand him. The gist of what he said, as far as I could remember, was that men were fallible creatures and prone to make mistakes easily. Several times he repeated the axioms that to err is human, and that one learns as long as one lives. He asked us to show understanding for those who had erred and to be generous to those in need. This certainly sounded like a church sermon, and we were beginning to realize why. As he continued, we became more and more convinced with each word that the rumors about Stalin's article were true. And, before long, he had told us everything.

"A lot of things have been happening lately," he recited. "Some of them good; some not so good."

Thereupon he launched into a lengthy recital of the good things that had happened. He repeated phrases which we knew by heart. Then, changing his tone to a lower key, he went on to expose what he termed were the "not so good." Here, for the first time, he mentioned Stalin and his article, "Dizziness From Success." In fact, without much ado, he announced that he was going to read it, and he did.

He read it slowly, word for word, as if he were afraid to leave out a single sentence.

We learned, as we listened to Stalin's article, that collectivization was a great success; more than fifty percent of the farmers in the USSR were collectivized. What this meant was that the Five-Year Plan for Collectivization of Agriculture was doubled. But then, to our disbelief, we heard that this success was not success at all for it was achieved by means of distortion of the Party line: the principle of voluntary collectivization had been violated and coercive measures had been applied. As a result, some middle-class and local poor farmers fell into the ranks of kurkuls. Brutal and criminal actions were often employed against them by the Party officials. The farmers were victimized through robbery, expropriation of property, and arrest. A compulsory collectivization of farm dwellings and farm animals such as goats, sheep, hogs, and domestic fowl had been carried out. As a consequence of such extortions, collectivization had been discredited, and farmers were hastily withdrawing from collective farms.

We listened with great attention, for our entire existence depended on those words. Not a single soul dared to move, or to utter a sound.

The representative finished reading at last. Without glancing at us, he took his handkerchief and started wiping the perspiration from his forehead. He did it slowly, as if trying to win time, or to figure out what to do next. Still not looking at us, he announced that he was going to read a resolution of the Central Committee of the All-Union Communist Party. Later I found out that this was published in *Pravda* on March 15, 1930. We learned that the Party resolved to stop the compulsory methods of collectivization; to stop the collectivization of farmers' dwellings and their domestic animals; and to make inquiries into the methods of expropriation of kurkuls.

It was hard for us to believe what we had been hearing. Again, there was much confusion. Was it true what the newspaper and the resolution said? What if this whole thing were a trick; a provocation? This was a distinct possibility. Only yesterday, these Party functionaries had used all the brutal means they knew or could devise to herd us into the collective farms. The Central Committee, we were told, had given orders to collectivize all of us before the first of May, at any price! Some of our villagers had lost their lives refusing to yield to the pressure. Thousands of others were labeled kurkuls, evicted from their houses, and banished to concentration camps far away. The majority of us had joined the collective farms as the only way to save our lives.

Now the Central Committee was telling us that it was a mistake; that the local authorities were to be blamed for these excesses because they acted overzealously and distorted the Party line. Where did the truth lie? Who was ultimately to be blamed for the loss of our freedom; for the thousands of deaths; for the destruction of our way of life?

CHAPTER 12

AFTER FINISHING the reading of the resolution, Comrade Representative raised his head and slowly scanned the hall. Then he drank some water, and repeated the previous gesture with his handkerchief.

The assembly was deathly still, all eyes watching him.

"There are things which are difficult to explain," he began haltingly, after looking at the paper he held in his hands. "What I am about to tell you is such a thing."

Then, stuttering, stammering, and often correcting himself, he told us that neither the Party as a whole, nor the Party representatives individually, could be held guilty for the forcible collectivization and for the terror that reigned in the villages throughout Ukraine. No, the Communist Party could not be blamed for these crimes, for it never advocated force or violence.

This statement of his sounded like a sarcastic remark or a bad joke. However, we had learned to take such statements in stride.

He continued: "The real culprits who distorted the Party line and brought so much suffering to your village were the Jews. Yes, it was the Jews who did it; not our dear Communist Party."

This was only the beginning. After some moments of hesitation, he went on explaining that the Jews, generation after generation, had been brought up in the belief that the Ukrainians were anti-Semites, and responsible for terrible and violent atrocities against them. This the Jews could not forgive nor forget. They know how to take revenge. It is a well-known fact, he continued, that the Jews, using the Communist Party as a springboard for their ambitions, have penetrated all branches of central and local governments, especially such branches as security and justice. Our local GPU, he pointed out, was entirely in their hands. They have been using these official positions for their own benefit. The Communist Party, announcing the policy of total collectivization and liquidation of kurkuls, had entrusted the local governments and special Party representatives such as Thousanders with almost unlimited power. The Jews took advantage of this power to take revenge against Ukrainians. They became overzealous in expropriating the grain from farmers, and causing starvation in Ukrainian villages. More than that, they pinned the labels "kurkul" and "enemy of the people" on the majority of the farmers without any justification and had them exiled to concentration camps or locked up in prisons.

What the representative had said we could not easily ignore. Such revelations and accusations were totally unprecedented. We had never heard such anti-Jewish rhetoric before from anybody, let alone official Party representatives. But, here, the official representative of the county Party organization openly declared that the Jews were to be blamed for every horror that had gone on in our village since the beginning of collectivization. His attempt to whitewash the Communist Party of all wrongdoings was something we expected. After all, he himself was a Party member! But why blame the Jews? This tactic was hard to fathom. Comrade Zeitlin might have been of Jewish origin, although we never knew for sure. But he was no worse than any other Party member or non-Party activist. Besides, he and others like him were just carrying out the Party's orders and instructions, acting on behalf of the Party. And why should only Comrade Zeitlin be held responsible for the acts of violence committed in our village?

There was something else. Antidiscrimination laws strictly prohibited anti-Semitism in the Soviet Union. Thanks to those laws, Jews were able to occupy key positions in the Party and government. Anti-Semitism was a punishable offense. The slightest derogatory remark or even a joke that might have been construed as such could have brought severe punishment. Yet, now the representative of the county Party organization was officially propagating anti-Semitism. Why? He seemed to be actually inciting a pogrom against the Jews. Was he acting on his own initiative, or on behalf of the Party?

The old axiom "Divide and rule" seemed to be one of the motives behind his speech. The representative also might have had a traditional Russian slogan in his mind: "Kill the Jews and save Russia."

There is no doubt that he wanted to make Jews the scapegoats for the crimes committed by the Communist Party during the collectivization and to incite the farmers against them, in this way diverting their attention away from the real problems and actual culprits.

But the Party representative had no success with such tactics in our village. His anti-Jewish rhetoric encountered our disdainful silence. Later we learned that he traveled with his anti-Jewish speech throughout all the villages of the county. But wherever he went, despite his efforts, he failed to provoke any pogroms.

Comrade Representative finished his speech, collected his notes, rushed to the exit with eyes cast down, and disappeared without a backward glance. We never saw him again. The member of the village soviet took his place at the rostrum.

What happened next was a spontaneous riot.

"We have had enough of you!" somebody yelled as the member of the village soviet tried to say something.

"Away with you!" someone else shouted angrily. "We have been listening to you for too long!"

The member of the village soviet desperately wanted to speak, and he started to yell at the top of his voice, waving his arms over his head, but the shouting did not stop. As a last resort, he grabbed the drinking glass and started ringing it with his pencil, but his voice and the ringing were both drowned out in angry swearing and cursing by the enraged crowd.

Suddenly a young man ran to the stage. The frightened and bewildered member of the village soviet, with his arms outstretched in a defensive position, backed up to the side stage door and disappeared outside.

"You heard what Comrade Representative said," the young man shouted. "We have been duped. Let's get our horses and cows out of that stinking collective farm before it's too late!"

"Let's do it now!" echoed the crowd.

"Right now!"

The young man jumped down from the stage and ran to the exit, and like stampeding cattle the audience rushed after him. Windows were broken, and children climbed out of them. Others used the stage side door to flee.

Once outside, they were in a great hurry to reach their destination.

"Hurry!" a man urged his wife. "Hurry up, or someone may take our cow!"

And they started running.

"How about our wagon?" a woman asked. "How shall we find it in this darkness?"

Others expressed similar worries:

"It's so dark outside! How can we recognize our horse and cow?"

"Run!" a man's voice urged.

"Let's go there quickly!"

And they ran as fast as they could, struggling in the deep snow, by way of shortcuts through orchards to the main road.

When my mother and I managed to extricate ourselves from the crowd stuck in the doorway, I noticed numerous houses burning in the village center. Flames rising high into the night sky were casting red reflections on the snow. Somebody shouted that our Hundred was on fire. I looked around and saw the flames engulfing the house which we had left just minutes ago.

The village was in an uproar. We could hear angry voices everywhere. Men and women were shouting, arguing. Now and then someone would be heard yelling and swearing. Some women were crying; others laughing out of sheer despair. Even the dogs, aroused by the noisy commotion, were barking furiously. From time to time, shots rang out through all this tumult. Who was shooting, no one could tell.

I was following my mother. It was difficult for her to run. She would often fall and almost completely disappear in the deep snow. But again she would struggle to her feet and try to run, and would fall again. She too was in a hurry. She was anxious to find our cow, horse, and wagon before someone else got them.

As we were approaching the village center, we met the first rioters who were returning home with their spoils: their own cows and horses. But not all of them were satisfied and happy. Those who could not reclaim all their belongings were even crying. Some of them had found their horses, but not their cows, and vice versa. Others found their horse equipment, but not their wagons. An elderly couple, who could only find their wagon, were trying to pull it themselves, but the wagon was too heavy for them. They stopped in the middle of the road, waiting for someone to help them. The old woman cried bitterly, telling everyone who would listen that they could find neither their horse nor their cow. But the majority who had found their precious possessions were quietly passing by and proceeding to their homes, as if they were afraid of losing them again.

We finally reached the collective farm. First we ran to the cattle barn. We knew where our cow was. Since the time we were forced to sign up for the collective farm, more than a month ago, we had visited her almost daily. Mother would often collect some scraps of food and secretly sneak into the barn and watch our cow munch contentedly on whatever she would give her. She would cry each time she visited the barn. Our cow meant much to us. Her milk was the main nourishment that kept us alive during the past few years. Without it, we would not have had much hope for survival.

Fortunately, we found our cow in her place. I left Mother to guard her while I rushed to the stable. But there I had no luck; our horse was gone. Then I ran to the yard where I knew our wagon had been, but it too was missing. There was no use wasting my time trying to find them, so I ran back. Hurriedly we headed home with our cow, thankful to at least have her back with us, but saddened by the loss of our horse and wagon.

Early next morning, we were awakened by the noise of heavy shooting somewhere in the village. It sounded as if a real battle was being waged there. Even artillery guns roared from time to time just as had happened a few weeks ago, when the guns were deployed in the fields north of the village, and the shells were flying over our heads, landing somewhere in the Tiasmyn River.

But even the shooting could not prevent my brother and me from going back to the collective farm to continue our search for our horse and wagon. We left home and, after dodging the main road, soon reached the church ruins. It was as far as we could dare to go. From behind the ruins, we noticed a few military vehicles in place in the square. Soldiers were patrolling the square and the streets. We could see guards at the village store and at the post office, and we could hear rifle shots far away on the outskirts of the village. We also noticed bodies lying in the blood-stained snow.

We did not know what actually had transpired in the village center during the night, but we were sickened by what we saw, and certainly not eager to pursue our initial undertaking. We decided to head back home as fast as we could.

Upon our arrival, there was nothing left for us as a family to do but to wait for what might happen next. We, the villagers, found ourselves in a very precarious and dangerous situation. We had just ruined the collective farm; some buildings were destroyed; and the greater part of our farm animals and implements were reposessed by the villagers. By our rioting, we had demonstrated our unwillingness to be members of the collective farm, and yet we had no assurance that we had won the battle. And we were still not sure if the Party representative had really meant what he had said last night at the meeting. Did he say it just to distract us from what he really had in mind? If so, what was it? There must have been a reason for everything he said.

There was also something else that bothered and worried us a great deal: were we still members of the collective farm after all that had happened? None of us, as far as I knew, had formally requested to have our membership discontinued. In that case, what was our status now? Would the Communist Party leave us alone now?

While we all waited anxiously for something to happen, news started spreading. More than twenty farmers had been shot to death in the morning following the riot. They were slaughtered while trying to take back their animals and farm implements.

The other tragic news was that another twenty people had been arrested the same morning. The young man who had actually started the riot in our Hundred was among them. All the wives, children, and other family members of the killed and arrested villagers were evicted from their homes and banished from the village on the same day. They were taken by military vehicles to the railroad station where the county Party and government officials and a train were ready and waiting for them.

A week or more passed after the riot with no further official reaction to what had happened. The all-important question of whether we were still considered members of the collective farm kept nagging us more and more. The uncertainty of what was ahead almost drove us to despair. It was a matter of life or death for us. This was the time when our farmers used to start spring sowing and planting. Now the majority of them could not do that because of the simple reason that they owned no land. On joining the collective farm, their land was collectivized and pronounced "socialist property," and as such, it was protected by the state law. During the riot, some of the villagers were able to reclaim their animals and their implements, if they were found intact. But how could they reclaim their land? There simply was no way; the land was no longer theirs. They could work that land, but there was no guarantee that they could harvest the crop. There was no guarantee that they would even live long enough to reap the harvest. In the middle of April, about two weeks after the riot, we were finally summoned to a village general meeting, which took place in the church. During the night of the riot, someone had tried to restore it: the altar and the icons, much to our great surprise, had been saved, and were put in their original places. The Communist decorations and propaganda articles had been thrown out. The night of the meeting, however, it was a theater and propaganda center again. Red was the dominant color. A red flag was installed in place of the altar. Wherever one looked, the slogan "Death to kurkuls" could be seen. Portraits of Communist leaders hung in the place of the holy pictures again.

The meeting hall was already full when Mother and I arrived. No one spoke. The people looked haggard and worried; their faces showed exhaustion, malnutrition, and weary indifference. Everyone seemed gloomy and serious, and indeed, there was good reason for it. They knew that their future would be decided at this meeting.

Soon the officials arrived. Most of them were strangers to us. Some of them looked urban: well dressed and well fed. They were, no doubt, intellectuals. Some, obviously, were workers from factories, but the rest—the majority of them—were peasants like us: haggard, dressed in rags, and hopelessly sad. Utter silence fell in the hall as they entered. The member of the village soviet who conducted the last meeting in our Hundred and who had survived the riot appeared on the podium and announced that the new Thousander would speak.

"Here is our new Thousander, Comrade Cherepin!" he shouted.

At this time, Comrade Cherepin was already standing at the rostrum, slowly measuring the audience with an indifferent look. He was a short, broad-shouldered man, whose bald head and spectacles made him look professorial. His outward appearance was deceptive, however, as we later learned. Eventually, we came to know him as a sadist who would not hesitate to expropriate the last pound of grain from us, or throw a baby out a window into the snow.

His speech was typical of what was expected from a Communist official addressing a rural audience: his voice was quiet, his tone patronizing, and his language simple. Like the speakers before him, he discussed all the revolutions in the world history, which didn't mean a thing to us. He made references to all the founders of Communism; he described the miserable life in the capitalist countries abroad; and finally, he proclaimed that Paradise was to be found only in the Soviet Union.

"Where else in the world do farmers have free meetings like this one?" he asked. "Nowhere!" he answered his own question quickly. "Only you have this privilege because you live in the Soviet Union!"

He stopped abruptly, as if he had run out of words. Then he changed his voice to a lower key, and continued:

"Some unpleasant things have happened in this village. Are we really to assume that they were done with your approval?"

"No!" he replied, after a pause, during which he seemed to think about something.

"Not all of you approved of what had happened! What happened was the work of enemies of the people—the kurkuls. Yes, indeed, the kurkuls have done this!"

Comrade Cherepin's Ukrainian was intelligible if his strange accent was disregarded. Nevertheless, it was difficult for us to follow the thread of his thoughts. He asked rhetorical questions and he was evasive; he spoke about what had happened without actually saying what did happen. Of course, we knew what he was speaking about, but we wondered why he didn't name the things specifically.

After a while, he became more specific. He told us that because we let the kurkuls influence us, and because we had done what we did, we had lost the right to live! Yes, those who oppose the Communists have no place in this world, but we still had a chance to prove ourselves worthy of living in the Communist society by joining the collective farm. With this statement, he referred to those who had not yet joined. Those who had misappropriated "socialist property," i.e., taken their animals and implements from the collective farm, should admit their grave mistake and return it all immediately. Those of us who were seriously thinking about leaving the collective farm for good should send a written request to the Board of Managers. He also informed us that only horses and agricultural implements would be collectivized. Members of the collective farm would have the right to retain their dwellings, their cows and small animals such as hogs, goats, sheep, and fowl as their own possessions.

And finally he gave us his warning: "Let it be known once and for all that if anyone raises his hand against the Communist Party and the Soviet Government, his fate is certain death!"

But that was not the end of the meeting. Comrade Cherepin, upon finishing his speech, had one of his propagandists read Stalin's new article, "Reply to Comrade Collective Farmers," dated April 3, 1930.

According to this article, the permission given to farmers to leave the collective farms was not the sign of abandoning the policy of collectivization. It was merely a matter of tactics. He maintained that, like a shooting war, the war against the class enemies could not be successfully waged without firmly securing the positions already gained, regrouping the forces, providing the front with reserves, and bringing up the rear. Stalin stated that "only dead souls leave the collective farms"; also, that those leaving the collective farms are hostile to Communist ideology; but that not all those leaving the collective farms are hostile or dead souls. They are farmers whom the Communist Party failed to convince in the righteousness of the Communist cause "but whom we will, no doubt, convince tomorrow."

Stalin also announced in this article that the government decided to exempt all the collectivized draft animals from taxation for a period of two years. Cows and small animals such as hogs, goats, sheep and fowl were also exempt from taxation regardless of whether they were in a collective farm or in private possession of collective farmers. That meant that those who had planned to withdraw from the collective farm should think twice before they did it.

The meeting broke up shortly before midnight. It was raining outside and very cold. On the way home, we made the decision to remain in the collective farm. There was no other choice.

Contrary to our expectations and the promises given by the Party representative at that meeting, no serious changes for the better took place in our lives after the riot. The forcible collectivization was renewed and intensified, and the taxation in kind and money continued with new zeal and vigor.

Our village was completely collectivized sometime at the beginning of 1931. But this early completion of collectivization did not mean that our villagers accepted the system of collectivized agriculture willingly. They never did. Our village was half ruined; more than one third of our entire population was physically exterminated or banished from the village. Any food we had was confiscated. By the end of 1931 we faced mass starvation. There was no way to survive but to stay in the collective farm where we had been promised some food for our daily work.

Yet the struggle of the farmers against collectivization did not terminate with our forced joining of the collectives. On the contrary, we became even more stubborn in the following years. During the harvest of 1930 and 1931, the government used the newly organized collective farms to expropriate as much of the grain and other agricultural products as it wanted. There was talk in our village that more than three quarters of the total crop of 1931 had been taken by the government. We heard that in some neighboring villages the whole crop had been taken. It was easily done, without any opposition. There was no bargaining over the price. It was the government who set the prices, not the farmers.

As one would expect under such circumstances, our villagers had no interest in working in the collective farm. Consequently, the crop acreage was greatly reduced, and besides that, a large portion of the crops—both grain and vegetable—went unharvested.

The fate of those animals who found themselves in the collective farms was not to be envied either. The Communist officials expropriated them without first preparing a proper place to house them, or enough forage to feed them. Consequently, many of them died from lack of food and gross neglect.

Besides this, small animals like pigs, sheep, and goats, as well as fowl, were stolen, or found their way to the dinner tables of the almighty Communist officials.

The horses especially were in a sorry predicament at that time. Communist propaganda did its best to convince everybody that horses would soon be replaced by tractors. Thus the horses suddenly became unwanted at the collective farm as useless eaters. It seemed that in the fall of 1930, nobody knew what to do with them. Finally, somebody made the decision to free them from the confines of the collective farm which could not feed or care for them. They were turned loose in the open fields and woods to roam and search for food. Soon a disease struck. The combination of sickness and lack of proper care caused the death of hundreds of horses in our village. The pattern was the same throughout Ukraine. Carcasses dotted the fields and woods. This tremendous loss posed a serious problem for the officials of the collective farms, for horsepower still determined agricultural production.

CHAPTER 13

I N THE collective farm, our personal existence became completely dependent upon the dictates of the Communist Party, and on the whims of the local officials. Every detail of our life was supervised. Our daily routine was subject to the strictest regimentation. We had to obey orders without any protest, and without giving any thought as to their sense or purpose. A vast system of secret police, spies, and *agents provocateurs* watched our every move.

We were always suspected of treason. Even sadness or happiness were causes for suspicion. Sadness was thought of as an indication of dissatisfaction with our life, while happiness, regardless of how sporadic, spontaneous, or fleeting, was considered to be a dangerous phenomenon that could destroy the devotion to the Communist cause. You had to be cautious about the display of feelings at all times, and in every place. We were all made to understand that we would be allowed to live only as long as we followed the Party line, both in our private and social lives.

By this time—after only two years of compulsory collectivization —normal human relations had broken down completely. Neighbors had been made to spy on neighbors; friends had been forced to betray friends; children had been coached to denounce their parents; and even family members avoided meeting each other. The warm traditional hospitality of the villagers had disappeared, to be replaced by mistrust and suspicion. Fear became our constant companion: it was an awesome dread of standing helplessly and hopelessly alone before the monstrous power of the State.

The Communist Party organization, the general membership meeting, and the Board of Managers were the collective farm's governing bodies. The Auditorial Commission and the kolhosp court carried the auxiliary functions of controlling and punishing. The Komsomol and Komnezam (this organization of poor farmers continued its existence even after collectivization) gave organizational support to the Party. Other organizations, duplicating village-wide ones, as well as all kinds of secret and nonsecret agents, agitators, propagandists, and activists, were used by the governing bodies to check the pulse of the members of the collective farm.

The local policy on the collective farm was determined by the leader of the Party organization. All other kolhosp officials were merely executors of that policy. The Party leader was a local dictator, holding a position similar to that of political commissar of a Red Army unit. The chairman of the kolhosp Board of Managers could not issue any directive without the approval of the Party leader, as the commanding officer could not issue any order without the approval of the political commissar.

According to the kolhosp statutes, the general membership meeting was supposed to be the highest organ of kolhosp self-administration. In reality, it was only an organ through which the Party organization could pipe its policy and decisions on all important questions.

The visible executive organ of the collective farm was the managing board. It was elected by the membership meeting for a two-year term. There were nine board members, including the chairman. Personal merit, knowledge, and farming experience were to be the qualifications of the candidates, but in practice democratic principles were circumvented. Only one candidate was permitted per office, and he was chosen from among either Communist Party members or trustworthy Party followers. Since votes were taken by a show of hands, and any open opposition to the Party would mean persecution of the voter, it was not difficult to secure the managing board for the Party.

The prerequisite for the chairmanship of the board was membership or candidacy in the Communist Party. Professional qualifications for this post were not considered, for most of the appointees were city dwellers who could not distinguish rye from wheat, or the harrow from the plough. Loyalty to the Party and to its policy in dealing with the farmers were valid enough recommendations for this office. In our village, a native was never appointed kolhosp chairman, although quite a few of them were appointed to such positions in other villages.

The election of the chairman was the model for the election of the members of the managing board and all other officials. The candidates for board membership did not have to be members of the Party, but they had to be "non-Party Communists," that is, faithful followers of the Communist Party ideology. They were also known as "activists."

The other supposedly independent institutions within the kolhosp framework were the Auditorial Commission and kolhosp court. The former, consisting of the members of the collective farm elected at the annual membership meeting, controlled the functions of the board and thus determined its policy. It also controlled the fiscal policy of the board, including budget, production, distribution, and annual income. However, all the reports to the members of the collective farm sent by this commission had to be scrutinized and approved by the Party organization prior to the meeting.

The kolhosp court, although called a comradely court, became in reality a dreaded punitive institution.

The Komsomol organization occupied the most powerful niche in the kolhosp structure, with the exception of the Party itself. Its members occupied positions comparable to that of full-fledged Communists. But the Komsomol also served as a trusted and reliable force for initiating new policies. If the Party was planning a certain campaign or a propaganda move, the Komsomol was the starting point or switch. When the switch was turned on, it put the entire political machine in motion.

All members of the collective farm were assigned to Brigades and Links. These were meant to be for work purposes only, but we soon felt their impact on every aspect of our lives.

There were eight Brigades in our collective farm. At first, they were organized on territorial principles, and thus one brigade might have corresponded roughly to one village Hundred. The members of the First Brigade, for instance, belonged to the First Hundred. Each Brigade of that time was comprised of approximately one hundred households, or about two hundred able workers.

The Links could be compared to the Tens. Each Link within a particular brigade was made up of ten or fifteen households, or from eight to thirty able workers, the number depending on the type of work it was assigned to do.

The labor tasks on the farm were therefore distributed among brigades, and the latter, in turn, allocated certain jobs to each link.

The nature of work on the farm, of course, depended on the agricultural seasons.

Theoretically, the brigade leader was to be elected from among the brigade members, and every competent farmer, according to the statutes, had the right to be elected to this position. But, in reality, the Board of Managers made appointments which were in fact suggested or approved by the Party organization. Many of these brigade leaders were not native villagers, but were sent to our village by the county government. Link leaders usually were native villagers. They were appointed by the brigade leaders, but the lists of the prospective candidates were approved by the Party organization and by the Board of Managers.

The brigade leaders became the most important link between the higher officials and the people, and consequently, they gradually assumed unlimited power over the members of their brigades. The members of his brigade could not leave the village or use their time as they wished without the leader's knowledge and permission. The members of the brigade, for example, could not plan a wedding or any other kind of special occasion without the leader's consent. Every move had to be agreed upon and coordinated in accordance with his wishes.

The link leaders were trustworthy helpers of the brigade leaders. Character or skill were not requirements for such a position: personal loyalty was the only quality that counted.

As members of the collective farm, we found ourselves under a dual government. The village government continued its functions. The Hundreds, Tens, and Fives with their commissions, propagandists, agitators, and all kinds of other functionaries, continued their activities. They were occupied, as previously, with collectivization of those villagers who still remained outside of the collective farms, and with the collection of food for the state. The Sunday and evening meetings were still called regularly, and although we were now members of the collective farm, we still had to attend them. The commission never left us alone; it visited us regularly under one pretext or another. We still received visits from the officials, the propagandists, and agitators, and from Komsomol, Pioneer, and Komnezam delegations. We were still told to deliver food, to pay various taxes and dues, and to "voluntarily" buy state bonds; and we still were asked to contribute "voluntarily" to many state funds plus a multitude of international funds that helped Communist Parties abroad.

All these claims and demands on us doubled and intensified when we joined the collective farm, for, in addition to the all-village government, the kolhosp administration was, in reality, another local government. When there were no village or Hundred or Ten or Five meetings, we could expect a kolhosp membership meeting, or a brigade meeting, or a link meeting. At such meetings, the village officials would be replaced by the kolhosp officials. Almost every day we would have some kind of meeting or political indoctrination lecture in the field during the working hours. The agendas of the kolhosp meetings were almost identical to those of the village meetings. As a consequence, certain problems discussed at the Hundred meetings in the evening would be brought up the next day at the brigade meeting in the field.

We had to study the speeches of Party and government leaders, as well as new legislative enactments or executive measures. For example, when a speech of a prominent leader was delivered, it was officially sent through channels from the All-Union Center, through the Union-Republic governments down to the localities. As soon as it reached the village, it went down to the villagers through a dual channel: through the village government and the kolhosp administration. This speech would then be read and studied at the village subdivisions in the evenings and on Sunday, and then again read and explained at the brigade and link meetings in the field. This was the procedure with everything the central or local government wanted us to do or know.

The kolhosp court in our village was one of the innovations that came with the new order. Previously, all cases had been tried at the county center. Now, our village was to have its own court.

The officials called it the comradely court. In the beginning, it did not have any impressive or offensive punitive power. Its activities were limited to disciplinary action. It could only impose small fines or forced labor of not more than a week on the farm or at the communal works.

But this court soon began to try all cases, including those of criminal, civil, and political nature. In the hands of the Communists, the court became an inquisitive organ. It was given jurisdiction over all the villagers.

The judge of this court served at the pleasure of the Party. During a court session, the judge was flanked by the village Party leader, and the chairmen of the village soviet and the Kolhosp. The activity of the court, therefore, was directed by these officials until the concluding statements were prepared. At that time, the hitherto ignored members of the court read the verdict.

Among the matters which came before the court were insults to officials, jokes or anecdotes about members of the regime, damage to farm implements, thefts of farm property, absences from meetings and propaganda gatherings, delays in paying taxes, and the like. The verdict of the court depended largely on how much damage had been done to Party policy.

The punishments handed down by the court were harsh. Failure to arrive at work on time was punishable by a forced labor sentence of one to three months. More severe sentences were imposed on those whose "offenses" were of a political nature. Opposition to Party policy and insulting its executors were considered high treason. The kolhosp court usually submitted such cases to the Superior Court, or the state security organs, or both, with recommendation of a death sentence or a term in a "corrective labor camp," as the concentration camps were known. Such recommendations were, no doubt, wholeheartedly accepted because those charged with such offenses never returned to the village.

Sessions of the kolhosp court were held almost every Sunday evening, with each session dealing with four or five cases. Court attendance by all villagers was obligatory. As it was impossible to accommodate all villagers at the court session at the same time, a schedule of court attendance by Hundreds was established. Usually, inhabitants of three Hundreds would be ordered to each session; punishment for failure to attend was a fine in money, or forced labor. The Court also tried those who failed to attend its own sessions.

I witnessed many of these court sessions. I still remember one in particular: it was on an evening in the spring of 1931. The setting was the former church. The organizers of the kolhosp court insisted on ceremony. The Thousander, Comrade Cherepin, was the first to appear on stage. After a pause for silence, he solemnly announced:

"Comrades, the kolhosp court!"

A hush came over the audience. Three farmers whom we all knew appeared on the stage: the judge was Sydir Kovalenko, a poor farmer who could hardly read or write. Two people's assessors[16] followed; no prosecutor or defense counsel appeared. How these individuals became members of this court was a mystery to us all. They were just ordinary poor farmers without any Communist Party or Komsomol affiliations whatsoever.

When the members of the court had taken their places, the chairmen of the village soviet and the kolhosp appeared on the stage.

As soon as these officials sat down, the judge announced the first case. Two defendants appeared, each escorted by a militiaman. The judge began the reading of the indictment, and from it we learned that the defendants had been accused on three counts. The charges were agitation against the Soviet regime, attempting to undermine the authority of Party and government officials, and the spreading of Ukrainian nationalism.

This was the culmination of a rather amusing incident. I had witnessed the seemingly insignificant event that had led to this case, and I feel it is worthwhile to relate it in all its details.

There is a proverb that might best explain the mishap—"What the sober man retains—the drunkard reveals." Being drunk, the defendants just spoke what they had thought, and what they thought was not in accordance with the Party line.

Since the start of collectivization, the necessities of life had almost completely disappeared from the shelves of the village store. Kerosene, matches, salt, and other common goods had become scarce. It had been announced one Sunday that a supply of herrings had arrived at the store, and that each person would be allotted one pound. Therefore, on that Sunday, a long line stretched along the square in front of the store. Petro Zinchenko, one of the defendants, wanted to buy his ration of herring. He was an honest and hard-working man, but he had the reputation of being a Sunday drunkard. Aside from this one weakness, he was a likeable and intelligent man. This Sunday, like every Sunday, he was drunk.

---

[16]People's assessors—instead of a jury, Soviet courts of law have so-called people's assessors, usually three in number. They are elected by a universal vote for two years, but the elections are usually fictitious. The candidates are approved by the appropriate Party organization. Although these assessors have equal rights with the judge in passing a verdict, in reality they are nothing but mute witnesses to the court procedures. The kolhosp court, although not a regular court of law, had at that time two people's assessors.

"Listen, Kitty," he said to a young woman standing in the line close to the store door, "if you let me stand ahead of you, our wedding will be held right after we buy our herring."

The young lady dissented.

"Well, I understand," Petro continued. "You don't want to marry me without the Church's blessing." He pointed toward the ruined church cupolas. "We'll be married there, in the church . . . under the portrait of our dear and wise leader and teacher, Comrade—"

"Shut up, you ass!" she shouted. And, of course, she did not let him take the place in front of her.

But Petro was not discouraged. He changed his tone and disguised his voice so cleverly that it sounded like that of Comrade Cherepin.

"Hey, you—enemy of the people!" he said to the young woman, "Who gave you the right to stand in the herring line ahead of a hero and invalid of the Revolution, and a member of the Komnezam?"

Her answer was still no.

The situation became embarrassing. Petro's joking used to evoke laughter from the people. He was more witty than ever now. His imitation of Comrade Cherepin was expert. However, this time no one dared to laugh. He was openly ridiculing the Soviet regime, and everyone feared the presence of secret agents.

"Comrade enemy," he continued, addressing the same lady, "in the name of our beloved Communist Party and dear government, I arrest you for refusing to cooperate with a hero of the proletarian revolution in his quest for a quick purchase of his ration of herring granted him by this same beloved Party and government."

The woman did not cooperate with him. But Petro, still in a joking mood, shifted his attention to another woman, an older one.

"Look, Granny, did you see that?" he asked, pointing at the younger woman. "I helped build this Communist paradise complete with its annual herring sale, and she—she won't even let me buy the herring before she does; may I stay in front of you?"

But Petro had no better luck. The older woman was not exactly in a joking mood either.

"You've got your paradise. Away with you!" she mumbled.

"What?" shouted the surprised Petro.

"I meant," shouted the woman, "that as long as you wanted this paradise, you've got it. Enjoy it! The end of the line is back there."

Petro jumped closer to the older woman.

"My dear," he exclaimed, "for years I've been looking for an angel in this paradise, and I've finally found her, in the herring line of all places!"

As the older woman struggled against Petro's attempt to kiss her, another drunkard weaved his way toward the line, swinging his arms and singing loudly.

He was middle-aged, and like Petro, was known for his wit. His name was Antin. He had been a Communist partisan during the Civil War. He also had the reputation of being an educated man; we all knew that he could read and write.

Petro left the old lady and went to meet Antin.

"Ah," he shouted to Antin, "birds of a feather flock together! Long live the drunkards of paradise!"

"Hurrah!" shouted Antin, embracing his friend Petro.

"Long live the herring eaters!" Petro responded with a long hurrah.

"Listen, Comrade-Sir," started Antin, "you are a bourgeois-capitalist-counterrevolutionary-imperialist shark . . ."

"Thanks," replied Petro. "Thanks for the honor."

"You want to buy a herring, don't you?" continued Antin. "And isn't that a counterrevolutionary desire?"

Petro laughed and then took his turn.

"You're an old, skinny, dirty pig, Antin. You are even more than a pig; you are an enemy of the people. The worst and skinniest enemy I ever saw in my whole long drunken life!"

"The honor is mine," answered Antin.

"How dare you come to the annual herring sale like this?" Petro continued, gesturing toward Antin. "How could you come to the public place with such dirty trousers on your socialist legs?"

The old man smilingly fingered the holes in his trousers.

"I ask you, is it permissible in the socialist paradise, under the leadership of our dear and beloved, our wise and almighty, our teacher and leader, great Comrade . . ."

"Shut up, you stinking rat! I feel like vomiting!" shouted Antin.

"That's exactly what I mean, continued Petro. You feel like vomiting when I speak about our dear and beloved . . ."

"I'll kill you!" Antin raved.

Petro wished to mention this leader by name, modified by the adjectives which the propagandists used for Stalin. A vigorous protest from Antin did not stop him.

"You'd better give me a direct answer about your trousers," Petro demanded. "How is it possible for you to expose your socialist bony knees to the public, as if you were a peasant of a capitalist country?"

"You are wrong, Comrade Red Partisan,"[17] Antin said. "My trousers are neither dirty nor torn. It's a new fashion."

"Aren't they lovely?" Petro continued. "And you mean those holes aren't holes?"

"That's right, comrade-sir, they aren't holes," Antin answered. "They are just delicate openings for ventilation."

Petro sighed. "Do the creators of this fashion have this kind of ventilation also?" he asked.

"I'm not sure about their trousers, only their heads."

The two men, weary of their dialogue, returned their attention to the herring line. Petro, again imitating Comrade Cherepin, shouted:

"Comrades, my compatriots! From now on, comrades, you are entitled to receive an annual ration of one whole herring! We'll call it the Red Herring, for those of you, comrades, who won't be able to consume the ration yourself will be urged to deliver the surplus to our dear Party and government, which will then distribute them among the starving laboring people of the capitalist countries. Comrades, join our socialist competition for the collecting of surplus herrings for the laboring classes of the capitalist world."

There was no laughter in the crowd during or after his herring speech. The people, aware of the danger, turned their backs on Petro.

Seeing that his humor no longer had any effect on the people, Petro enlisted Antin in a new mode of entertainment, dancing and singing.

They sang the new anti-Communist folksongs created by the villagers themselves during collectivization. They sang a few more of them before realizing their failure to cheer the people, and finally elbowed their way through the line singing:

> *Oh, Communists; oh, Communists,*
> *You are dirty traders—*
> *You've sold our Ukraine*
> *For Muscovite treasures.*

[17]A Red Partisan was a participant in the Communist partisan (guerrilla) warfare during the Civil War of 1918–1921. This title became synonymous with being a Soviet patriot, and, as such, it secured all kinds of privileges for its bearer.

It was at this point that someone turned them in; now they were the defendants, attended by militiamen, standing before the kolhosp court.

I had no knowledge at that time of either the judicial system or of the procedures of law; nevertheless, this court struck me as a tragicomic parody of justice. After reading the indictment in which there was no mention of their specific crimes, Judge Sydir started the interrogation. He read the questions with a trembling voice.

"Your name?" he asked Petro, without raising his head from the piece of paper which he held close to his eyes. The question came as a complete surprise to Petro.

"What?" he retorted, open-mouthed with astonishment. (It so happened that Petro and Sydir had been neighbors and friends for as long as they had lived.) "Don't you know me anymore?"

Sydir was painfully embarrassed, and seemed at a loss what to do next. He turned to Comrade Cherepin. From then on, Cherepin conducted the court proceedings almost single-handedly. Other voices spoke only when Comrade Cherepin asked questions.

"You heard the judge," Comrade Cherepin angrily hissed at Petro, looking at him as if he were a troublesome insect. "Your family name, given name, and patronymic."

"But he knows my name! All know . . ." started Petro.

"Your name!" repeated Comrade Cherepin, raising his voice.

Petro first looked helplessly around as if trying to find out what was happening, then obediently answered. A stream of other questions followed.

"Date and place of birth?"

"Occupation and place of work?"

"Nationality?"

"Membership in the Communist Party?"

"Name of parents?"

"Their social status before the Revolution?"

"Did they have hired hands?"

This was the beginning of a long and exhaustive interrogation. Petro had to relate a detailed biography, from infancy to the present day. Comrade Cherepin was especially interested in what Petro's parents, grandparents, relatives, as well as his wife's parents, grandparents, and relatives did before and during the Revolution and Civil War. Were they civil or military servants under the tsarist regime?

Were they rich or poor? Did they exploit hired hands? Did they oppose the October Revolution?

To us villagers, this kind of interrogation was a strange and frightful phenomenon. Not many of us knew our exact date of birth, nor the birthdays of our relatives. The deceased grandparents and other family members were dearly remembered, but probably not one of us knew whether they had had hired hands or not. So at first we couldn't understand what Petro's ancestors had to do with this trial. But, as the interrogation progressed, it struck us with staggering clarity that we had to answer now for what our ancestors had done.

Petro knew approximately how old he was, but he did not know when he was born for the simple reason that his birth had not been recorded.

Comrade Cherepin interpreted this as contempt of court. Then Petro could not give a detailed account of his whereabouts and activities before and during the October Revolution and Civil War. This was interpreted as an attempt by Petro to hide his counterrevolutionary activities. As the interrogator delved deeper into Petro's personal life, it was revealed that his father was a noncommissioned officer in the tsarist army during World War I. No one in the village, including Petro himself, knew exactly what rank his father had held, but he was considered a sort of hero by the villagers for not many farmers could attain even this kind of rank in the tsarist army. However, he had been killed in action on the front lines and forgotten in the village. Even Petro thought there was nothing special in having rank, whatever it had been, to make a fuss about. But Comrade Cherepin was of another opinion.

"So, so . . . your father was a noncommissioned officer in the tsarist army, eh . . .?" he deliberately emphasized the word "officer." At that time it was anathema. "Tell me," he continued, after a pause, "how many poor farmers were noncommissioned officers in the tsarist army?"

"How should I know?" Petro responded.

"Not many," Cherepin said, staring at Petro. "Only those farmers could get promotions who loyally served the tsar and his regime. Isn't that true?"

"My father was—" Petro wanted to say something.

"You were not invited to talk!" Comrade Cherepin cut him short. "We know your kind; we still remember that time. Your father was promoted because he was loyal to the tsar; and having been promoted, he was that army slave driver we all hated. If he hadn't been killed, he would have become a counterrevolutionary; an enemy of the people."

"But—" Petro tried to speak again.

"Shut up!" Comrade Cherepin shouted angrily.

"But, he was killed three years before the Revolution," Petro managed to shout.

Comrade Cherepin did not take time to interrupt him. Now he sat staring at Petro in disgust. After a moment of silence, he leaned toward Sydir, the judge, and whispered something. The latter promptly ordered Petro to sit down.

Then he called the defendant Antin. Antin also had to answer a multitude of questions, but his interrogation did not last long. Soon Comrade Cherepin turned to the judge who automatically ordered Antin to sit down, and announced that Comrade Cherepin was to speak. This was supposed to be the prosecutor's charge, but in reality it was another political speech filled with stilted phrases. From that speech we understood the charges against Petro and Antin were accusations of agitation against the Communist Party and the Soviet government and of spreading Ukrainian nationalism. Of course, they were labeled counterrevolutionaries and enemies of the people. He singled out Petro as a son of a former tsarist noncommissioned officer and someone who could become a saboteur at any time. Thus he recommended that their case be submitted to the People's Court and to the state security organs.

When Comrade Cherepin finished speaking, somebody started to applaud, and others followed. After all, we had received a thorough lesson in applauding. Then it became quiet, as in a church.

"What crimes did they commit?" somebody shouted from the rear of the room.

"What did they do?" someone else asked from another area.

The audience grew animated. More voices demanded to know the defendants' crimes. Sydir, the judge, like an obedient dog, looked at Comrade Cherepin. The assessors shifted uncomfortably in their chairs.

But Comrade Cherepin was ready to deal with any emergency. Without paying any attention to the judge he slowly rose to his feet, and in a matter-of-fact manner, offered an explanation.

"Whereas the defendants' crimes consist of their anti-Party agitation, as well as their mocking of the Party and government and me, your Party representative; and whereas they propagated Ukrainian nationalism; and whereas the mention of their specific crimes publicly would mean repetition of the defendants' crimes against the Party and government, this court is of the opinion that naming their crimes publicly would be harmful to the Party and government."

That was all. This statement was rather confusing to us but somehow we got the message.

"Do you have any other questions?" Comrade Cherepin casually asked.

There were no more questions.

Then we were surprised to hear that the defendants were to be given the chance to speak in their own defense. Comrade Cherepin whispered something to Sydir, the judge, who then announced that the defendant Antin would speak first.

Antin, holding his soiled cap, and shifting from one foot to the other, did not know what to say. He only repeated over and over that he did not remember what he had said or done on that Sunday morning because he had been drunk.

Then, it was Petro's turn. Although at first he was confused, he quickly regained his composure. First, he looked hard and long at the officials before shifting his gaze to the members of the court with a sympathetic gesture that showed he realized their plight. For some reason, he then glanced at Antin's ragged shirt and his own feet which were wrapped in rags. Then he started to speak.

"Comrades . . ." he said, using the official title.

"We aren't your comrades," interrupted Comrade Cherepin. "You are a defendant here!"

"And who is asking the questions here?" Petro shot back. "I thought Sydir was the judge!"

Someone burst into laughter. Sydir, the judge, who all this time was sitting as straight as a ramrod in his chair, now gazed at the members of the court, and found them looking at him and then at each other.

But this atmosphere of confusion did not last long. Comrade Cherepin jumped to his feet.

"I am asking the questions here!" he shouted with arrogance. "And what I am asking must be answered, for I am the representative of the Party."

After a deliberate pause, he continued:

"We have had enough of your wit," and pounding the table with his fist, he shouted, "Proceed, Comrade Judge!"

Petro was allowed to finish his plea. It was not a plea for forgiveness. He only stated that if Antin were guilty on some counts, it was only because he had involved him. He asked the court to let Antin go free. The court then adjourned for deliberation.

Shortly afterward, the stage curtain was raised to reveal the court and officials.

Sydir, the judge, announced in a frightened voice that inasmuch as the crime went beyond the jurisdiction of the kolhosp court, the case under consideration would be transmitted to the superior judicial organ, whatever that was, and to the state security organs. The defendants were to remain in custody.

That was the last time we saw Petro and Antin, the village jesters, poor farmers, and staunch supporters of the October Revolution.

After the case of Petro and Antin was closed, a few minor cases were tried. A quiet farmer had to answer why he did not meet the state delivery grain quota. We believed this was a show trial, since the overwhelming majority of the villagers could not deliver theirs either. It was his misfortune to be chosen as the scapegoat to show the consequences. He was labeled "an enemy of the people," and his case was also to be submitted to the higher court and the state security organs.

This also happened to two other farmers. One was accused of selling his horse before joining the collective farm; another was to be punished for calling a member of the Komsomol a janissary.[18]

The next case was different. Two wretched farmers were called to the bench. They were ragged. Their faces were bearded and covered with dirt. They did not speak to each other; it was clear that they were not on speaking terms. One of them had a favorite fishing spot that he considered his own. When he came there early one morning he found it occupied. A neighbor of his had also found this spot attractive. An argument ensued. The first farmer wanted to have his favorite fishing spot back; he claimed that he was used to it; he had improved

[18]Janissary (or *Janizary*) was a soldier of an elite Ottoman (Turkish) army unit. The Janissaries were exclusively recruited by forced levy of Christian children. They were known for their implicit obedience. In Ukrainian, this word is synonymous with henchman.

it; and had been fishing at that particular spot for years. But the other farmer was also stubborn and saw no reason why he should yield to his neighbor. After all, he argued, the river, the fish, the water, the air, in fact, everything belonged to all the people. Wasn't that what the propagandist had told them at the Sunday meeting? The first farmer was not impressed by such an argument and landed a square blow between the other's eyes. A fight followed, and the intruder consequently found himself with a bloody nose and two black eyes.

He therefore decided to take revenge and complained to the village soviet; that was how they both landed in the kolhosp court.

The interesting part about it all was the verdict. It was pronounced by Comrade Cherepin personally. He probably considered it a matter too serious to entrust even to Sydir, the judge.

Comrade Cherepin announced that inasmuch as the rivers, land, and forests belonged to all the people, both the plaintiff and defendant were guilty of trespassing on public property and therefore had committed treason. They were each convicted to two weeks of forced labor.

Panas Kovalenko (not related to Sydir, the judge), a poor farmer, now a member of the collective farm, did not know what the word *zhlob* meant. Nevertheless, it brought him to the kolhosp court, and consequently, cost him his life.

The incident that brought Panas to the court had its start in the kolhosp field a few days before. Spring seeding and planting had begun, and one day Panas was harrowing. It happened that on that day the county Party officials were visiting the kolhosp, and during their inspection trip through the field they spotted Panas. He noticed them also. They were standing on the road debating something. It was obvious that he, Panas, was the subject of their discussion, for one of the officials pointed at him.

Then, as Panas with his harrow came closer to them, Comrade Cherepin, who accompanied the officials, ordered him to stop. As soon as Panas did so, the officials approached him.

"What are you doing?" Comrade Cherepin asked, standing at attention like a military man.

"You see what I'm doing," was Panas's answer.

"What do you mean? Can't you talk?" Comrade Cherepin, asked angrily.

"Yes, I can. Can't you see what I'm doing?" answered Panas, with a slightly raised voice.

Then an official interrupted:

"Comrade Cherepin wants to know what you call the kind of work you are doing right now?"

"I'm harrowing," answered Panas, looking at the strangers and Comrade Cherepin with amusement.

The official held a booklet in his hands, and he immediately started to look something up in it, turning the pages rapidly. When he found what he was looking for, and had read it carefully, he looked at the harrow and at Comrade Cherepin. The same official asked Panas:

"Do you always harrow this way?"

"How else could I do it?" was his answer. "For hundreds of years my ancestors did it this way; so do I."

"You mean, you are using only one harrow for harrowing?" continued the official.

The phrase in the booklet to which the official had referred stated that it would be kolhosp policy to harrow a field three times in succession. However, in Ukrainian, this phrase could also be interpreted by someone ignorant in the matter of agriculture to mean "to harrow with three harrows piled upon each other." Such a misinterpretation was made by these Party officials. Now, seeing Panas harrowing with one harrow only, they froze in consternation. This was an obvious violation of the Party instructions, and therefore an inexcusable crime.

When the officials expressed their bewilderment and Panas remained so calm, the highest official became angry. Turning away from Panas, he addressed Comrade Cherepin, who stood at attention.

"Comrade Cherepin," said the Party official, "the Party and government sent you here to see that all goes well and smoothly according to the Party's instructions. Yet you have failed the Party!" Comrade Cherepin listened to him with his usual intent, unwavering gaze. The county official, pointing to the booklet he held, continued:

"In these instructions,"—he waved the booklet high—"it is explicitly stated that harrowing should be done with three harrows. Yet, as you see for yourself, this man harrows with only one. Can you explain why the Party's instructions are ignored in your kolhosp?"

While the ranking official was speaking, all the others eyed the harrow, then Comrade Cherepin, and Panas, in turn. The situation became embarrassing. The officials looked at them as if they were the worst of traitors, and without waiting for an explanation, they turned away and went to their car, leaving Comrade Cherepin and Panas alone in the field. This abrupt withdrawal brought about an argument between the two of them.

Comrade Cherepin loudly accused Panas of violating the Party's instructions about harrowing. Those instructions clearly called for harrowing with three harrows, Comrade Cherepin contended. That meant that three harrows were supposed to have been put together, one on top of the other. He knew for certain that he had passed these instructions to all brigade leaders, and he also was sure that Panas knew about them, but nevertheless, he, Panas, had ignored his instructions entirely. There was no doubt but that he did it on purpose. He did it in order to diminish the importance of the Party management of agriculture, and thus to sabotage the socialist system of agricultural economy.

On his side, Panas wanted to explain that the instructions should be understood as harrowing three times, and that he had intended to do this. However, he couldn't do it at that particular time, for first, there were not enough harrows available in the collective farm, and second, the horse was too weak to pull three harrows hitched one after another.

But this explanation did not help Panas. Comrade Cherepin insisted that he did it deliberately. More than that, he called Panas a traitor, a saboteur, and, of course, an enemy of the people. That was too much. Even Panas, a poor farmer, could not take it anymore.

"You *zhlob,* leave me alone," he shouted in a rage.

That was an unexpected twist of events for Comrade Cherepin. No one could dare call him names. He was the Party representative! Whatever he was doing was in the Party's name. And whoever was dealing with him, was dealing with the Party and government embodied in his person. Consequently, those who were against him were also against the Party and government. Yet, this ignorant farmer dared to call him *zhlob.* To him this was inconceivable. He wouldn't stand insults from anybody, especially from a farmer. That ignorant farmer must be taught a lesson. He, Comrade Cherepin, an old revolutionary, old Communist, a partisan of the Civil War, would teach Panas how to speak to a Party and government official. That coarse farmer, that beast, must be punished so that he, and for that matter, everybody would be discouraged from such behavior in the future toward the Communist officials. That dirty farmer would remember his lesson as long as he lived.

"You will have to explain that to the court," Comrade Cherepin said through set teeth, trying to control himself. "You'll be notified in due course. But remember, I'll get even with you sooner or later!"

Panas was left alone. He knew that Comrade Cherepin meant what he said.

Well, what is *zhlob,* anyway? This question struck Panas with all its mystery as soon as Comrade Cherepin had left him alone. He thought he knew that word. To him there was nothing in it that could bring a man to court. He had heard it used many times. More than that, he himself had often been called it. But he never thought it an insult.

True to Comrade Cherepin's word, Panas was now standing before the kolhosp court. Cherepin became so carried away by his tirades that we thought he had forgotten the court case entirely. Then, after an hour or so, he finally launched an attack against Panas. With the voice of an individual who had suffered a gratuitous insult, he let all know that during the performance of his official duty, he had been humiliated and discredited by the Citizen Panas Kovalenko. All noticed that he did not call him "comrade," an address that was supposedly reserved for a loyal citizen only. We all knew this was a bad omen. As far as we were concerned, Panas was already convicted.

Having mentioned Panas's name, he paused, looking at the audience as if asking for sympathy. Then Comrade Cherepin started to speak again. He now described Panas' crime in a high-pitched voice. With each word the crime grew greater and greater, and Panas smaller and smaller.

"This creature,"—he pointed at Panas viciously with both his hands—"not only ignored the Party's instructions, but also insulted me, your Party and government representative. And, remember—insulting me, he also insulted and disgraced the Party and government as well; he thus insulted our dear and beloved leader and teacher, our dear Comrade . . ." The name of the Party leader was drowned in spontaneous applause.

Comrade Cherepin looked around complacently. Panas gazed at his feet. When the applause faded away, Comrade Cherepin solemnly declared his verdict: Panas's crime was of such a serious nature, that he recommended that the case be submitted to the state security organs and to the superior court.

All would have gone smoothly for Comrade Cherepin except for one question: how could Panas insult the Party, government, and Comrade Cherepin all at once?

"How did he insult you?" somebody shouted from the corner.

"What did he do?" someone else asked.

The hall came to life. Many wanted to know what actually had occurred between Comrade Cherepin and Panas. Somebody even asked whether there were witnesses to the incident, whatever it was. At first, Comrade Cherepin quietly gazed over the hall. Then he got up, drank some water, looked into the empty glass as if he wanted to see whether he had emptied it, slowly put it down, deliberately coughed into his fist, and casually rang for silence. The hue and cry disappeared, and a deathlike silence reigned immediately. No one dared move. We all waited for what he would say.

But Comrade Cherepin was in no hurry. He looked straight at the audience as if trying to hypnotize everyone in the hall. Then he spoke:

"Since the nature of the crime of Citizen Kovalenko is such that it discredits our beloved Party and government and myself, as your Party representative in your village, I do not think it advisable to repeat it here publicly."

For a moment he became quiet. Then, in a clear voice, he added:

"I repeat my demand—and this is the demand of our beloved Party and government. As there is no doubt of the defendant's malicious crime, his case must be submitted to the higher court and to the state security organs."

He finished his pronouncement and deliberately paused as if in expectation of some opposition. Then he said something to Sydir, the judge. This was his order to start the court hearing. We knew that Panas was convicted before the court hearing even started. Sydir, as in previous cases, was at a loss for words. Bewildered and helpless, he looked now at the defendant, now at Comrade Cherepin. Then after Comrade Cherepin whispered something in his ear, he called the defendant and said:

"As Comrade Cherepin stated in his patriotic speech, you were disrespectful to our Party and government, and also to Comrade Cherepin." Then, continuing in a fatherly tone of voice, "Now, tell us, what did you have in mind?"

"Nothing, Comrade . . . I had nothing in mind," Panas eagerly answered.

Sydir, the judge, looking at Comrade Cherepin, corrected Panas: "Nothing, Comrade *Judge.*"

Panas reluctantly repeated what the judge had said. But the matter of addressing the judge by the defendant was not settled with this. Comrade Cherepin interrupted, and corrected both of them: "Nothing, Judge."

Panas duly repeated this also.

The judge then resumed the interrogation.

"And why did you say that?" he asked politely, like a father admonishing his child for some mischievous behavior.

"What?"

"You know what!"

"Oh, you mean *zhlob?*"

That was it! Inadvertently, Panas revealed what Comrade Cherepin was reluctant to pronounce publicly.

Panas' answer caused a sensation among the audience. Somebody actually giggled. Sydir, terrified, called for silence, but no one listened to him. The crowd grew more and more animated. Even Comrade Cherepin seemed a little restless, but he did not wait long. He quickly rose to his feet, and rang for silence, but the noise continued. For a few seconds he stood speechless, as if deciding what to do next. Then he raised his head, and with all his might he shouted:

"The Party and government won't tolerate any riots here!"

All became quiet in an instant. Comrade Cherepin deliberately stared at the audience for a moment, and then he started to talk slowly, savoring each word:

"As you, comrades, all saw and heard personally, he did it again," pointing his finger at the defendant. "This is typical of the enemy of the people. They take any opportunity to discredit our beloved Party and government. As you have noticed, I had no wish to reveal the nature of the insult, for I did not want to drag our beloved Party and government through the malicious slander in public."

Comrade Cherepin then stopped for a moment. The feeling in the hall was intense. We sat quietly with bowed heads. We knew only too well that those to whom the tag "enemy of the people" was attached were doomed. They never had a chance to defend themselves.

"I repeat," Comrade Cherepin continued, holding his head high, "I did not publicly reveal that slanderous insult, for I did not want to insult neither our beloved Party and government, nor you. I say 'you,' because the Communist Party and Soviet government are yours."

This was something new in his speech: he involved us in the whole case and it was rather strange to hear, for we hadn't felt insulted. On the contrary, our sympathies were with Panas.

Comrade Cherepin started again: "But he, the accused, used this noble court to publicly repeat his black deed."

We were preparing to listen to another patriotic speech, but then we suddenly heard Panas speaking.

"Good people," he desperately shouted, "you are out of your minds! I said nothing of such a nature that could not be repeated here!"

But no one spoke to support him. All kept silent. Comrade Cherepin was carefully surveying the audience.

"Yes, you did," he said, after a moment of silence. Then he started his own interrogation, completely ignoring Sydir, the judge, who was staring foolishly now at Comrade Cherepin, now at Panas.

"Tell me, how can you say such things to a Party functionary?" he asked Panas in an almost benevolent voice.

There was no answer.

"Have you nothing to say in your own defense?"

Panas mumbled something under his breath which no one understood.

"Did you willingly say to me, the Party representative, that I was a you-know-what?"

"Comrade Cherepin—" Panas started to say something.

"I am not your comrade!" shouted Comrade Cherepin. "How many times do I have to tell you that?"

"Well . . ." mumbled Panas.

"I haven't finished my statement," shouted Comrade Cherepin.

"I meant . . ." Panas tried again.

"What you meant does not count; only what you said counts," cut in Comrade Cherepin. After a pause, he continued:

"I mean, perhaps you didn't mean to call me and the Party and Government a you-know-what . . ."

"Well, I meant . . ." Panas started.

"I mean, perhaps you were a little bit excited? Is that what it was?"

It was obvious that Comrade Cherepin wanted Panas to admit

publicly that he did not want to call him names; that he was sorry for what had happened in the field.

"Yes, yes, that's what I meant; I didn't mean to . . ."

We could see that Panas was losing ground. He kept repeating, "I didn't mean to. . . ."

Comrade Cherepin was all smiles. He knew he had broken his enemy. After one of those meaningful pauses of his, he turned finally to Sydir, the judge, and whispered in his ear.

But in the hall a great wave of confusion arose again. This time they wanted to know what the word *zhlob* meant.

"What is *zhlob?*" someone shouted loudly.

Few, if any, actually knew what the word meant. Panas then explained that he did not know its exact meaning. He had first heard the word in the city; somebody had called him a *zhlob* when he was waiting in the bread line in front of a store.

There was no doubt that Comrade Cherepin had known precisely what that word meant; but he continued to insist that it had greatly insulted himself and the Party.

Actually, it was not so. I knew what that word meant, and I couldn't help shouting:

"Request permission to explain," I nervously intruded, and without waiting for permission, I blurted out:

"It isn't a Ukrainian word; it's Russian, and it means 'ignorant boor!' "

After my hasty explanation, it was clear to everyone that Panas was not guilty of what Comrade Cherepin accused him of, or any crime, for that matter. But it did not help him. Comrade Cherepin's insistence won, and the court ruled that Panas had insulted not only Comrade Cherepin, but the Party and government as well, and the case would be submitted to a higher court.

We never saw Panas again. From that time on, as if in memory of Panas, we called Comrade Cherepin "Comrade Zhlob"—behind his back, of course.

CHAPTER 14

ONE OF the strangest facets of life on the collective farm was the introduction of various campaigns to solve a multitude of problems. In the years to come not a day would pass that we were not involved in one campaign or another.

For example, as spring approached, a Seed-Time Campaign was launched. All had to take part in it: men and women; young and old; healthy and sick. This campaign, as it stretched through the entire season, merged into the second campaign: the Harvest Campaign. This was followed by the Autumn Seed-Time Campaign. The fourth one was the Winter Campaign that prepared for the opening of the new Spring Seed-Time Campaign.

While these campaigns were in progress, other campaigns were continually being forced upon the farmers. These included the Tax Collection Campaign, the Campaign for Voluntary Delivery of Food to the State, and many others. Whether running concurrently, or attached to each other like a string of curses, these campaigns burdened us with a nagging weight.

As these campaigns whirled above the heads and through the long working days of the members of the collective farm, other smaller harpings plagued us. These were neatly outlined as "Problems" and "Questions." There were such titles as "The Problem of Fertilizers," "The Question of Increasing the Fertility of Pigs," "The Problem of Raising the Cow's Productivity," "The Question of Eggs and Chickens," and on and on. The bombardment with such titles to boost agricultural output was, at best, naive; but for us each campaign, with its related or unrelated outlines of problems and questions, signaled a new search for scapegoats as excuses for failure.

The goals of the Party and government for the collective farm were couched in simple terms: what is bad must be made good; a few must be made many; a little must be made much; small must become big. There was no limitation to goals, and thus no end to the endeavors and human sacrifices in terms of sweat, anxiety, and humiliation.

The officials demanded not only cooperation and rapid fulfillment of quotas, but also a cheerful and enthusiastic approach to the assigned tasks. The slightest sign of indifference was suspect, for it indicated opposition to official policy, and consequently, sabotage, as it was interpreted by the Communist officials.

Of all the campaigns, problems and questions, the Horse Campaign remains clearest in my memory. This was the most peculiar and ridiculous, and for some, the most tragic one.

A complete turnover of livestock ownership was effected by the collectivization of agriculture. As the farmer joined the collective farm, he was expected to contribute his stock to it. Naturally, he preferred to enter the collective farm with as few animals in his possession as possible. Many, embittered by the policy of collectivization, slaughtered their livestock prior to their forced joining of the kolhosp. Others attempted to trade or sell their animals. But not all could be sold, and those unsold were taken into the kolhosp stables under the new collective ownership.

If death is better than life in a total misery, then the fate of the animals under collectivization was worse than that of those slaughtered by the farmers, for the kolhosp stables were slow highways to the grave. Provisions for the care of animals were slipshod, if not entirely lacking. Forage was not available for them, and the farmers, deprived of their ownership, were indifferent to the fate of collectively owned livestock.

The results were catastrophic. The combination of lack of care and disease that struck during the winter months killed hundreds of horses in our village. A serious problem then developed for the officials of the collective farm, for horsepower still determined agricultural production. It was this problem that brought about the Horse Campaign in our collective farm.

A rumor was circulated the day prior to the meeting that Comrade Cherepin, having returned from the county Party conference, had important news to communicate to the members of the collective farm. The stablemen predicted that this meeting would have something to do with horses. They ventured this guess because Comrade Cherepin had made an inspection of the horses immediately upon his return from the conference.

The former church was again the meeting place. When Mother and I arrived, the meeting was already in progress, and the hall was filled to capacity. The speaker, of course, was Comrade Cherepin.

The same words and slogans flowed from his mouth uninterruptedly. He exalted the class struggle, and the world proletarian revolution in a deluge of words. These were his favorite harangues which he juggled expertly while the audience waited for the main show to begin. After an hour or so, Comrade Cherepin finally changed topics and touched on his main point.

Reminding us all that the Soviet Union should overtake the capitalists countries of the entire world, especially the United States of America, he pointed out that horses carried hope for the future. The reason that led to the substitution of the word "horses" for "tractors," on which high hopes had been placed in the most recent tirades, had been determined at high Party levels. Zig-zags like this were not explained to the farmers.

"Horses, comrades, horses, and more horses," Comrade Cherepin shouted. "Our dear Fatherland is in want of horses; and our beloved Communist Party demands horses!" He stopped for a moment. Then, staring at his audience, he pronounced slowly but clearly, through clenched teeth: "We need more and better horses, comrades! This is our watchword at the present time."

The new watchword, however, had been placed in the old familiar straitjacket of doctrinal haranguing. Only a few weeks before, Comrade Cherepin had predicted prosperity for the present and coming generations if the members of the collective farms would "increase the fertility of the pig stock."

Another time, speaking about the "productivity of the cow," he stressed that if the farmers would solve the "milk problem"—and they had better solve it, or else!—the Soviet Union would become a country "of rivers flowing with milk and honey."

During previous meetings, the villagers managed a sympathetic blankness which dissolved after the meeting ended, when the listeners erupted into laughter or criticism, depending on the individual.

The absurdity of the "horse speech" was no different from that of other speeches. That horses were valuable in agricultural endeavors was recognized everywhere and by everyone. But, no member of the collective farms (to whom Comrade Cherepin was speaking) owned his own horse. They had all been collectivized. Now Comrade Cherepin's outburst suggested that the farmers should immediately produce more horses in some way. At least, this was how we understood him.

"We must solve the horse problem!" Comrade Cherepin reiterated. "And speaking dialectically, in order to have horses, one must at first have colts. Our future, comrades, depends on horses, for on horseback we'll reach our goals more easily and quickly!"

That was something to digest and to wonder about. None of us, of course, knew what the word "dialectically" meant. So this point was lost for us; for me, at least. But the second part of his statement was clear. All of us knew how to ride a horse. I even imagined Comrade Cherepin on horseback chasing the "goal." But, what was he trying to tell us?

In a lower voice, after a pause that he apparently gave to allow the importance of his statement to penetrate our minds, Comrade Cherepin continued:

"But, comrades, even this branch of our society has not been immune from the destructive power of our class enemies. This, the most vital factor in our existence became infested by the counterrevolutionary activities of the capitalist elements."

Pains of fear became pains of pity as attention fell on the stablemen. They were being blamed and doomed.

The voice of Comrade Cherepin boomed again, and the audience came to attention, each hiding behind the back of his fellowman.

"That the enemies of the people are at work in our kolhosp is an established fact. How many colts are there in our stables? You don't even know! And how many are to be born in the near future? Can you tell me?" He paused for a second. "No, you cannot!"

The audience sat in silence. Everybody now tried to avoid showing any sign of emotion. Immoderate display of feelings, for any reason, had been "rewarded" handsomely in the past. Now, facing Comrade Cherepin as he was throwing out accusations about the "low fertility of the kolhosp mares," the villagers sat speechless.

"Fifteen!" he shouted. "There are only fifteen colts on the entire collective farm!"

Comrade Cherepin's ignorance of agriculture and its vocabulary, now caused a situation which was absurd to the villagers but pitiful and tragic to his victims. Tossing around human terms while referring to the mares in the kolhosp stables, he asked how many of them were pregnant. The senior stableman to whom the question was addressed guffawed at the misuse of the word "pregnant." This was something unusual. The people had been conditioned to listen to Party dignitaries with the same attention once accorded the priest.

As the senior stableman laughed, Comrade Cherepin glanced at him, and then at the audience. He then deliberately took a drink of water. The stableman hesitated; his mirth disappeared quickly under the murky stare of the Party boss. He began to realize the gravity of the situation, but it was too late.

"You are laughing," Comrade Cherepin sneered at him. "To you, it is funny. My words amuse you. The words of the Party and government amuse you!" His voice was rising in anger. His eyes gleamed with fire.

The pale-faced stableman, searching for a way out of his dilemma, tried to say something. Raising his hands, he mumbled, "I . . . I only wanted to say that . . ."

"I am still a Party and government representative here," shouted the enraged Cherepin. Realizing that he was fighting for his very life, the stableman squeezed in a short apology before Comrade Cherepin could again shout him down.

"I laughed only because mares cannot possibly be called 'pregnant'; only women. . . . The mare is with foal!"

The stableman did not quite finish what he wanted to say. He probably could not find just the proper word. However, he again apologized for his "childish behavior," denied that he had laughed on purpose, and asked forgiveness for having interrupted such a worthy and patriotic speech.

When he finished his plea, he gazed with frightened eyes around him for some sort of help. The villagers all had their eyes riveted on Comrade Cherepin, and the accused was left pitifully alone. The audience remained silent, waiting for Cherepin to continue.

"As you see, comrades," Comrade Cherepin finally broke the silence, "the event which has just happened is an excellent example of what Comrade Stalin—" A loud and prolonged applause interrupted him.

"Comrade Stalin—" Somebody started to applaud again, but he ignored him, and continued:

". . . Comrade Stalin describes as the class enemies' sally."

He deliberately paused, looking complacently at the audience. Then his eyes turned again to the senior stableman.

"Would you be kind enough to tell me why there are no—or if there are some—why so few of these whatever-you-call-them mares? Why, eh? Would you explain that? No; you cannot! There is nothing to explain. Everything is clear."

The nervous stableman jumped to his feet, wanting to say something more, then reconsidered, sat down again, and raised his hand. But he was completely ignored. Comrade Cherepin continued:

"And how can segregated and firmly fastened mares ever become whatever-you-call-it?" He rushed past the last words, and went on.

"No, no, a thousand times no! Never!! And the class enemies know this. They know it very well. That is why the mares are separated from the horses; and that is why they are tied firmly in their stalls. This explains the low fertility of our mares, and that is why we don't have any colts in the kolhosp! That is why we'll never have enough horses in our kolhosp as long as this condition exists, and as long as these enemies of the people run our stable."

Comrade Cherepin finished his speech with an air of satisfaction and smug accomplishment. He drank some more water and sat down. As before, there was a complete silence.

The meeting remained in session for several more hours. Only after midnight, when about all of the Party members had given their speeches, made their condemnations, and heaped their abuse on the stableman, did it come to an end. Finally, the leader of the Komsomol read the final resolution. As far as I can recall, it read:

Considering the report of the Party representative, Comrade Cherepin, concerning the instruction of the county Party Organization to start the Horse Campaign throughout the county, we, the members of the Lenin Kolhosp, resolve to include ourselves in the above-mentioned campaign immediately. As we start the Horse Campaign, we do solemnly promise to our Party and its beloved and wise . . .

The end of the sentence was drowned in loud applause. But the silence was restored, and he repeated: "we promise to achieve a hundred percent pregnancy rate among our mares."

A storm of applause followed. The resolution was adopted unanimously.

The next day, all the stablemen were relieved of their duties and transferred to field work. The senior stableman was taken to the county seat, where he vanished.

The life of the horses was changed radically. In Comrade Cherepin's words, "to give the mares a chance to get pregnant," all horses were left in their stalls untied. This was an explicit order of Comrade Cherepin.

Although changes were brought about in the collective farm as a result of the Horse Campaign, the horses' difficulties had not been solved—at least, not at that time. The village jesters speculated that the horse problem remained in its disgraceful state because the Party and government instructions continued to ignore an important detail. No one in the Party seemed to recognize the importance of stallions.

CHAPTER 15

ONE MORNING, upon reporting as usual to the collective farm labor office for my daily work assignment, I was told that I had to drive the kolhosp chairman to the county seat. Without delay, I harnessed a horse to a farm cart, and as soon as the chairman was ready, we started our journey.

My passenger, Comrade Mayevsky, was an outsider. He had been sent to us by the county government. He was a large man in his early forties. His face was round and fat, and he was always clean shaven. We never discovered what he did prior to coming to our village, but it was quite obvious that he did not know much about village ways. His most prized possession was his revolver which he carried in such a way that half of it was always on display. In his office, he kept the revolver on his desk, and toyed with it whenever a visitor seemed to disagree with him.

Just after we left the village, Mayevsky fell asleep in the back of the cart, so our journey was a very quiet one.

We stayed in the county center only a short time, and by noon we were well on our way back to the village.

It was a beautiful day; the sun was shining brightly. A light breeze was blowing and larks were singing. As we rounded a curve in the road, a man came into my view. He was walking slowly in front of us toward the village. As I got closer, I recognized him: it was Vasylyk, a distant relative of mine and a neighbor.

This unexpected meeting created a difficult problem for me. Only a few days before, militiamen had visited our village, searching for him. Now there he was, only a few hundred feet away from me. In a couple of minutes I would overtake him, and I knew he would start a conversation with me. This would mean certain death, for in my wagon was the most ruthless official in the village.

I tried to slow down, but it didn't help for Vasylyk was walking too slowly. All of a sudden, I saw a narrow road on the right side of the road. On a sudden impulse, I swung the horse into it. I was sure Vasylyk would take the next field path to the left, since that was the shortest way to my home.

But now the road was very rough, and the rattling and bumping awoke Comrade Mayevsky almost immediately. I pretended that I had fallen asleep. This made him furious. He kicked me in the back with his boot, and ordered me to turn back to the main road.

I made another attempt to avoid Vasylyk by setting the horse into a gallop. But in spite of the speed with which we passed him, Mayevsky spotted him. He ordered me to stop the horse, and leaped from the wagon. Vasylyk saw him, realized his danger, and disappeared into the wheat. Mayevsky ran after him. Then I heard a shot; then another; a scream; and a third shot. . . .

Mayevsky returned to the wagon, his face glowing with satisfaction. "He wanted to escape," he said, wiping off his gun. Then, for some reason, he aimed the gun at the horse's head. There was a happy look on his face as he did this. "He made a big mistake," he continued, speaking more to himself than to me. "He did not know what it means to deal with a Red Partisan. Well, now he knows. . . ."

Putting his gun into its holster, he boasted: "Hundreds of counter-revolutionaries have tried to escape me, and all of them are dead now!" Then he looked at me.

"So, so," he sneered through his teeth. "So, so, you wanted to help him." Then he climbed back into the wagon, and after a moment or two, he was again apparently sound asleep.

Vasylyk's fate had actually been sealed on that February night when hundreds of our villagers were arrested and banished from the village. His father, although a poor farmer, was labeled a kurkul and, consequently, found himself and his family, Vasylyk included, among the arrested.

About a year had passed, when one day we received an anonymous letter mailed from the Arctic seaport of Arkhangelsk, informing us that Vasylyk had been shot to death while trying to escape from the concentration camp.

Then, one June night, as we were about ready for bed, we heard a knock on the door and a voice from outside. After a moment of hesitation, I opened the door. A miserable-looking figure stepped inside. There was no doubt in my mind that it was Vasylyk. Shaking my hand, he tried to smile. He looked totally exhausted. His clothing was torn and dirty, and his feet were wrapped in rags.

"We heard you were shot," my mother exclaimed on seeing Vasylyk. "And what happened to your mother and father, and to all . . . ?"

"I'm dead, indeed," he interrupted, trying to joke. "I'm only a ghost. Have you ever seen a ghost?"

The story he told us was truly a ghastly one. I shall retell it exactly as he told it to us.

That February night was cold and it was snowing. The column of sleighs loaded with the arrested farmers left the village under the guard of militia and soldiers of the security forces armed with rifles and machine guns.

Many tragic incidents happened along the way. A youth of about sixteen, tried to escape. He jumped off the sleigh and dashed into a backyard, but the machine gun crew opened fire and pinned him down. He was wounded, seized, and brought back to the column. Disregarding his wound, the guards tied him to the wagon by ropes. The wound proved to be fatal, and he died before the column reached the railroad station.

A GPU soldier was riding in a sleigh with one family. Ignoring all the people around him, the soldier started to make improper advances to a young girl. When he continued to annoy her, the girl's mother lost her temper, and struck him in the face. The soldier grabbed his gun, and shot the mother point-blank, killing her.

Upon reaching the railroad station, the girl was approached by the GPU officer who was in charge of the column. Speaking loudly enough to let everybody hear him, he informed her that her mother was killed by the soldier in self-defense. Her mother, an "arrested enemy of the people," he said, assaulted the guard with the intention of starting a riot among the convicted kurkuls. Thus, the action of the soldier was legitimate, patriotic, and even heroic. The girl and her two younger brothers were then taken away from the column and never seen again.

The news about the boy and the woman had not yet reached the rear of the column before several other incidents occurred. A few of the older men, among them my Uncle Havrylo, could not withstand the hardships and brutality and died before reaching the railroad station. A young couple committed suicide by slashing their veins.

As the snow continued to fall, some of the sleighs became stuck, and when this happened, the entire column had to stop. The men had to help the horses amidst the shouting and firing of the militiamen and the GPU soldiers and the screams and cries of the women and children.

A few miles from the railroad station, the column took a field road toward the railroad tracks. A freight train stood in the field on auxiliary rails. The front cars had already been filled with arrested farmers from other villages. Soldiers of the regular army stood guard at every car.

As soon as the column reached the train, the GPU officer passed the order that all had to remain in their sleighs. Guards took positions around the column. Without delay, the GPU agent moved from sleigh to sleigh with list in hand, calling the roll. Then the checked groups were escorted to the train immediately and herded into the cars, group after group.

When the first car was filled and locked, all realized that wives were separated from their husbands, and children from their parents. An angry murmur rushed through the column as the men claimed the right to be with their own families. A boy ran to the car that held his parents. A machine gun fired warning shots over the heads of the people, but the boy kept running. Three more shots rang out, and the boy fell dead.

At this point, the unrest turned into turmoil. Skirmishes broke out as people tried to escape. Several men broke from the column and ran toward the bushes that bordered the fields. A sleigh driver tried to escape as he urged the horses away from the station. Guardsmen opened fire, and the men running to the bushes fell and lay still. The man and his family on the sleigh did not escape death either. A machine gun caught up with them; he and his wife were killed, and his elderly mother and three children wounded.

Facing guns from every direction, the arrested farmers finally gave up, and order and silence were restored.

Group after group disappeared into the cattle cars. When the loading was completed, the doors were closed and locked, and a guard posted at each door. The dead were left behind in the field.

Vasylyk was in the last car. He was lucky enough to have his entire family with him, but it was torture for him to see his parents and his sister suffering under such horrible conditions. There were at least fifty people in his car, all herded into the cars that had been designed for livestock transportation. There were no beds or seats. The wooden floor, pierced by holes, was the only place where they could sit: there was no place where the sick could lie down.

It was dark inside the cars when the doors were closed. Only feeble shafts of daylight penetrated the cracks in the sides of the car. There was total confusion: those standing tried to find a place to sit down, and those sitting were trampled by the ones standing. There was shouting and arguing, and women were weeping for their husbands who were packed into other cars. Children cried for food; all suffered from the cold.

The lack of food and adequate clothing aggravated the situation. The arrested had been prohibited from taking any of their possessions, except for the personal belongings they could carry. And, since no one suspected that he or she would have to leave their home or village, the majority had failed to take their most needed belongings.

A pail in the middle of the cattle-car served as a toilet for all fifty people. A throng of people continually stood and waited their turn. Those who wanted to reach it had to literally walk over those sitting on the floor. This embarrassing situation increased the arguing and fighting.

The attempts to call the attention of the officials to the unbearable conditions were unsuccessful. Thus, hungry and cold, crowded together in the stinking cars, the arrested began their forced journey to an unknown destination.

The train was set in motion around midnight. When it crossed the bridge over the Dnipro River, all realized that it was heading north. The train moved slowly, and often stopped. At times, it stood still for hours. During one stop the door was unlocked and opened halfway. The first thing the arrested saw were two soldiers armed with rifles, ready to shoot. Another group of soldiers waited with sacks and buckets. The officer in charge announced that a loaf of bread would be given to every four persons and a herring to each. The water would be distributed from the buckets. The arrested were warned that those buckets were government property, and it was the responsibility of everyone in the car to see that they did not get damaged. A "supervisor" of the car had to be chosen who would be responsible for the distribution of the food and water, and for keeping order and "cleanliness" in the car which still had no proper sanitation facilities.

After these brief instructions, the soldiers shoved the sacks containing the bread and herrings and the buckets of water into the car and the door was locked again.

Immediately, the hungry people started shoving and arguing. Each had their own idea of how the food and water should be distributed. Opinions were expressed loudly. The strong pushed aside the weaker. The shouting and fighting were accompanied by the pitiful whining of the children.

Choosing a supervisor from among the group was a problem, for the position would naturally associate the individual with the officials. Nevertheless, one was chosen and the distribution of the food began.

Toward morning on the second day of the journey, a desperate cry of a woman woke up those who were still asleep: her husband had died. During the riot in the village square, he had been slightly wounded by a bullet in his leg. Afraid to be separated from his wife and then killed somewhere behind the walls of a GPU prison, he concealed his wound from the officials. A subsequent infection killed him. His corpse was removed at the next station stop. The sobbing wife of the deceased husband begged the officials for permission to be present at his funeral, but she was not even permitted to step out of the car. The men who carried the body away said there were many deaths on the train that night, and their corpses were piled up on the platform.

This first death affected the people in the car. The crying and shouting, as well as the quarrels and disagreements ceased. Everyone realized that the next dead one might be he or she.

The train moved forward slowly but steadily. It became colder. Contrary to everybody's expectations, the train did not stay long at the Moscow freight station. After a short stop, it gave a prolonged whistle and moved forward again. Those who sat close to the walls could see the lights of Moscow through the cracks.

The next stop was Alexandrov. By then, it had become unbearably cold, and the inmates of the train were suffering severely. Here Vasylyk lost his mother and sister. His mother who had fallen asleep sitting in the car, was stricken with a heart attack and never awakened. When her body was taken away, her daughter was permitted to step out of the car and follow the bearers. Vasylyk and his father were denied this privilege. When the bearers returned to the car, Vasylyk's sister was not with them; she was said to have been detained by a GPU officer.

As the train started up again, Vasylyk's father was silent. He expressed neither sorrow nor agitation; he just kept repeating from time to time: "My dear girls; my dear girls!"

The train began moving faster after Alexandrov. It passed many towns and villages without stopping. It was still snowing.

From signs and the names of the railroad stations, it was obvious that the train was moving in the direction of Archangelsk, a port on the White Sea. However, no one knew its exact destination.

On the twelfth night of the journey, the train stopped. No sign of a settlement could be seen through the cracks in the walls but increased activity by the guards suggested that it was not a usual stop.

In the morning, the door was opened, and instead of passing the usual daily rations of food and water to everyone, the guard ordered all to leave the car and line up beside it. Those who were not able to do so were carried out and placed on the snow. The usual chain of security troops surrounded the train and its cargo. The majority of the soldiers were from Central Asia.

As soon as the unloading was finished, the empty train left. To the arrested families who remained behind in the endless solitude, the disappearing train symbolized the end of everything. Vasylyk's first thought was that this would be his grave; that they would all be executed on the spot.

There was no sign of life around: no roads; no town; only a snowy plain which stretched for miles in all directions. Only a few snow-covered weeds and shrubs interrupted the monotony of the Artic expanse. In the distance loomed the silhouette of a forest, which would be the destination of the prisoners.

The officer in charge passed the warning that anyone attempting to leave the column would be shot. After roll call the column was set into motion. The sick who could not move were left behind on the ground under guard. No one ever saw them again. The children who could not walk were carried by their parents. Since there was no road, walking was extremely difficult and everyone had to follow in the tracks of the guards who led the way into the forest.

It was the coldest time of the winter in that region, and a blizzard blew violently from the north. Walking through the deep snow made the prisoners' feet wet, and soon they began to freeze. Many could not walk very far, and these were left behind.

Vasylyk's father had become sick during the train journey, apparently with pneumonia. Vasylyk helped his father along as much as he could, but in his sick and weakened condition, the old man collapsed. Another man in the column helped pull his father up, and Vasylyk began to carry him. It was difficult doing this through the deep snow, but he wouldn't leave his father behind. The officer in charge noticed them, and ordered Vasylyk to abandon him. He did not obey the order; he could not leave his father to die in the snow alone. The officer called the guards, and two huge Mongols came up and knocked Vasylyk down, wrestling his father away from him. Only then did he notice that his father was already dead. At gunpoint, he had to abandon his father's body in the snow.

After three or four long hours of difficult stumbling and walking, the column reached its destination deep in the woods.

It was peaceful all around: there was no sound, and no visible motion. The ground was covered by a blanket of snow. Huge, dark pine trees stood all around, their branches weighed down by snow and ice. Beneath and among them, at some distance, were several small huts, the only sign of human habitatation. Those facilities were built especially for the guardsmen, the inmates learned later.

The officer in charge explained that this place was to be their new home. He pointed out that as "enemies of the people," they should have been executed, but the government had decided to let them live in the hope that they would start a new way of life. He then said that the prisoners were to be divided into three labor groups.

The first group, consisting of the young and strong, would work in the forest as woodcutters; the second group would fence the settlement with barbed wire; and the last group was to build dwellings. This latter group included all the women and children. The officer assured the prisoners that the necessary tools would arrive at any moment. There was no food either, and even though he knew the prisoners had not eaten all day, he considered this a trifling matter. He was certain they could wait until the food arrived the next morning. Then he ordered the heads of families to make shelters and build fires for the night that was fast approaching.

It was only the dim hope of survival, and perhaps a return to their homes someday that kept these villagers alive as they prepared themselves for that first Arctic night in the forest. All who were still able to walk, rushed into the woods. Although they had no axes or other tools, by sheer determination they erected temporary shelters and fires were lit before nightfall.

Vasylyk joined a family of his acquaintances to build a shelter out of pine branches, but it didn't give too much protection against the Arctic weather. Everyone sat huddled around their fires all night long as a blizzard raged and the wind howled. The snow threatened to extinguish the fires.

Morning finally came and the storm had quieted. The officer then ordered all the prisoners to come to the middle of the camp. Everyone had to stand in line for the roll call, including the children and the sick. Many people had died during the night: some from exposure, others from exhaustion and starvation. The officer in charge ordered the corpses brought to the center of the camp and piled up in front of the line of prisoners, because even they had to be counted and identified.

After the roll call, a soldier read the list of assignments to various brigades. Then the food rations were distributed for the food and tools had arrived during the night.

Vasylyk was assigned to the brigade of woodcutters, and that morning was sent out into the forest to work.

He was still determined to escape and find and bury his father's body, for he was sure it was still lying in field where he last saw it. He also hoped that on the way back home he might find his sister who had been abducted in Alexandrov. However, his several attempted escapes were unsuccessful, as the guards were too watchful and experienced to allow an "enemy of the people" to escape easily, and he was severely punished for each attempt, but the punishments could not deter him from his intention and only increased his determination.

It took Vasylyk more than two years to finally escape.

In May 1932, while Vasylyk was still working as a woodcutter and his brigade were loading wood unto a train, he met a railroad man, also a Ukrainian, who had been exiled to the region earlier. This newfound friend gave Vasylyk clothing and a pair of shoes. Thus, disguised in more or less ordinary clothing, he was able to elude the guards.

Hidden in the locomotive as a stoker, he reached Arkhangelsk, which was in the opposite direction from his destination. From there, he sent us an anonymous letter, hoping to mislead the authorities. Then he started his journey homeward, traveling mostly by freight trains.

On the way, he stopped in Alexandrov to look for his sister, and the grave of his mother, but in vain. The cemetery attendants could not remember burying a woman of his mother's description. He was also unable to find his father and had no success in locating his sister. He finally realized that his search for his family was futile.

A new acquaintance, introduced to him by his Ukrainian friend, advised him to go to Moscow. The friend said that it would be much easier for him to outmaneuver the militia in that large city. So Vasylyk decided to try his luck there, although it was prohibited to enter Moscow without special permission. He got there by catching a moving freight train.

But Moscow was not the place for Vasylyk. He could not speak Russian well and looked too much like a Ukrainian farmer, all of whom were being hunted like rabbits. Besides that, it was impossible for him to find work. Every place he applied for a job, he was asked to present identification papers. Therefore, to avoid being captured and arrested again, he decided to return to his homeland, Ukraine.

Having had experience in traveling by train without tickets, he reached Kiev safely. There he repeated his endeavors to find work, but was again unsuccessful. He was recognized everywhere as a farmer, and farmers were prohibited from leaving their villages without official permission.

He finally decided to return to his native village. That is how he arrived at our home. Vasylyk lived with us for a few weeks, but, eager to work and to avoid staying in one place for long, he decided to move to the town. After another unsuccessful attempt to find work in town, he returned to our village only to meet his death at the hands of Mayevsky.

CHAPTER 16

AS SOON AS we returned to the village, Comrade Mayevsky woke up and ordered me to stop near the village soviet. He then informed the first militiaman we met that I was under arrest and ordered him to put me in the jail.

Since the eviction of the kurkuls, my Uncle Havrylo's house had become the office of the village soviet. Surrounded by neat auxiliary buildings and beautiful trees, it was very attractive from the outside, and roomy enough inside to accommodate the village government. Its location in the center of the village was another reason for its being chosen. Having settled down comfortably in the new office, the village officials established a hitherto unknown institution in the village, a jail. My uncle's pantry had been quickly remodeled with everything used for storage purposes thrown out, and a hole made in the wall for a window.

Once in jail, I realized that I would be charged with helping an "enemy of the people" escape from "Soviet law and the will of the working people." When my eyes became accustomed to the darkness in the room, I could recognize my fellow prisoners, about twelve farmers. I knew most of them personally, including Dmytro, my neighbor and a distant relative. It so happened that while plowing a field, he had run across a stone, thereby damaging the plow. Although this was a very common occurrence, the brigade leader said Dmytro had done it on purpose to slow down the work and lessen the output of the collective farm. At first, Dmytro thought that the brigade leader was joking, but when he realized that the man was serious, he lost control and punched the leader in the nose. As a result Dmytro was put in jail.

Only about five years before, Dmytro had married a beautiful girl, and three years before his arrest, he had become a father. He told me that had been the happiest moment in his life. Now his happiness, and probably his life, were coming to an end.

A similar incident led another neighbor of mine to be sent to jail. The horse with which he had been working in the field stumbled and sprained a tendon in its foot. This too was a common occurrence, but Comrade Cherepin thought differently. He claimed that the horse's foot was sprained because of carelessness and had my neighbor put in jail with no hope of returning to his sick wife and four children.

I also met the father of a school friend there. I called him "Uncle Petro". In the village he was known by his last name, Shost. I was not surprised to see him in the jail because he was one of the farmers in our village who had refused to join the collective farm.

Shost was poor, and in a way he typified the Ukrainian farmers of that day. He owned about fifteen acres of black land, two plowhorses, a cow, one or two pigs, and perhaps a dozen fowl—chickens, ducks, and geese. His farm buildings were quite rundown, and his house was old. The interior was divided into two sections: one was used for storing grain and farm produce, and the other part served as living quarters. This consisted of only two rooms: the front room was a combined living room, kitchen, dining room, and washroom. The other room was a bedroom where the whole family slept. The furniture was crude and primitive. There was a bench along one wall, and a table with a couple of homemade chairs stood in a corner. Icons were hung on the east wall, and on the front wall were the family photographs.

Seldom was a real bed to be found in a farmer's quarters, and this was true of Shost's. The sleeping space for his family was a wide wooden bench and the oven top. The floor was clay; the roof was thatched; and the interior was whitewashed.

Shost never hired help, for his farm was only big enough to support his family. In the years when his harvest was small, he would do other work to earn enough to see his family through the winter. He would journey to nearby towns and work on the roads or do other jobs, eating and sleeping with the other laborers in hovels in order to stretch his small wages and buy more food for his family.

With the coming of spring, he always returned to his beloved land. He believed in the land as he believed in God. Day and night he labored in the field and found happiness in watching his crops grow. One way or another he kept bread on the table.

He was an honorable man, and like all Ukrainian farmers, he had great self-respect and an intense love of freedom, both inherited from the Cossacks.

When the Communist government started the collectivization of the villages, Shost showed himself to be a strong and obstinate man. He refused to join the collective farm. For generations, his land had been the property of the family of Shost, and he intended to give it to his son when old age forced him away from his plow. Then eventually, his grandson would own the land, and so on, as it had always been.

The Shosts had survived many wars and foreign occupations on the same piece of land. They had grown up on the land and went out into the world, sometimes never to return, but they always thought of this farm as their home. Asking farmer Shost for his land was like asking for his very life.

To break his spirit, the village officials and the collective farm organizers hesitated at nothing. The most powerful weapon in their hands was the tax. They levied taxes payable in kind and money. Every time Shost thought he had paid all that was required, more items were taxed, and more of the produce of his land was taken from him.

Finally, the day came when he had no more money or grain. His horses were taken, then his cow, and then his implements. Shost resisted, a broken man, but not a beaten one. One day, men in uniform came and arrested him. He had been declared a kurkul and, of course, labeled an "enemy of the people."

Now he was in jail. He asked me to continue my friendship with his son, Ivan, if I should be freed from jail. He believed I would be freed because I was still a minor. In case something happened to his wife, he begged for my mother to take care of Ivan and his daughter Varka. Those were his last words to me. Then I heard his heavy breathing and sobbing.

It was already dark when we heard the clattering of keys and then the voice of a militiaman calling the names of those who had received food from home. Only then did I realize another tragic aspect of prison life.

When I had spoken of being hungry, I was told by my fellow prisoners that there wasn't any chance of getting food unless somebody brought it from home. I was also informed that there was no regulation with regard to food or other comforts of the prisoners. The food and the sleeping commodities were the concern of the prisoners themselves. If someone had a family, he had the hope that he would receive his daily meal; but those who were alone were left at the mercy of their fellow prisoners. It was a time of famine in the village. The only food available to the villagers, and thus to the prisoners, was vegetables and fruit.

When the militiaman finished calling out names, and locked the door, leaving the cell in darkness, I could sense that not all the inmates had received their supper. I didn't receive mine, but I did not expect it, for I knew that my mother had not yet heard of my imprisonment.

Fortunately, I was not in the jail long. Sometime after midnight, I was awakened, and ordered to leave the jail. My mother was waiting for me outside. On the way home, she told me that when I failed to appear at home after sundown, she had become alarmed and decided to search for me. She found my whereabouts easily, but it wasn't that easy to find Comrade Mayevsky, who had ordered my arrest. She finally found him in the company of a young woman, and asked for my release. He refused to listen to her, constantly repeating that there was no difference between a minor and an adult "enemy of the people." But, after my mother's persistence, he finally agreed to write a note to the village militia authorizing my release. Mother thought he had done it only to show his mistress the power he had in the village.

I told Mother about the murder of Vasylyk and, after some discussion, we decided that early the next morning, my brother and I would look for his body and bury it properly.

It was extremely dangerous for us to do this. Vasylyk had been the son of a kurkul, and the political atmosphere was such that anyone who associated with people of this group was treated like a kurkul himself.

But Mother disregarded the danger for us all. Vasylyk had to be buried in a decent way, no matter what might happen to us.

Long before daylight, Mother awakened us and gave us her final instructions. And, as we were about to leave the house, she placed a piece of paper in my pocket. She told me that it was a prayer, and that I was to read it over Vasylyk's grave after burying him. She warned me that I had to destroy it as soon as I had read it, for it was a dangerous piece of evidence. Then she kissed us and we left the house on our sad mission.

As we approached the place where Vasylyk had died, a beautiful day dawned. The eastern horizon became red, and the sun emerged like a huge ball of fire. The wheat fields were silent, except for the morning song of the quails.

It did not take us long to find his body. It was lying not far from the road in the midst of the tall wheat. The ground around him was stained with blood, and flies, ants, and other insects were swarming on and around his body. We immediately started digging. It was a difficult job for two young and hungry boys to dig a grave in the hard ground, but we finally managed to do it. We dug the grave slantwise, so we could roll the corpse into it with a minimum of effort. On the bottom of the grave we spread some straw. Then we wrapped the body in a blanket we had brought from home, and slid it into the hole in the ground. We quickly covered the body and hole with earth; made a cross from wooden strips Mother had provided; read the prayer she had given me; and then, after destroying the piece of paper, wended our way back home with heavy hearts.

CHAPTER 17

THE YEAR 1932 witnessed the last battle of collectivization: the battle for bread, or to be more specific, for the crop of 1932. On the one side was the Communist government; on the other, the starving farmers. The government forces resorted to any means in getting as many agricultural products from the countryside as possible, without regard to the consequences. The farmers, already on the verge of starvation, desperately tried to keep what food they had left, and, in spite of government efforts to the contrary, tried to stay alive.

It may be of help to the reader to remember that up to the end of 1931, the Communists fought their war against the farmers under the guise of fighting against "the kurkuls as a social class." But by 1932, the situation had already changed: the so-called kurkuls had already been physically liquidated, and collectivization had been completed except for a small number of farmers who were still clinging to their freedom. Thus, the battle now was fought between the Communist forces and the collective farmers; the Collectivization Campaign now changed into the Grain Collection Campaign.

The long and cold winter of 1931–1932 was slowly giving way to spring. By April, the snow had already melted away, and the weather became damp and drizzly. Often a heavy fog would descend upon our village, as if attempting to cover and hide the misery of our existence. Then cold winds would chase away the fog and bring cold torrential rains in their place.

Around this time the plight of the villagers became desperate. This was the memorable spring of 1932 when the famine broke out, and the first deaths from hunger began to occur. I remember the endless procession of beggars on roads and paths, going from house to house. They were in different stages of starvation, dirty and ragged. With outstretched hands, they begged for food, any food: a potato, a beet, or at least a kernel of corn. Those were the first victims of starvation: destitute men and women; poor widows and orphaned children who had no chance of surviving the terrible ordeal.

Some starving farmers still tried to earn their food by doing chores in or outside the village. One could see these sullen, emaciated men walking from house to house with an ax, or a shovel, in search of work. Perhaps someone might hire them to dig up the garden, or chop some firewood. They would do it for a couple of potatoes. But not many of us had a couple of potatoes to spare.

Crowds of starving wretches could be seen scattered all over the potato fields. They were looking for potatoes left over from last year's harvest. No matter what shape the potatoes were in, whether frozen or rotten, they were still edible. Others were roaming the forest in search of food; the riverbanks were crowded too; there was much new greenery around: young shoots of reed or other river plants. One might catch something, anything, in the water to eat.

But the majority of those who looked for help would go to the cities as they used to do before. It was always easier to find some work there, either gardening, cleaning backyards, or sweeping streets. But now, times had changed. It was illegal to hire farmers for any work. The purpose of the prohibition was twofold: it was done not only to stop the flow of labor from the collective farms, but also, and primarily, to prevent the farmers from receiving food rations in the cities.

There were some villagers who saw their salvation in the cities' marketplaces. There they brought for sale their best clothes, from prerevolutionary times, their family heirlooms, handicrafts, women's jewelry which had been passed on from generation to generation, homemade shirts, towels, tablecloths—all embroidered with traditional Ukrainian designs—handwoven Ukrainian rugs, and other valuables. These they sold for next to nothing, or bartered them for something edible. But many of the hungry villagers didn't go to the marketplaces with the intention of selling or bartering something; they had nothing to sell, and no money to buy anything. These public places were their last resort for finding some food. They became permanent residents there. I saw many such villagers when I went there occasionally for my mother. They wandered in the midst of the market crowds with outstretched hands, with tearful eyes, begging passers-by not to let them die. But most of the time the city dwellers would hurry past them, with eyes downcast, as if afraid or ashamed to even look at them. Soon, these starving beggars became such an everyday sight that the city people became used to them, and no longer paid any attention to them. The rejected hungry multitudes turned to scavenging. They would go over garbage and trash, taking anything that had been discarded: corncobs, apple cores, fruit peelings, even bones. At night, the hungry and starving slept right in the marketplaces under tables and benches, in bushes, or backyards.

Some of them would be mugged or even murdered during the night; others would be picked up by the militiamen on night duty, loaded onto trucks, taken out beyond the city limits, and dumped somewhere to fend for themselves, with strict orders not to return to the city. Yet many of them would return in spite of the danger; others would dejectedly go back to their villages, resigning themselves to death; some were in such a weakened state that they died where the militia had dumped them.

Many of the doomed tried to save themselves by going to the railroad stations and railroad tracks. Those who had something valuable to sell came there with their wares in the hopes of finding buyers among the travelers. Others came empty handed, just to beg for a piece of bread or a morsel of food. But one could also still find a few bold souls who came to the station intending to travel to some more distant cities, usually in Russia, where there was no famine. However, such an undertaking was a very difficult and risky one. Train tickets were sold only to those who had written permission from the collective farm. It stated that its bearer was permitted to travel to a certain destination. The GPU men and the militiamen were constantly checking travelers' documents. Even those who were returning from Russia to Ukraine with legal travel documents were searched. Any food found in their baggage was confiscated.

By this time our village was in economic ruin. Poverty was universal. We had never been rich, it is true, but economically, we had always been completely self-sufficient and had never gone hungry for so long. Now starving, we were facing the spring of 1932 with great anxiety for there was no hope of relief from the outside. Deaths from starvation became daily occurrences. There was always some burial in the village cemetery. One could see strange funeral processions: children pulling homemade handwagons with the bodies of their dead parents in them or the parents carting the bodies of their children. There were no coffins; no burial ceremonies performed by priests. The bodies of the starved were just deposited in a large common grave, one upon the other; that was all there was to it. Individual graves were not allowed, even if someone were still physically able to dig one. This strange ordinance originated with Comrade Thousander who was supposed to have said: "There is nothing wrong with a common grave," implying that the Soviet man who lives and works in a collective can also be buried in a collective grave.

Looking back to those events now, it seems to me that I lived in some kind of a wicked fantasy world. All the events which I witnessed and experienced then and which I am now describing, seem unreal to me because of their cruelty and unspeakable horror. It is simply too difficult to associate all those happenings with real life in a normal human society.

I shall never forget the celebration of May Day in our village in 1932. May Day is an important Communist holiday, and the village administration would not miss it. On this day the Spring Sowing Campaign was to be launched officially, even though spring sowing and planting had been going on since the beginning of April.

Our collective farm specialized in growing potatoes, tomatoes, cabbage, onions, and other vegetables which required much care and many workers. On the eve of May Day, to attract attention to the launching of the Spring Campaign, the collective farm administration made a special announcement: A hot meal was to be distributed from an outdoor kitchen in the village square to the participants of the celebration, which was to take place in the morning. After the celebration and their meal, the collective farmers were to go straight to their field work.

I came to the square with our school. It was an established custom that the village school, which in my village was a nine-year school, was the focal point of such celebrations. We had to sing and recite poems, play games, and show everyone that we were very happy. It took quite an effort on our teacher's part to explain to us each time how to look happy, and it was particularly difficult for us to imitate "happy youngsters" this year. Many of our schoolmates had already died, and many others were sick from starvation and could not partici-

140

pate in the celebration. Nevertheless, nobody could ignore the Communist holidays. We students had to participate like everyone else, and we had to smile and laugh whether we wanted to or not.

On the way to the square, we had to sing the songs we had learned for this occasion. We also carried a huge red flag and the usual Communist slogans such as "Long Live the Communist Party," "Long Live the Soviet Regime!" and "We thank the Communist Party for Our Happy and Prosperous Life!"

The first thing I noticed upon reaching the square were some kettles hanging over the fire. Around these kettles was a cordon of militia deputies guarding them like some treasure. All of the militia were armed with shotguns. The village administrators stood close to the kettles, which were being tended by several women. The huge crowds of hungry participants were kept at some distance from the kettles by a row of tractors.

The scene I saw in the square is impossible to forget. There were literally hundreds of emaciated people staring at one focal point: the kettles steaming with hot food. Some of the onlookers stood on their own, others were so weak that they had to be supported by relatives or friends. Many others could only lie on the ground. The crowds were strangely quiet and orderly but tense with expectation, waiting for something to happen.

When Comrade Thousander mounted a tractor to begin the celebration with one of his usual harangues, all the protruding eyes that had been fixed on the steaming kettles and the smoke from the fires turned to him. He started by congratulating all of us on the holiday. Then he reminded us that in celebrating May Day, we must (and he emphasized *must*) show solidarity with all proletarians, whatever that meant. At the end of his long speech, he announced that with the celebration of the May Day, the collective farm began its Spring Sowing Campaign. The best way to celebrate these two great patriotic events, he admonished, was to take part in the socialist competition for speedy fulfillment of one's work norms in the field.

By this time, his hungry audience began growing impatient. The hundreds of pairs of eyes had lost interest in him long ago, and again kept their hungry stare on the kettles. They could wait no longer. Very slowly but persistently, the multitude began to advance forward, getting closer to the kettles.

"And now"—Comrade Thousander was shouting his finale to his

hungry audience—"now, thanks to our dear Communist Party, we are able to celebrate these two events with our traditional hot buckwheat porridge!!!"

The hungry and ragged crowd did not wait for him to finish his last words. Men, women, children, all who could, rushed to the kettles, shouting, shrieking, cursing. Hundreds of feet trampled over those who were weaker or who lay on the ground, and tried to crawl to the kettles.

But no one managed to get to them. At the moment it seemed that the threatening crowd was about to overrun the area with the kettles, a shot rang out, then another. . . . This however did not stop the stampede. Then a desperate man mounted one of the tractors and started shouting something. A third shot sounded. The man on the tractor wavered a second and then fell. This third fatal warning signal caught the attention of the crowd, and the tumult subsided.

Comrade Thousander, who had stood on the tractor speechless and helpless during the uproar, now regained his composure. Surveying the crowd contemptuously from his high position, he shouted angrily, "Stop behaving like wild animals!"

"You'll have to wait your turn in lines," he continued. "The first ones to receive the meal will be those who are able to work in the field." Saying this, he stepped down from the tractor and took his place by the kettles to supervise the distribution of the food.

Slowly order was restored. The hungry ones were properly lined up. Some were standing; some lying in their waiting lines, all holding food containers: bowls, pots, and cans. Comrade Thousander nodded benevolently, signaling the May Day meal to begin. Each person received two large scoops of buckwheat porridge. No one was forgotten or omitted.

After the meal was finished, Comrade Thousander mounted the tractor again to make an important announcement. From now on, he said, the members of the collective farm who worked in the field would receive a pound of bread, and two hot meals daily. Then he ordered those who were able to go immediately to the field and start working.

There were not many who left for the fields. The buckwheat porridge could not perform miracles. Many were too weak to walk for a longer distance, or even get up. They remained sitting or lying in the square, licking the remainder of the porridge from their containers.

We, the pupils, and our teachers, were the last ones to receive our portions of the porridge. While the hungry crowds were gulping their shares, we had to sing patriotic May Day songs, thanking the Communist Party and the Soviet government for granting us a happy and prosperous life. All the while we endured the hunger pangs torturing us and envied those who were already eating their porridge.

The man shot and killed on the tractor was dragged away from the place where he had fallen and left lying in the square in open view. I noticed after a while that a starving dog approached him, and after some careful sniffing, started licking the blood off his wound.

CHAPTER 18

THE BATTLE for the Ukrainian wheat crop of 1932 started almost two months before the harvest.

At the end of May, some strangers appeared in our village, and little by little, we began finding out who they were. The Party had mobilized 112,000 of its most active and reliable members in order to organize a speedy harvest of the new crop, and to secure its swift and smooth requisitioning and final delivery to the State. Soon these members became known to us as the Hundred Thousanders, or just Thousanders. There were nine of them in our village, one for each Hundred, and one who was to become the village Thousander: the leader of the entire group. The former Thousander, Comrade Cherepin, along with his entourage, were transferred to another village. In no time at all, these new Thousanders took over our entire village like tyrants, imposing their wills and their demands upon us.

The name of our new village Thousander was Livshitz. We called him Comrade Livshitz, or simply Comrade Thousander. Nobody knew where he came from, but it must have been one of the big cities. He had urban manners, and although he spoke broken Ukrainian, he tried to speak in a polished and polite way. His hair was dark, with no signs of graying, although he must have been in his fifties, and he was of average height. We believed he was married for he wore a plain gold band on his finger, but we heard nothing about his wife or family. He was a typical town dweller; there was nothing unusual in his appearance. However, the look in his eyes, and the way he talked to us betrayed his hatred toward us, the people over whom he was to rule.

Comrade Livshitz and his colleagues assumed their authority in the village without delay. The next day we heard that they had reinstated the village administrative system established by Comrade Zeitlin, our first Thousander in 1930. We were again caught in the meshes of the administrative units of Hundreds, Tens, and Fives. Again, we were subjected to endless meetings and sickening propaganda speeches. Once more we were forced to participate in "socialist competition" between those administrative units. We had to resume "path-treading," this time for not turning in "hidden hoards" of food and so forth.

The new Thousander, in addition to regular secret informers of the GPU, established a spy network which was very naive, but at the same time very effective. This was the network of *silkors,* or village correspondents. The spy network was organized as follows: ordinary villagers, usually members of the Young Communist League and schoolchildren, were appointed by the village Party organization, or by the Thousander personally, to act as reporters. The ostensible purpose of their contributions to the press was to report about what was going on in the village. But, in reality, these *silkors* were instructed to look for traitors and saboteurs. They were particularly instructed to denounce those villagers who were hiding foodstuffs from the state, and those, who in one way or another, demonstrated hostility toward the Party and the government. In other words, they were taught to spy on their fellow villagers, and then report their findings and observations to the local newspaper. What these *silkors* did not know was that their reports were passed on to the appropriate government agencies, usually to the GPU and militia. If a given report seemed to contain some worthwhile information, a GPU agent or a militiaman would be dispatched to the village to investigate the matter further.

Thus the stage was set for a new drama to be performed by a new cast under the directorship of the new Thousander. A prelude to this drama took place in our neighborhood: it was the eviction of Stepan Shevchenko from his house.

Stepan was a poor farmer. He had a nice family consisting of his wife and two children: a boy of nine and a girl of seven. They were all healthy and seemed to be content with their lot. Although he was a poor farmer like the rest of us, Shevchenko differed from us in one way: he had categorically refused to join the collective farm, and what was most amazing to us, he somehow managed to survive in spite of it, or so it seemed, until June 1932.

He paid off all his taxes in kind and money for the year 1932, and apparently thought that the government would leave him alone, at least for a while. But he was overly optimistic.

One day, he received a requisition order demanding him to deliver 500 kilograms of wheat to the state. He delivered it in full. But no sooner had he done so when he received another order. This time they demanded twice as much wheat, something they knew he could not deliver because he had none left. His explanations were of no avail. The officials persisted and threatened him with Siberia. He knew that they meant it, so he was forced to sell everything he had of value, including his cow, to buy the order of wheat. He naively believed that now his troubles were over. Yet his fate had been sealed when he refused to join the collective farm. The demands of impossibly high quotas of grain were only excuses for ruining him. Sure enough, he soon received the inexorable third order: 2,000 kilograms of wheat immediately! This he could not do. He had nothing more of value to sell with which to buy any more grain. He and his family were already left destitute.

One fateful day, the Bread Procurement Commission paid him a visit. They searched his premises for hidden grain, but found nothing. Nevertheless, he was labeled a kurkul, and he and his family were ordered to leave their house immediately. The house and all that belonged to the Shevchenkos was confiscated and was to be turned into "socialist property." Upon hearing this proclamation, Shevchenko and his family put up a desperate struggle. Their cries and screams and the shouting of the officials attracted our attention. My brother and I ran there to see what was going on.

Shevchenko was struggling hand-to-hand with a few commission members; he tried to wrench himself free from them while shouting that he wouldn't leave the house which he had built with his own hands and by the sweat of his brow. He was pleading with them to leave him alone, for he was poor and had no more grain. His wife clung to the doorpost, resisting all attempts to be pulled away. Their frightened and helpless children just stood there, crying bitterly. Comrade Thousander did not participate in the struggle; he was smoking and watching his men carry out his orders.

After they subdued Shevchenko, they tied his hands behind his back and led him out to a waiting cart. His wife, still struggling, had to be carried out of the house by her hands and feet and thrown into the cart. There was nothing left for the children to do but meekly follow their parents. One of the men drove the one-horse cart with its pathetic load to the village center. After a while, the rest of the members of the commission emerged from the house. Comrade Thousander locked it with a padlock; then they all left as if nothing had happened.

We learned later that Shevchenko's house was to become the headquarters for the First Hundred. The previous headquarters, had been burned down during the riot. Shevchenko had become the innocent scapegoat for that crime because the house that he had worked so hard to build was needed to replace the destroyed building. We found out later that the Shevchenko family, together with other evicted victims, were taken from the village center to the railroad station and transported somewhere, with no trace.

Some village wit who still preserved his sense of humor, nicknamed the newly arrived Party Representatives the "Morticians." This nickname caught on, and soon the comrade Thousanders became known among us as the "comrade Morticians." Of course, no one would have dared to use that nickname openly. Yet a better title could not have been invented, for our village under their administration was full of starving people: some who died; others who were about to die. This specter of death was obvious to anyone entering the village. Yet, the Thousanders and a multitude of other diverse Party and government representatives, continued their search for grain from house to house unabated, in spite of seeing the victims of starvation with their very own eyes. In most cases, instead of finding grain in the households, they found the bodies of starved farmers. Even after such gruesome discoveries, they did not stop their search. The Party representatives' mission puzzled us. Collectivization had been completed and was no longer an issue. What then were they looking for in our village? Was it that the government needed convincing proof that we had all indeed perished? Bizarre as it may be, this seems to be the best answer to this question.

One Sunday in June we were summoned to a Hundred meeting. The meeting was to be held at Shevchenko's house. When my mother and I arrived the meeting had already started. Upon entering, I noticed that the interior had been completely remodeled: the walls that once partitioned the house into two rooms and a kitchen had been torn down. Now the place had become a large meeting hall with a raised platform and a rostrum at which the village Thousander, Comrade Livshitz, was making a speech. Portraits of Party leaders decorated the walls, and a long banner was hanging from the ceiling with the slogan, "The Struggle for Bread Is a Struggle for Socialism!" Another slogan on the right wall proclaimed, "Death to Kurkuls!"

I looked around me at the audience. It was not large; the hall was only half-filled. There were about thirty people present, all pathetic-looking: some were emaciated, walking skeletons; others, on the contrary, were swollen from starvation. All were silent, depressed, and apathetic.

Comrade Thousander was speaking about the Joint Resolution of the Council of Peoples' Commissars and of the Central Committee of the Communist Party of the Soviet Union concerning the grain delivery quota from the 1932 crop. The gist of his speech was the victory of the collective system of agriculture over the independent one. Based on that victory, he asserted, and by the annihilation of the kurkul elements in the villages, the USSR had achieved a great development of grain farming, a great expansion of acreage under crop, and great gross yields of grain. In 1931, the delivery to the State was increased to almost 2.5 times the amount delivered in 1928 when independent farming prevailed. Comrade Thousander reiterated that the Soviet Union had overcome the grain farming crisis thanks only to a realization of Lenin's Party policies. Then he announced that in 1932 Ukraine, as a whole, and our village too, would have to deliver the same quota of grain as last year.

Having finished reading and interpreting the Joint Resolution, Comrade Thousander went on to praise collective farming. He tried hard to prove that through collective agriculture the USSR would soon catch up with, and overtake, America and Europe in grain farming. The increase in grain delivery from the crops of 1930 and 1931 served as good proof of it, he said. He concluded by demanding that the grain procurement quota for 1932 be fulfilled at any cost. It was to be done as soon as the crop was harvested instead of waiting until January 1933, as the resolution indicated. By doing so, we the villagers, would prove our loyalty to the Communist cause. With this the meeting closed. There were no questions; no discussions. One could see that Comrade Thousander and his stooges were in a hurry to leave. They wanted to avoid hearing about the starvation among us.

Comrade Thousander's pep talk did not make much sense. His

figures for the total grain delivery quota for the entire Ukraine, and for our village in particular, did not mean anything to us, or matter much. Our grain bins, we knew and understood only too well, were empty. We also knew that attributing the increase of the 1931 grain delivery over that of 1928 to the superiority of collective farming over individual farming was deceitful. We knew very well from our own experience that the increase was due to other factors. To increase grain delivery in 1930 and 1931, all stocks and reserves, and even seed for sowing, were ruthlessly confiscated from the farmers without any regard to their needs.

Comrade Thousander's announcement that in 1932 we had to deliver the same quota of grain as in 1931 was a hard blow to us. We simply could not fulfill his demands. The 1932 grain quota was not based on the actual amount of grain sown, cultivated, and harvested; it was based upon an unrealistic government plan.

The farmers were either unused to or not interested in working in the collective farms. There was a shortage of manpower and draft animals. Because of famine, many villagers were either too weak to work or had left the village altogether in search of food. As a result, much collective land stood idle. A great deal, if not half, of the grain crop was lost in fields during reaping; such losses occurred during the harvest of 1931, and even more losses were expected during the harvest in 1932. Besides that, the farmers had no more grain reserves for sowing in the spring of 1932. Their corn bins stood empty or had been used for firewood. Thus Moscow's demand to deliver the same grain quota in 1932 as in previous years was not only impossible, but promised to be catastrophic.

While Comrade Thousander and his cohorts went on with their campaign for collecting and delivering the grain of the 1932 harvest to the state, the life of our villagers took a turn from bad to worse. Those in the most deplorable conditions were the villagers who could not plant their vegetable gardens, as well as those who were not able to work at the collective farm. As mentioned already, farmers who did work there received either one pound of bread or one or two pounds of flour daily. In addition, two times a day, they were fed a hot meal, usually some soup thickened with flour. It was hardly enough to sustain a working-person's life, but it was better than nothing. The working villagers still had the problem of feeding and supporting their dependents, for whom they received no extra food. The children, the

149

elderly, and the sick had to be sustained on what those working would bring them from work surreptitiously.

Faced with starvation, the villagers tried everything possible to save themselves and their families. Some of them started eating dogs and cats. Others went hunting for birds: crows, magpies, swallows, sparrows, storks, and even nightingales. One could see starving villagers searching in the bushes along the river for birds' nests or looking for crabs and other small crustaceans in the water. Even their hard shells, though not edible, were cooked and the broth consumed as nourishment. One could see crowds of famished villagers combing the woods in search of roots or mushrooms and berries. Some tried to catch small forest animals.

Driven by hunger, people ate everything and anything: even food that had already rotted—potatoes, beets, and other root vegetables that pigs normally refused to eat. They even ate weeds, the leaves and bark of trees, insects, frogs, and snails. Nor did they shy away from eating the meat of diseased horses and cattle. Often that meat was already decaying and those who ate it died of food poisoning.

CHAPTER 19

WE COULDN'T help feeling that we were pawns in some lethal game. Each of our moves to escape death met with an official countermove; each of our measures to avert it was opposed with official countermeasures. In their opposition and retaliation against us, the officials often resorted to actions that would have been ridiculous but for their unbelievable sadism.

One of these which I still vividly remember was the campaign for the delivery of dog and cat skins to the state. Spring was already being heralded by nightingales singing in the flowering orchards. But this year it did not bring the usual joy to our people, for starvation had reached its culmination point. Since anything edible was being consumed by the villagers, dogs and cats had become a very desirable commodity. One such spring day we heard gunshots reverberating some distance from us. The sounds were coming from the east, and as the shooting approached closer, it was accompanied by the loud barking, whining, and yelping of dogs. At the same time, we heard some men shouting and laughing. This sounded very strange at a time when all the people in the village were downcast and silent. Suddenly, shots rang out in our own backyard, somewhere behind the barn, followed by the sound of a dog yelping and whining. We immediately recognized our dog, Latka. I ran out, and as I came to the place, I saw our Latka lying on the ground in a pool of blood, dead. Three gunmen stood beside her, looking down at her, talking and laughing. I broke out crying and tried to pet my dead dog. But my lamentations made no impression on the killers. One of them pushed me aside, took our Latka by her tail, and dragged her to the main road where a horse-driven cart already loaded with the bodies of other dogs and cats waited. Then all three of them mounted the cart and drove away. After a while, we heard the sounds of more shouting in the distance, and of animals crying out in their death throes.

Soon we had an explanation for this seemingly senseless slaughter of pets. Our village had received an order to deliver a certain quota of dog and cat skins. The requisition was addressed to the village hunters, even though not a single shotgun was left in our village after the confiscation of all guns. So, the problem now was how to fulfill this new quota? Help came from an unexpected quarter: the Thousanders! They benevolently decided to do the dog and cat hunting for us, although no one had asked them. Thus our village became the hunting ground for the Thousanders. All nine of them came to our village carrying their own shotguns, in addition to their revolvers, which we knew they always carried. The Thousanders started their hunting season without asking our permission or even informing us of their intentions. Beginning at the eastern end of the village and moving west, they systematically and indiscriminately shot each dog and cat they saw.

The carcasses of the poor dead animals were dumped in the main yard of the collective farm. But skinning them proved to be more difficult than killing them: it was a slow process because there were not many qualified skinners. The piles of carcasses were guarded by two men appointed by Comrade Thousander personally. It was rumored that he was concerned about the possibility of our starving villagers stealing them one by one. A week or more passed, and the carcasses still had not been skinned. The piles began decaying and emitting a foul smell. Finally, we heard that Comrade Thousander personally ordered and supervised the distribution of the carcasses to those who wanted them!! The carcasses were distributed in a matter of hours. Hunger is the best relish indeed, as the proverb says. The question remained as to what this campaign and its consequences meant to all involved. Did the government really need the skins of the dogs and cats? It might have. Yet, the officials were not in a hurry, it seemed, to skin the dead animals. Could it not have been a part of the general plan to starve the farmers into a complete submission to the government? The fact that the Thousanders came to our village armed with shotguns indicated that this campaign of dog and cat killings was planned and prepared ahead of time. Was the extermination of dogs and cats perhaps a means of depriving the starving farmers of one last possible source of food?

One day, at the beginning of 1932, an alarming piece of news spread: "They are killing the nightingales!" In Ukraine, the nightingale is a national symbol. A nightingale conjures up an image of the Ukrainian village with its orchards, fields, and whitewashed houses. Each village household claims one or two nightingale families in its orchard as its own. We used to listen to the singing of nightingales in our village like city folk listen to concerts. Nobody, not even mischievous boys, chasing other birds, would ever harm the nightingales. A legend handed down between generations of villagers asserted that the death of a nightingale would bring calamity to the household or estate in which the nightingale had died, or (if such a crime were conceivable) been killed.

But hunger is merciless, and it made the starving people merciless to any creature, including nightingales. Disregarding the legend, starving wretches started hunting nightingales together with other birds. Their nests were plundered of their eggs and their broods.

Like the dogs and cats, the nightingales also became prey of the Thousanders, even though this time there wasn't any official campaign for them.

In the twilight hours or at dawn, we now heard shotgun blasts instead of the singing of the nightingales. In their hunt for the nightingales, just as in their extermination of our dogs and cats, the Thousanders were thorough and systematic. This time, they started in the village center. We heard that they split into two groups: one moved westward; the other eastward. In a few days they reached our place, and I had a chance to see them in action. They would stealthily and noiselessly approach a tree in which a nightingale was singing and wait for the appropriate moment. Then one of them would aim at his target and fire. There usually wasn't a miss; they were skilled marksmen. For each successful shot the lucky hunter would be congratulated by his companions.

We watched this senseless nightingale hunt with feelings of helpless outrage. We could find some justification if a villager, half-demented by hunger, resorted to killing the beloved birds in his great despair. But there was no excuse for killing them in such a cruel, well-organized manner, and with such lightheartedness, as if for sport or target practice. In seeking an explanation for this newest exploit of the

Thousanders, some villagers thought that it was an act of revenge of these city dwellers against us villagers. But then the question arose, revenge for what? We didn't feel guilty of anything against them or the government which they represented. No matter how we tried, we could not understand what was going on.

One factor was clear: the song of the nightingales was very effectively silenced, and it took quite some time until the nightingales reappeared in our village, much to our great silent rejoicing.

CHAPTER 20

THE FIRST half of June 1932 brought us some relief, and deaths from starvation became less frequent. The early fruits and berries began ripening, and many of the vegetables we grew were ready for consumption. Those who did not have their own gardens and orchards stole from others whatever and whenever they could. At night they would descend on the gardens like swarms of locusts, pilfering everything in sight: green onions; young potatoes; half-grown root vegetables such as carrots, beets, and parsley; strawberries and fruits. Soon, many gardens were completely devastated by them.

Thefts, burglaries, and robberies that were seldom heard of in our region became common occurrences now. A murder or suicide ceased to be a sensational event. Lawlessness was the result of the complete reorganization of communal life and the dissolution of human relationships. The local government, which was supposed to care for law and order became, in the hands of a few Communists, the instrument of our oppression and was either unable or unwilling to give us the protection that as citizens we ought to have had.

For instance, we heard that two brothers, Fedir and Vasil, good friends of mine, were beaten to death and thrown into an abandoned well. It was rumored that they were killed by their neighbor for stealing a cooked meal from his house. Another boy was beaten to death for stealing strawberries from someone's garden. A young woman met with the same fate for stealing vegetables. In all these and similar cases, no investigations ever took place, no trials were ever held, and no penalties were ever inflicted on those who were responsible.

The kolhosp crop was not safe from the starving farmers either. As soon as night fell, the kolhosp vegetable fields would be swarming with villagers, ravenously hungry. They grabbed everything they could find in the darkness. They dug up potatoes; pulled out young cabbage-heads and root vegetables. This was the time when the heads of grain began to fill out. They became great hunger quenchers for the starving people who flocked to the wheat fields, broke off the heads of wheat, and often ate them right then and there. The wheat heads were also taken home and dried; their grain, even though green and not yet ripe, was used to cook gruel and porridge. Those who worked in the kolhosp fields endeavored surreptitiously to get hold of some vegetables or a few heads of grain to take home and feed to their children and their nonworking family members. But this soon proved to be an unreliable source of food. Comrade Thousander eventually put an end to it: he organized a brigade of "Communist vigilantes" and entrusted them with guarding the kolhosp fields. The vigilantes had been recruited from among the Communist activists, the Komsomol, and also from the schoolchildren. Years later I came across the following statistics provided by Pavel Postyshev, Ukraine's Moscow-appointed ruler at that time:

In 25 regions of Ukraine, 540,000 children engaged in the protection of crops and in picking of fallen grain, and 10,000 children in the fight against wreckers.

The vigilantes guarded the kolhosp fields day and night. Each worker was not only closely watched in the field, but also bodily searched at the end of each day. This was done on the explicit order of Comrade Thousander who was afraid that the collective farmers might have succeeded in hiding some vegetables or heads of grain under their clothing, even after having been watched so industriously.

Furthermore, to safeguard the 1932 crop against the starving farmers, the Party and government had passed several strict laws. In compliance with these laws, watchtowers were erected in and around the wheat, potato, and vegetable fields. These were the same kind of towers that can be seen in prisons. They were manned by guards armed with shotguns. Many a starving farmer who was seen foraging for food near or inside the fields, fell victim to trigger-happy youthful vigilantes and guards. If some starving person was caught alive while searching for food there, he was severely punished. If he was convicted of theft of "socialist property," no matter how negligible the amount might have been, he was evicted from his house and banished to a labor camp somewhere in northern Russia.

One of the cruelest laws of all was enacted on August 7, 1932. This law decreed that all kolhosp and cooperative property such as the crops in the fields, community surpluses and storehouses, livestock, warehouses, stores, and so forth, were hereupon to be considered as state owned. The protection of such property from theft was to be enforced in every possible way. The penalties for theft were execution by firing squad, and confiscation of all property of the guilty one. The alternative sentence was no less than ten years of penal servitude in a labor camp, as well as confiscation of property. There could be no amnesty for these so-called felons, convicted of theft from the kolhosp.

This law, as already mentioned, was aimed at the starving farmers. No other interpretation is possible. Only those poor, hungry wretches in quest of food were driven and forced by hunger to steal from the communal, and now state-owned, property. And the state, instead of providing them with food, at least with some meager rations, forced them to steal that "forbidden fruit" and thus become criminals. Not only petty thievery of a potato or a couple of heads of grain from the communal fields was considered a grave offense against the state: it was considered a great crime to even glean the already harvested fields, to fish in the rivers, or to pick up some dry branches in the forest for firewood. After the passage of this law, everything was considered socialist, state-owned property, and thus everything was protected by law.

CHAPTER 21

THE long-awaited harvest of 1932 finally arrived. Its beginning was loudly heralded by endless political speeches.

Sometime in the middle of July, we witnessed the arrival of a combine and two harvesters and, the next day, a small military unit in two trucks. The trucks were parked next to the harvesting machines, and the military found accommodations in the school building. We soon learned that these military people were prohibited from leaving the school premises or associating with us. Sentries were standing around the premises day and night. During the time the military stayed in the village—about two months—we never saw them in the streets or talking to villagers.

The soldiers were followed by a group of students and a group of laborers. The students came from the Teachers' College, the only institution of higher learning in the county seat. The laborers were from the machine-building factory there. This was the plant, as we often heard, under whose patronage our kolhosp had been formed. These two newly arrived groups were lodged in what had been the parochial school before the church was destroyed. These newcomers were also completely isolated from us.

It was announced that the next Sunday (which was a workday at that time), the wheat harvest campaign would be officially inaugurated. Early in the morning on that day, all the kolhosp members had to appear in the village square. We also heard the rumor that during the inauguration, a hot meal would be distributed. That did the trick! When we arrived, the square was already overflowing with people, even though the day had just dawned, and the sun was barely over the horizon. People in the kolhosp worked not by the clock, but by the sun: from sunrise to sunset.

Just as during the May Day celebration, kettles were hanging over the fire in the center of the square. Around the fire stood a few Thousanders with shotguns slung over their shoulders. A little farther from them were the soldiers in their two trucks. A group of students, and a group of laborers stood separately on either side of the combine. All these official representatives and participants looked solemn. They tried to avoid looking at us, the ragged and hungry collective farmers.

We all stood at some distance from the kettles, quietly, with our eyes fixed on the boiling and steaming porridge inside them. This time, no one lay on the ground weak or dying, as it had been during the May Day celebration. Those people had died already. In and around the square this time stood the ones who were the fittest survivors of the rigors of hunger. They managed to survive by not shying away from eating anything edible and organic, no matter how distasteful, unpalatable, and revolting it was.

Comrade Thousander mounted the combine to start what was inevitable at such occasions: the political speech. This time, however, it was surprisingly short. Nevertheless, he took some time reminding us that only collective farmers had the opportunity to celebrate the beginning of harvest in such a well-organized, dignified way. Talking about the harvesting machines and the combine on which he was standing, he took the opportunity to boast that only the farmers of the Soviet Union could afford to have such advanced agricultural machinery. Finally, he urged us to be thankful to the Communist regime for the soldiers, the students and the laborers, who had been sent to give us a helping hand in harvesting the new crop. Of course, he failed to mention why all this additional help was needed. He did announce that the collective farmers would receive two pounds of bread and two hot meals daily throughout the harvest season. He concluded his speech with the slogans "Long Live the Communist Party" and "Long Live the Collective Farms" and after that, he invited all of us to receive our rations of the hot porridge.

This time the crowds lined up in a well-organized manner and proceeded silently towards the food. Most of the farmers shuffled forward with bowed heads and avoided the eyes of those who were ladling the porridge into their containers. They felt humiliated for being fed like beggars in the presence of all the newcomers from the city.

It took quite a while to feed the large crowd. Comrade Thousander grew impatient and gave the order to move to the fields while many still thronged around the kettles. The first thing to be set in motion was the combine. A red flag was hoisted onto it, and banners were attached to both of its sides. Their slogans proclaimed the farmers' enthusiasm for being able to deliver so promptly their grain quota to the state. The engine of the combine was started, and it began to move forward slowly. It was huge and impressive. At some time, and under other circumstances, the novelty of seeing such a huge machine in motion would have attracted much attention from the villagers. This time, however, the hungry people were more preoccupied with their porridge. Many people, after licking the rest of the porridge from their bowls, hoped to get a second serving.

Meanwhile, the military trucks began moving, following the combine. Next came the harvesters and after them, in a long column, the horse-drawn kolhosp carts, about two dozen of them, with city laborers and farmers. The cavalcade was followed by the rest of the farmers on foot, some of them still finishing up their food.

It was obvious that all aspects of the harvest campaign—its opening with a celebration, the march to the field, and even the beginning of reaping itself—had been planned and carried out with military precision. As soon as the procession reached the wheat field, the combine turned off the road to the left, and started its job of cutting and threshing the grain. The military men jumped off their trucks and rushed to their assigned places. The trucks lined up so as to catch the threshed grain pouring from the combine.

On the other side of the road, the horse-driven harvesters also went into action simultaneously. The women following the harvesters quickly and skillfully bound the reaped wheat into sheaves, while the men picked and loaded the sheaves onto their carts and brought them to the threshing machine operated by the students and laborers from the city.

At the beginning, everything went smoothly as planned, but then, in spite of all the careful planning, trouble began.

According to the regulations concerning the delivery quota, the new crop of grain had to be taken straight from the threshing machines to the main collecting points, in our case, to the railroad stations. In no time at all, the first military truck was filled with grain and immediately left for the station. The second truck was soon also filled with grain before the first had a chance to return. There was no other choice but to use the ordinary carts for transporting the grain, even though these carts were not suitable for the task. Comrade Livshitz had promised the county Party organization to dispatch a "Red Column" transport with as much grain as possible and as promptly as possible. He had to keep his promise. The grain delivery plan had to be fulfilled on time. So he ordered the carts filled with grain, disregarding the losses that might be incurred. The carts, piled high with grain, lined up in a column on the road, red flags decorating them, and their sides plastered with placards proclaiming that the farmers of our village voluntarily gave this grain to the state. This so-called Red Column first made a detour back to the village and from there went on to the railroad station.

The Red Column also had the task of performing a propaganda stunt: it had to pass through all the neighboring villages on its way, spreading the word that the farmers of our village were happy to deliver the first yield of their new crop of grain to the state.

In the meantime, the operation of the threshing machine had to be completely halted since there were no more horse-drawn carts to carry the sheaves. Seeing this, Comrade Thousander quickly and easily solved the problem. If there were no horses, then people could substitute for them. So, he rushed the students, laborers, and all who were in the field to the harvesters to bring in the sheaves. "Don't just stand there," he shouted. "You and you—move, and fast!" And move they did. As soon as the sheaves were ready, they would be grabbed and dragged to the thresher. One could see the people with their bundles of sheaves of ripe and dry wheat scurrying like ants for more than half a mile to the threshing machine. Needless to say, much grain was lost on the way.

Thus began the harvest of 1932 in our village. The next day, two more trucks arrived from the MTS, and the harvesting proceeded more or less without trouble. The state delivery quota was the first priority, and no one dared even mention the needs of the local farmers.

From the very start of the harvest to the end, not a single pound of wheat had been distributed to the village inhabitants. Nothing was left for them. We were told that all the grain had to be transported to the railroad stations. We also learned that there it had been dumped on the ground, covered with tarpaulins, and left to rot.

CHAPTER 22

SOMETIME by the end of August, the Grain Collection Campaign reopened with even greater intensity. Day and night we were reminded that we were still lagging behind in the fulfillment of the grain delivery quota. Endlessly long meetings were again conducted daily. All this was beyond our comprehension. We had been members of the collective farm for more than two years. This meant that we had no land of our own and therefore, logically, we could not have any grain of our own. Since collectivization had been started, the state Bread Procurement Commission had crisscrossed our village several times and requisitioned all of our grain reserves. As a result, our villagers were slowly starving to death. Anybody who came to us could see that. But the Thousanders and the other Party and government representatives pretended not to. They continued searching our homes and taking every single grain they could still find.

At about the same time—the end of August—it was rumored that we villagers would no longer be permitted to shop in the village store. One day we were summoned to a Hundred meeting and informed about the new law the government had passed to combat speculation in general consumption goods. Farmers who had not fulfilled their quotas of delivering grain and other produce had no right to buy their commodities in the state-owned stores. In order to buy such commodities one had to show an official certificate from the village soviet proving that its holder had fulfilled all quotas. Since all stores at that time were state owned, and nobody in our village had been able to fulfill the quotas, no one could buy anything. As a result we were deprived of the simplest necessities of civilized life. Most of us could not afford, for instance, the luxury of a kerosene lamp for lighting the house because we could not buy kerosene. We had to eat the little food we had, mainly vegetables, unsalted. We had to bathe ourselves without soap, for we were deprived of the right to buy it. I won't even mention other staples, such as sugar and so forth, for we had not seen them in our village for two years.

Later on, this law proved to be even harsher than we at first thought. The villagers would go to the neighboring cities where they could buy household goods from black marketeers. The law defined the customers of the black market system as speculators and established prison terms or detention in concentration camps for them of from five to ten years, without the possibility of parole or amnesty. As a consequence, for buying a needle, a spool of thread, a pair of stockings, or a pound of salt on the black market, a villager, if caught, was convicted of speculation and sentenced for up to ten years at hard labor somewhere in the Russian north.

A reprieve finally came. In September 1932 we received an advance payment in kind: a meager ration of 200 grams of grain of wheat per labor day. A month later, we received some potatoes, beets, and onions. This was all the food that was supposed to sustain our lives until the next harvest. Not a single villager who worked in the fields could have accumulated more than 200 labor days. The work norms were so high that it was rare for anyone to receive even a full labor day for twelve or more hours of work during the harvest season. Such a day's work was credited with only three quarters of a labor day, or even half. Thus for 200 labor days, a family of five received only about eighty pounds of grain, wheat, or rye, or sixteen pounds of grain per person.

It should be noted here that the rural populace in Ukraine depended almost exclusively on bread at that time. Villagers were completely deprived of meat, fat, eggs, and milk products. Nor were there any grocery stores, bakeries, or market stores of any kind in the village. In order to stay alive until the next harvest, we had to have at least two pounds of bread per person daily. Instead we received the equivalent in grain for less than one and a half pounds of bread per person for an entire month. We were promised that we would be getting more grain at the end of the year, but these promises were never kept.

It was the same story with payment in money. At the end of

December, the members of the collective farm were paid 25 kopeks (about five cents in American money at that time) per labor day. A family with 200 labor days received 50 *rubles* as payment for all of 1932. With this money, one could have bought only about three loaves of bread on the black market.

In normal times we lived off of our gardens. They provided us with potatoes, cabbages, beets, beans, carrots, and other vegetables. Our traditional ways of preserving and storing these vegetables gave us enough food to carry us through the entire winter with no great hardship, provided we had plenty of bread. Even in the winter of 1931–1932, with the great scarcity of grain, we somehow managed to survive because of our vegetables. But the year of 1932 had not been normal. That spring we had a massive famine during which the people consumed even the seeds for planting, so there was nothing left with which to plant the vegetable gardens. Most gardens remained overgrown with weeds. The meager allotment of food received from the collective farm as advance payment was soon consumed. With no additional help forthcoming starvation set in.

Famine or no famine, the Bread Procurement Commission continued to work. Sometime in November 1932, we were told that the grain delivery to the state had begun to lag behind schedule. The Government ordered all advance payments of wages in kind stopped; grain which had already been distributed returned and all the seed and forage reserves requisitioned.

This order gave a great impetus to the activities of the Bread Procurement Commission. Previously, grain quotas were met by taxation of villagers according to acreage under cultivation. Since the taxation was too high, the grain reserves had already been used up in previous years. Nevertheless, the government continued to levy new quotas. The village officials were only too willing to comply with the government's demands, and a new method of collecting the grain from the villagers was introduced. This was known as "pumping the bread out," a term used by both villagers and officials. The village quota was divided equally among the Hundreds, which divided their quotas among their component Fives, which in their turn divided their quotas among their five householders. Therefore, if a Five's quota had been two thousand pounds of grain, for example, then its five householders would have to deliver their share of four hundred pounds each.

The village officials worked fast, and they did their job well. At the next meeting, we were told that the village as a whole; that is, all village subunits, all functionaries, all school teachers and pupils, and, of course, all the farmers as individuals, were to compete with one another in the collection of foodstuffs. Consequently, the meetings lasted longer, the functionaries became more aggressive and brutal, and the farmers sank deeper into despair.

But still the collecting of foodstuffs did not advance as quickly as the officials desired. Something drastic had to be done, so in time, the official line of reasoning acquired a new tone: the farmers were now considered too ignorant to understand such a highly patriotic deed as collecting and delivering food to the state. The Party and the government meant well for the farmers, and if they did not appreciate what the Party meant for them—well, that was the farmers' fault. The farmers were to be treated like children, and that put the Party and the government in the position of parents. The farmers had to follow the Party and the government without asking questions. There was no alternative. And, as unruly children are punished by parents, so would the unruly farmers be punished by the Party and the government.

In accordance with this philosophy, the commission no longer tried to enlighten us in the matter of food collection. There was another way. To put it in official terms, this was "direct contact of officials with the masses of people." In plain language, it meant that the Bread Procurement Commission was ordered to visit the farmers individually at their homes.

The commission members would go to a certain house and inform the householder about the amount and kind of food he should deliver. If he didn't have any grain, the commission would proceed with a thorough search for "hidden bread." Of course, anything found would be confiscated.

The Thousanders and their lieutenants could now do whatever they wanted without regard to the formalities of the law. They could use all their tricks or threats to lure or force the farmers into their traps. Going from house to house, searching, and carrying off everything they wanted satisfied their greed and criminal urges while allowing them successfully to serve the Party and the government.

At times, those officials exhibited a sort of childish behavior that flabbergasted us. Often they would entertain themselves by playing with their guns. Sometimes they fought duels in jest. That was how we learned that all of them carried guns. On their daily rounds, they sometimes shot at anything that moved. Occasionally, they even went so far as to stage mock executions of one or another of the villagers.

I witnessed the following scene: a neighbor of ours could not deliver the required quota of grain. Comrade Thousander, the head of the commission, decided to "teach" him how to obey orders. He announced that our neighbor would be shot for "opposing the Party's policies." The execution was to take place immediately in the garden behind the man's house. No doubt Comrade Thousander was expecting our neighbor to plead for mercy and promise to deliver the grain quota. The commission members suspected that he had "hidden grain" somewhere. But, our neighbor could not be so easily frightened.

"As you wish," he quietly announced to the surprised officials. "I am ready; let's get it over with." And he led the way into the garden. Then he was blindfolded and asked for the last time whether he was willing to deliver the grain quota. His answer was that he had nothing to deliver. Comrade Thousander raised his gun and fired—over our neighbor's head. Then the blindfold was removed, and our neighbor was asked the same question. The answer was still the same. The blindfold was put on once more: the bullets flew over his head again; but he would not change his story. By now, the officials' laughter had changed to rage. Not being able to accomplish anything at the time, they left, promising to return and give him a "real lesson."

What had once been a "tax in kind," then a "bread collection for the whole state," and later "expropriation of bread for construction of the socialist society," now became robbery. Free of any restraints, the commission went from house to house, day and night, searching for "hidden bread." Each commission had its experts for this purpose. The experts responsible for searching for grain in the ground were equipped with special screw-type rods. The long rods sharpened at one end were used for probing haystacks or tacks of straw, and the thatched roofs of the farmers' houses. The commission members searched everywhere: they drilled holes in the gardens, backyards, in the earth floors of the houses, and in the farm buildings. They looked for grain under beds, in the lattices and cellars. They never missed checking inside the stoves and ovens, on and under shelves, in trunks, and up the chimneys. They measured the thickness of the walls, and inspected them for bulges where grain could have been concealed. Sometimes they completely tore down suspicious walls or took apart or demolished cooking and heating stoves and ovens. Nothing in the houses remained intact or untouched. They upturned everything: even the cribs of babies, and the babies themselves were thoroughly frisked, not to mention the other family members. They looked for "hidden grain" in and under men's and women's clothing. Even the smallest amount that was found was confiscated. If so much as a small can or jar of seeds was found that had been set aside for spring planting, it was taken away, and the owner was accused of hiding food from the state.

One day, the commission came to our house leading a horse with them. Why? we wondered. The horse searched for grain in the ground. The "search expert" led it all around our backyard. At first, we couldn't figure out the reason for this ceremony. Later we found out that a horse presumably would not step on a covered pit; it would abruptly stop before it, or jump over it. That would be a signal for the commission to grab their shovels and start digging for hidden grain. Fortunately, we had no covered pits.

As 1932 neared its end, we often heard explanations of why the officials continued searching our homes for grain. They were very simple: since we were still alive, we must have been eating something to survive. We had not fulfilled the grain delivery quota, and yet we had been complaining that we had nothing to eat. But we were still alive! That meant that we had to have food—but where? It had to be somewhere. The officials felt that they had failed in their duties to find the hidden treasure of food. This made them frustrated, angry, and all the more vicious and cruel to us.

We were being watched day and night. We were cautioned, for example, that the village windmills were being closely scrutinized. Those who wound bring some grain to the windmill for converting it into flour could be sure that they would be visited by the commission even before they returned home. But such cases were very rare because we had no grain at that time. The village windmills stood idle.

Aside from wheat and rye, other cereals such as millet and buckwheat were also staples of the Ukrainian diet. To prepare the millet or buckwheat grain for cooking every household had its own mortar, a simply-designed wooden contraption that separated the grain from the husk. One day, sometime at the end of November 1932, it was announced that all mortars had to be destroyed on the explicit order of Comrade Thousander. The following days witnessed the senseless destruction of this device. Members of the commission, armed with axes, went from house to house, hacking the mortars to pieces without giving us an explanation of why it had to be done. Those of us who still had some millet or buckwheat grain had to find some other way to remove the husks.

Smoke curling from the chimney could also cause trouble for a household, as it was a reliable sign that something might be cooking inside. The officials instructed their men to carefully observe our chimneys. In our Hundred, for example, a special smoke watcher was appointed. His duty was to watch all Hundred homes day and night and to inform the Thousander about each and every house from which smoke was emitted. Especially closely watched were the houses of those villagers who were suspected of "hoarding bread." The houses with the telltale sign of smoke would be visited by commissions without delay. If cereal was being cooked, the houseowner would be subjected to a lengthy interrogation, and a thorough search would be made. The usage of grain before the fulfillment of the quota was considered illegal, and was severely punished. Since our village had not yet fulfilled that quota, by cooking our gruel and consuming it, we "misappropriated socialist property for our personal gain." Even the smallest amount of cereal had to be delivered to the state.

A house with smoke coming from its chimney was also in danger of becoming a target for thieves. Robbers at that time were interested only in food, cooked or raw. We often heard that terrible crimes had been committed for a couple of potatoes or a pot of buckwheat gruel.

There was also another way used to find out whether a villager had grain or other agricultural produce: that of arrest and jail. As I had mentioned before, the prisoners in the village jail did not receive food from their jailkeepers; their families had to feed them. One of the Thousanders was struck by an ingenious idea: how about throwing those suspected of "hoarding food" into jail and then wait to see what happened?

The idea was enthusiastically accepted, and soon we started hearing of arrests without any reason; arrests made just to find out what kind of food, if any, the arrested would receive from home. The trick didn't work. There really was no food in the village. Bringing food to jail would have meant exposing the family, including the arrested family member, to obvious danger. Thus no one wanted to do that, even for the sake of one's own father.

In November 1932, the suffering of our villagers began to approach the magnitude of last spring's famine. The first famine had been marked by unspeakable suffering, and yet, it had not been without a ray of hope: it was spring, and we all prayed that the new vegetables and fruits would sustain us until the summer harvest. The situation this autumn, however, was different. The harvest of 1932 was good, but the government took everything. The collective farmers were left without bread, except for that meager payment in kind that they received as advance compensation for their work. By the end of November, we were at the end of our resources. We were without food, and we had no money with which to buy any. The dried and preserved wild berries, the edible roots, the cabbages and pumpkins, the beets, the fruits had already been consumed. There was no hope of getting a new supply of them. We faced a severe winter with freezing temperatures, and great snowstorms which we knew would last until the end of March or even longer. Again, as in last spring's famine, a multitude of beggars roamed the village, pleading to be rescued from death. They begged for morsels of bread, for scraps of food, for peelings and discards. Once again, one could see famished people, dressed in rags and tatters, roaming over the potato field searching for leftover potatoes. Once more, starving farmers, like walking skeletons, searched the forest and explored the river with the hopes of finding something edible. And again, they went to cities, railroad stations, and the railroad tracks, in hope of getting some food from the passengers.

Compared with other villagers, my family and I were in better shape to survive the winter. We had learned from the difficulties experienced during last spring's famine to make extra preparations and to take special precautions to stay alive. Our main problem was how to hide the little food we had from the X-ray eyes of the officials. It was difficult to outwit them, but our survival instincts made us inventive.

The threat of imminent famine sharpened our minds; it freed us from the fear of being caught and made us ready to fight for our lives at any cost. While preparing for the long winter, we knew that we had to outsmart our persecutors if we wanted to stay alive.

Hiding food was not an easy task. The prospect of intolerable hunger forced us to take risks we would otherwise have never dared. After much worried thinking and discussion, our mother finally hit upon an idea: it was very simple, but extremely risky.

"Why not enlist the help of the government?" she remarked, as if it were obvious.

We did not understand what she had in mind.

"What do you mean?" I asked, completely baffled. "You mean to ask the government for help? You know that instead of helping us they have already taken everything we have!"

"No, not that," she answered quietly, as was her way. "I mean we should hide whatever food we have in a pit on government land."

We had to agree with her. It was an excellent idea. Its logic was clear: no official would even think of someone daring to hide food from the government on the government's own land. Any personal use of government property was severely punished by law, but we dared to defy that law, and by doing it we saved our lives.

As we anticipated, the Bread Procurement Commission searched all over our backyard and garden, but did not bother to cross the boundary to the government property—the adjacent sand dunes.

During harvest time, my brother and I had not been idle. No matter how carefully the crop was guarded, we were able to collect enough wheat grain to sustain our lives until at least the next spring. We were agile young boys with nimble feet; we knew each path, each bush, and we knew how to avoid being caught. The only problem that remained was how to hide the grain. However, that problem had now been solved by our mother.

We buried some potatoes and grain in several places in a strip of land adjoining the woods. That land was a useless sandy dune overgrown by bushy willows and sallows so it was very easy for us to disguise our hiding places. In the winter, these hiding places were covered by snow, and we left them undisturbed. But when spring came and the snow melted, this hoard was our only means of existence. We would open our hiding places during the night, take out some potatoes and grain, enough for a few days, and then close and cover them up again. Our nightly visits to those hiding places are among my unforgettable experiences. Those potatoes and that grain were the greatest treasure that was ever hidden in the ground.

During the wintertime, we ate the food that was hidden elsewhere —in the tree hollows, for example, or in the roof thatching. We hid the grain in small bags in many places so as to be able to remove one bag at a time. Upon removing it, we immediately cooked and ate it. Both the cooking and the eating were done at night. We still had some potatoes, sauerkraut, and pickles which we received as advance payment in kind for our work in the kolhosp. This was our only solid food, but as days passed, these resources began to diminish rapidly, and we trembled at the thought that the commission might some day catch us eating our cooked wheat.

CHAPTER 23

WE LOOKED toward the approaching winter of 1932–1933 with great trepidation, as if awaiting the arrival of the Judgment Day. It came with nature's crushing wrath. The particularly severe winter conspired with the Communists against the farmers.

In our region, winter begins at the end of November when the heavy rains stop and the first frost sets in. The puddles freeze and the mud hardens. Heavy grayish white snow clouds chase each other across the sky.

This change of weather is accompanied by an icy east wind which blows along the valley and forces people to retreat into their shelters. It is the time when our villagers hurriedly finish their work in the fields and retire to their deserved winter rest. In the past, when the field work ended, our villagers were not forced to go out in bad weather. They would set aside enough food and firewood so that the cold days and nights indoors meant little hardship.

But the winter of 1932–1933 was different from any of the previous ones. Although nature followed her usual pattern with the exception of unusual cold, the life of the villagers did not take its normal course, for in step with the winter, a great famine approached.

The scarcity of food alarmed us as early as November while we were still working in the fields of the collective farm. The small advance received from the kolhosp had already been consumed. We had been told that we would receive more food as soon as the field work was completed. But we never did.

Then came the taxes. Taxes in the form of eggs and milk were obligatory only to those who owned fowl and cows. But each household had to meet a quota of meat, approximately 250 pounds annually, regardless of livestock holdings. Farmers without livestock were forced to pay this obligation to the state with money. Thus the annual earnings of a collective farmer from his work on the collective farm were insufficient to meet his obligations to the state, let alone for his subsistence.

However, even if the villagers had had money, it would have been impossible for them to purchase food. For, in fact, the trade in foodstuffs and other consumer commodities was officially prohibited. On November 6, 1932, the Council of People's Commissars and the Central Committee of the Communist Party jointly issued the following resolution:

> Because of the shameless breakdown of the grain collection campaign in various counties of Ukraine, the Council of People's Commissars and the Central Committee of the Communist Party of Ukraine order the local Party and administration authorities to eradicate sabotage of grain, which has been organized by counterrevolutionary and kurkul elements. The opposition of a number of Communists, leaders of this sabotage, must also be stamped out, and the passive and indifferent attitude towards this sabotage on the part of some Party organizations must be liquidated. The Council of People's Commissars and the Central Committee have decided to blacklist all those localities which conduct criminal sabotage and to apply against them the following reprisals:
>
> 1. To suspend the flow of all merchandise and all state and cooperative trade in these localities; to close all state and cooperative stores; and to remove all supplies of merchandise.
> 2. To prohibit trade in essential foodstuffs, which trade heretofore had been conducted by collective farms and individual homesteads.
> 3. To suspend all credits destined for those localities and to withdraw at once all credits already given to them.
> 4. To overhaul the personnel of the administrative and economic organizations and to remove all enemy elements therefrom.
> 5. To do the same on collective farms by removal therefrom of all enemy elements engaged in sabotage.

This resolution obviously deprived the farmers not only of the foodstuffs grown locally, but also of commodities such as matches, salt, kerosene, fish products, sugar products, canned food, etc., as I mentioned before. The trade in foodstuffs and consumer goods was prohibited throughout Ukraine, for there wasn't a single village that had fulfilled the grain delivery quota.

Anxiety turned to panic when the first disquieting news came that the kolhosp storehouses were empty, that the grain had been taken away from the village, and that none had been left for the local populace.

The long winter had just begun. It would be six months from December before we could gather vegetables in our gardens again; it would be eight months before we could get bread from the new crop of grain. Already, some of us were on the verge of collapse from starvation. We clung, nevertheless, to the hope that the government would help us, but as time went by, that hope faded.

Meanwhile, the cold became more intense and the snow fell slowly, continuously, threatening to block the road from the village to the county seat and other neighboring towns. Yet the members of the Bread Procurement Commission continued in their task, relentlessly tramping from house to house, confiscating everything edible they could find in their attempt to meet the state quotas. Even the smallest amounts of grain and meat were forcibly seized from the villagers.

We had to do something. No one wanted to lie down passively and starve to death. One of the first steps undertaken by the villagers was a mass exodus to the neighboring cities where they hoped to find jobs and food. All—young and old—tried to reach the cities as they had tried before during the last spring famine. Many did not make it, and their frozen bodies became roadmarkers for others on the snowed-in route to the county towns. Those who were strong enough to reach the cities failed to find a paradise of plenty, even though the food rationing there slowed down the onslaught of famine somewhat. The food rations were so small that the city dwellers could not help the starving farmers.

Jobs were as scarce as food. Some of the younger huskier men found jobs at the sugar plants, state road construction projects, or woodcutting. Others were hired to carry water from the community wells. But the elderly men and women and the children who desperately sought out the cities with the hope of earning their daily bread were less fortunate.

As the exodus of villagers to the cities increased, the government confounded the farmers with an ordinance prohibiting a villager from appearing in any city without a proper certificate. Any emigration out of Ukraine was also strictly prohibited.

It was precisely at this time, the end of December 1932, that the government introduced a single passport system for the entire country in order to prevent the starving farmers from leaving their villages for the cities. This meant that all Soviet citizens over sixteen years of age, permanently residing in the cities, had to be registered with the militia in order to get their Soviet passports.

No person lacking a passport was permitted to live in a given city or be employed and receive food rations. All but the farmers had to have passports. This meant that a farmer could not stay in a city longer than twenty-four hours without being registered with the militia. Thus, not having passports, the farmers could not be employed in a city, and most importantly, they could not have food rations.

The passportization was supposedly directed against the kurkuls, as Soviet propaganda proclaimed: "Passportization is a mortal blow against the kurkuls!" This murderous slogan revived the old question: *"Who is a kurkul?"* All villagers had been collectivized by this time. There was not a single independent farmer left in our village by the end of 1932. Could the members of a collective farm be kurkuls? It was difficult for us to understand such logic. But, at this point, such faulty reasoning didn't matter to us anymore.

Now it began to dawn on everyone why there wasn't any food left in the village; why there weren't any prospects of getting any more; why our expectation that the government would surely help us to avert starvation was naive and futile; why the Bread Procurement Commission still searched for "hidden" grain; and why the government strictly forbade us to look for means of existence elsewhere. It finally became clear to us that there was a conspiracy against us; that somebody wanted to annihilate us, not only as farmers but as people —as Ukrainians.

At this realization, our initial bewilderment was succeeded by panic. Nevertheless, our instinct for survival was stronger than any of the prohibitions. It dictated to those who were still physically able that they must do everything to save themselves and their families.

The desperate attempts to find some means of existence in the neighboring cities continued. Many of the more able-bodied villagers ventured beyond the borders to distant parts of the Soviet Union, mainly to Russia, where, as we had heard, there was plenty of food. Others went south, since we had also heard that there, in the coal mines and factories of the Donets Basin, one could find work with regular pay and food rations.

However, few of the brave adventurers who set out for these lands of plenty reached their destination. The roads to the large metropolitan centers were closed to them. The militia and the GPU men checked every passenger for identification and destination. These courageous men and women doing their utmost to stay alive, achieved quite the contrary. We can only guess what happened to them when they were arrested; it was either death or the concentration camps. If they managed to escape the verdict of death in the "people's" courts, receiving the questionable reprieve of hard labor, they never began their sentences. The combination of hunger, cold, and neglect took their lives on the way to the camps, at the railroad stations, or in the open box cars rolling north and east, in which they froze to death.

The ones who escaped the roadblocks set up by the militia and GPU often became the victims of outlaws who terrorized the railroad lines and the open markets. The lucky ones who managed to return to their villages after these terrible experiences, and those who remained in the village, gradually lost their spirit and belief in salvation from their plight. Weakened by lack of food, freezing for lack of fuel, they simply had no more stamina left. The farmers sank deeper and deeper into resignation, apathy and despair. Some were convinced that starvation was a well-deserved punishment from God for believing in Communism and supporting the Communists during the Revolution.

We heard that a few of those who came back had somehow managed to acquire food—mainly flour—but few of them were able to bring their treasures home. Those provisions, obtained under great hardships, had been confiscated by the state agents, or stolen by outlaws.

All of these events convinced us that we had lost our battle for life. Our attempts to escape, or to secure food from other sources, were for the most part unsuccessful. We were imprisoned in our village, without food, and sentenced to die the slow, agonizing death of starvation.

CHAPTER 24

AT THE END of 1932 when all the vegetables and bread had been consumed news reached the villages of our region that special stores had been opened in the county town with plenty of everything. It was even rumored that foreign goods were available there. However, we also learned that the only medium of exchange for these goods was foreign currency and gold or silver, the latter two in any form or quantity.

Little by little, more information about these stores trickled into our village. The stores were known under the name of Torgsin, which is an abbreviation of the Russian words for "trade with foreigners." It was said that this store was selling all the necessities of life: groceries, clothing, medicines, and so forth.

We knew that Torgsin had existed for sometime now, but only in the large metropolitan cities where many foreigners lived. Now, these stores were coming to us. Yet, as unsophisticated as we were, the aim of the Soviet government was clear to us. These stores were intended to strip us of the last remnants of our gold and silver. Family heirlooms such as crosses, icons, earrings, wedding bands, watches, and anything else that might have contained some precious metal were much coveted by the regime. The Communist government, suspecting that the farmers still possessed gold and silver coins from prerevolutionary times, wanted to get hold of them. For generations, families had accumulated such treasures as silver teapots, sugar bowls, cream pitchers, salt and pepper shakers, and other silver pieces. It used to be a fashionable custom among young village women to have one of their upper front teeth crowned with gold whether or not it was dentally needed. The government wanted these too.

Hunger accomplished everything that decrees and threats could not. The last reserves of precious metals, meager as they were, were pried or dug out from their hiding places. They became the only means of survival.

To own gold was now everybody's dream; it became synonymous with life itself. Gold could buy bread . . . just imagine. Even we lowly villagers could buy bread, and plenty of it very easily if we only had that magic gold. But the question was how and where to get it? A few of us had some, but the majority had never even seen it.

As the news about this fabulous store spread, we began to hear horror stories about armed robberies and murders. Wearing gold jewelry openly, or having a gold tooth, was flirting with death. Murders committed for a pair of earrings, or a ring, or whatever else was made of gold or looked like gold, soon became everyday occurences. A girl lost her finger along with her ring when the robber who was unable to remove the gold ring simply cut off her finger. Thieves armed with tongs would forcibly extract the teeth from those who had gold crowns. These crimes had a tremendous demoralizing impact on our lives.

Gold fever resulted in the complete destruction of our cemetery. Our village was very old; its beginnings dated back to the sixteenth century. Through all those three centuries or more, our cemetery had been the burial place for people from all walks of life: the prominent and rich as well as the common farmer. It was the custom to bury the dead with all their personal possessions such as jewelry, weapons, and crosses. Now, the graves were opened and looted of all the valuables they contained. At first, the grave plundering took place secretly at night, but soon, it was done openly in broad daylight. There actually was no need of hiding this horrendous crime for the government did not mind the pillaging of graves. Nobody was ever punished for this crime as far as I know. The cemeteries, after all, were looked upon as a part of religious tradition, something the Communists were bent on destroying. So, like the church and the independent farmers, our cemetery had to go; grave robberies were officially ignored and tolerated, if not actually encouraged.

In many cases, the remains of the buried were desecrated after the graves had been dug up. One could see human skulls and bones scattered all over the cemetery, and the plots which once held them were torn up, leaving empty, gaping holes. Even the wooden crosses marking the graves were carried off and used as firewood.

The cemetery looting turned out to be of some use: the opened graves soon received new bodies; the victims of starvation. This was a bizarre stroke of good fortune, since the starving villagers did not have sufficient strength to dig new graves for their dead relatives and neighbors. Now they only had to drag their bodies to the cemetery and drop them into the looted open graves.

There were a few villagers who had some pieces of precious metal in hiding and could realize their dream of trading it for food. We happened to be among those lucky ones. One evening my mother revealed her secret to us: she had two gold medallions. They had been her parents' presents to her when she was still single, some half century ago, or more than thirty years before the October Revolution. At that time, it was the fashion for young women to wear gold coins as medallions. Mother no longer wore her most precious possessions, but kept them well-hidden for a rainy day. Even her children, knew nothing of their existence. We were in the direst of straits. The famine by this time was reaching its height; we had to have some food if we were to stay alive. Mother asked us, as she always did in important matters, as to the best way, in our opinion, to utilize these medallions. We decided unanimously that we should take one of them to the closest Torgsin in the county capital. We agreed to make this trip as soon as possible, for the snow had not yet sealed off our village completely. Later on, the intensity of the winter elements would make it impossible for us to leave the village at all.

One morning in late January 1933, while it was still dark, Mother and I set out along the main street through the center of the village for the county town. We followed the street to the main road which led straight into the town.

It was a memorable trip. Soon the sun rose and started to shine in all its brilliance in the vast blue sky with the white snow cover reflecting its light. The landscape was very calm and silent. We met nothing that was alive: there were no birds, cats, or dogs; not even their traces in the snow signaling life. And we didn't meet a single human being. I had the eerie sensation that we were indeed walking in the kingdom of death.

The only sign that people were still alive was the smoke rising from distant chimneys. However, not many houses showed this signal. The majority of them, buried in deep snow drifts, hid the horrible sight of their inhabitants suffering and dying from starvation.

Soon, however, as we slowly made our way through the snow toward the village center, graphic evidence of starvation became visible. We noticed a black object which, from afar, looked like a snow-covered tree stump. As we came near, however, we saw that it was the body of a dead man. Frozen limbs protruding from under the snow gave the body the appearance of some grotesque creature. I bent down and cleared the snow off the face. It was Ulas, our elderly neighbor whom we had last seen about a month ago.

A few steps further, we saw another frozen body. It was the corpse of a woman. As I brushed away the snow, horror made my blood turn cold: under her ragged coat, clutched tightly to her bosom with her stiff hands, was the frozen little body of her baby.

We finally left our village behind and stepped onto the open road which led to the county seat. However, another ghostly panorama now opened in front of us. Everywhere we looked dead and frozen bodies lay by the sides of the road. To our right were bodies of those villagers who apparently had tried to reach the town in search of work and food. Weakened by starvation, they were unable to make it and ended up lying or falling down by the roadside, never to rise again. The gentle snow mercifully covered their bodies with its white blanket.

One could easily imagine the fate of those people whose bodies were lying to our left. They most probably were returning from the county town, without having accomplished anything. They had tramped many kilometers in vain, only to be refused a job and a chance to stay alive. They were returning home empty-handed. Death caught up with them as they trudged homeward, resigned to dying in their village.

The wide open kolhosp fields, stretching for kilometers on both sides of the main road, looked like a battlefield after a great war. Littering the fields were the bodies of the starving farmers who had been combing the potato fields over and over again in the hope of finding at least a fragment of a potato that might have been overlooked or left over from the last harvest. They died where they collapsed in their endless search for food. Some of those frozen corpses must have been lying out there for months. Nobody seemed to be in a hurry to cart them away and bury them.

The actual seven miles' distance to the town proved to be very laborious for us. After we left our village, a cold wind started blowing from the north, and clouds appeared on the horizon. It was difficult, especially for Mother, to walk against the wind, but we stubbornly persisted, and after about six hours of struggle with the wind and snow-covered road, we arrived at the entrance to the county town. Here yet another horror awaited us.

Our county seat at that time had no sewage system, and the raw sewage was collected, usually at night, by a special sanitary brigade. There was no special dumping ground for the cargo of the horse-drawn sewage tanks. They were usually emptied outside of town, along the sides of the roads. The road from our village to the county seat seemed to have been their favorite dumping ground; consequently, both sides of the road for a considerable stretch were thickly covered with raw sewage. This was in itself, a most distasteful sight and unpleasant in normal times, but we had become used to it. Now, as we slowly trudged along these littered roadsides, our stomachs turned over anew. Scattered here and there throughout the sewage were frozen corpses. They were lying singly or in groups, or just piled up one on top of another, like debris after a disaster. Some were covered with snow, showing only arms and legs protruding; others were covered by freshly dumped raw sewage. The infants were invariably pressed to their mothers' bosoms under the cover of homemade coats.

These dead were farmers from the neighboring villages and their families, all victims of starvation. Deprived of all means of existence, the farmers saw their only chance of survival in escaping to the city where they hoped to find some job, some food, and some help. Despite the prohibitions on leaving the boundaries of their villages, they moved in throngs to the county seat, swelling and annoying its population and the city management. They appeared on the doorsteps of houses, begging for a crumb of bread, or even a piece of potato peel, usually in vain. The city inhabitants, with their own meager food rations, could not give the villagers sufficient food to save them from starvation. There were simply too many of them. They were standing or lying in the city streets, in the marketplaces, at the railroad stations, under fences, in backyards, in the ditches by the streets and roads. They became such everyday sights that the city people mostly passed them by, ignoring them and their pleas. Thus, after fruitlessly trying everything and going everywhere, the villagers and their families met their inevitable deaths. The dead lay undiscovered or ignored for days, like driftwood.

Often the starving people would be rounded up like cattle by the militiamen, taken beyond the city limits, and left to their fate. The dead, and those barely alive and unable to walk anymore, were all loaded onto trucks or horse-driven carts, and hauled away somewhere outside the city limits. They were dumped into ravines or in the dumping grounds for sewage along the roadsides. Weren't these people entitled to at least a decent burial in the cemetery, even in common graves?

When mother and I finally arrived at the Torgsin, there was already a great crowd of starving people there. Emaciated and skeletonlike, or with swollen, puffed-up bodies, human beings stood around in the streets, leaned against the telephone poles and walls, or lay on the sidewalks and in the street gutters. They were patiently waiting for some merciful shoppers to share a pittance of their purchases with them. Others were begging noisily, shouting and crying; the rest held out their hands quietly and silently. Here and there among the crowds we could see rigid bodies of the dead, but nobody paid any attention to them. . . .

We were informed at the entrance to the Torgsin that all shoppers were required to first go to the office across the street for an appraisal of their valuables. Having found the office, we were directed to an official inside. The official, a fat man behind iron grates, took Mother's medallion without even looking at us, weighed it quickly, and tossed it into a drawer. He then handed us a form, requiring our name, address, and the type of our valuable. Afterwards, we received a receipt indicating the sum we were authorized to spend: exactly 18 rubles. Another hour passed as we stood in line waiting to enter the Torgsin. Finally we were inside.

What a sight it was. I could not believe my eyes; it was like a dream. Here was everything we needed and more. There were things we had never even heard of nor seen in our lives. There were even groceries known to me only from books I had read. All the items were tastefully arranged and exhibited in cases under glass. Looking at these splendid assortments of foods, I began to feel dizzy. For months, I hadn't even seen ordinary food. I had forgotten the taste of real bread. Now, everywhere I looked were these wonderful things to eat.

I was completely overcome by hunger pangs; they were so violent that I could hardly manage to stand upright. Savage hunger gnawed at my stomach, and there was a choking sensation in my throat, as if someone's hands were squeezing and twisting my neck. In my agony, I was about to burst out crying, but at that moment, I felt my mother's hands on my shoulders. She understood my emotional state. Perhaps she felt the same way. As I looked at her, she smiled at me and said: "Have some pride, my son!" These words calmed me and gave me strength to overcome the physical weakness.

We decided to buy only the basic and most essential products, so, when our turn came at the counter, we quickly selected what we needed without much hesitation and difficulty. We bought some butter, salt pork, lard, two loaves of bread, sugar, and a few miscellaneous items to make up exactly 18 rubles. Most of these items were neatly packed in cans, boxes or bags. To our astonishment, we discovered that the labels on all of them bore the trade mark "Made in USSR," meaning they were destined for foreign markets.

After we finished shopping, we left the store as unobtrusively as possible and started our trip back home. We did not fear robbers during daylight, for we were in the same position as the rest of the starving villagers, and moreover, looked like them: thin and haggard, dressed in rags, with beggars' sacks on our shoulders. No one in his right mind would have suspected that in those potato sacks we carried a few pounds of salt pork and other staples which to us were the greatest treasures on earth.

Already on the way home, we could not resist the temptation to eat some of the bread and salt pork. It tasted heavenly. Mother suggested that we not eat too much for fear we would become sick. Now it was getting dark, and we were afraid to walk home the same way we had come. Consequently, we decided to go to a railroad station in the hope of catching a train to a station just three miles away from our village. This would shorten our walking distance and it would keep us in a safer populated area.

As we approached the station, a freight train slowly passed to our right. We noticed people gathered around something on the tracks. We joined them, and saw a pile of mangled human bodies in a pool of blood. Somebody said that it was a suicide; a woman carrying a child had jumped under the oncoming train. The onlookers began leaving the scene one by one, and the crushed bodies of the mother and her child remained lying there without any further attention. No one shed a tear or showed any emotion for their tragic end; all were too numb.

We walked to the station building. There were great crowds of people there also, both inside and out. They had come, as did all of us, from the surrounding villages. This was their last hope to find some food. They hoped that some sympathetic traveler would throw them a piece of bread from the train window. Some had hopes of finding a job. Still others brought with them the best of their belongings with the prospect of exchanging them for food, or selling them for money. They sat patiently on the cement floor of the platform, wet from snow, exhibiting their wares: beautifully hand-embroidered Ukrainian national costumes made of homespun materials, along with homemade richly embroidered tablecloths, embroidered towels, handwoven rugs. Some of them had been kept in trunks or in the hopechests of women for decades or even centuries as family heirlooms. But these valuable articles found no buyers at this time. Very few passenger trains passed by, and local people were not interested in buying anything but food. Except for Party and government officials, and black marketeers, all were hungry or starving.

Most of those who were crowding the station's waiting hall inside were trying to buy tickets somewhere north of Ukraine, to Russia, where there was no famine. But their efforts were futile. Train tickets to Russia were officially prohibited to Ukrainian farmers with few exceptions. Only those with special certificates permitting them to leave the collective farm for a specific place could buy a train ticket to Russia. Nevertheless, the starving people tried their luck. They had nothing more to lose and nothing else to do, especially now that the fields, rivers, and forests were covered with deep snow. As a result, they flocked to the railroad stations because each train was bringing some ray of hope, some good news. Above all, there was the possibility that in spite of all prohibitions, one would somehow be able to board the train to the north. They kept dreaming of the impossible. They had thoughts of traveling on the roof of the train, or underneath the railroad car, on the steps, on buffer platforms, and on the bumpers.

But, for the most part, these dreams were never realized. The crowds in and around the railroad stations would be rounded up periodically by the militia and GPU men, loaded onto trucks like stray animals, and dumped somewhere outside the town limits.

We had better luck in obtaining train tickets because we were going south, not north. Soon we were on our way home, but the horror pictures of starvation were not over.

There were very few people in the car we entered as there wasn't much traffic to the south—to the interior of Ukraine. There were many vacant places, and soon after we occupied our seats, a woman entered our compartment followed by two small emaciated boys. What a pitiful sight they were! Their faces were skin and bones; their eyes were bulging, dull, and listless. They were unkempt; their clothes were ragged and dirty.

After they sat down, I noticed that the woman held a baby under her coat at her bosom, and that the baby was dead.

"It's a girl," she said quietly, without showing any emotion. "She died yesterday. My poor baby; she was hungry, and kept crying . . . and then suddenly she stopped. . . . We stayed overnight outside. They threw us out of the waiting hall. It was very cold. The boys huddled under my coat like chicks under their mother hen. . . ."

We didn't know what to say and just kept watching her silently and with sympathy.

She put her dead baby on her knees and started to unwrap the dirty rags in which it was bundled. Then, as if realizing that the baby was dead, she bundled it up again, held it tightly to herself, and pressed her cheeks affectionately against the baby's cold and rigid face. She started crying and talking to her dead baby:

"I am sorry . . ." she sobbed, tears rolling down her face and dropping onto the baby, "It's not my fault. Heavens, I tried; I did all I could. . . . They labeled me an enemy of the people. . . . They threw us out wherever we went." Then she started kissing her baby tenderly, its eyes, its forehead, its cheeks.

"Don't worry, my baby, you won't be alone for long; soon we'll follow you; soon you will be again with your Mama and your brothers. . . ."

Mother could not listen to her lament any longer, and afraid of bursting out crying in front of her, she got up and started towards the door, motioning me to follow her. Once in the corridor, she gave vent to her emotions. Crying, she asked me to cut three pieces of bread and give it to the woman and her boys. We returned to the compartment and I handed the bread to them. Words cannot describe the sensation the sight of bread made for these starved human beings.

185

After eating half of her portion of bread, and saving the rest for her boys, the woman calmed down somewhat and was able to tell us her sad story more coherently. It was a typical story of other Ukrainian families of that time, but incomprehensible to those who did not live through those experiences of suffering and tragedy.

A year before, we learned, this woman's husband was labeled a kurkul and "an enemy of the people," and was banished somewhere to the north. She never heard from him again. He never saw his baby daughter who was born after his banishment and was now lying dead in her arms. She had worked hard on the collective farm, but received only a few pounds of grain and some vegetables which amounted to practically nothing and were gone by the time winter had set in. Hungry and cold, with no prospect of getting food and firewood, she heard somewhere that there was no famine in Russia.

She had a little money, so she decided to try to go north to Russia with her children. In spite of hardships, she finally reached the railroad station and for two days tried to buy a ticket to a city in Russia where some of her neighbors had gone. They actually had written to her that there was no famine there, proving that hearsay was true. However, she was unable to buy a ticket since she did not have the necessary certificate from the collective farm. Now, since her infant daughter had died, she decided to go to another city not far from her village. She had heard that some kind of a children's shelter was located there; perhaps she would be able to leave her boys there. What would happen to her after that did not matter. She was only concerned about her two boys' survival.

I went out into the train corridor and stood there a while looking out the window. The train rolled on the tracks with its rhythmic motion. Snow-covered fields, trees, and telegraph poles rushed by. But even here, the otherwise peaceful scenery was disturbed: all along the tracks, groups of starving people were standing, sitting, or lying. They had trudged a long way to the railroad tracks hoping for a miracle; maybe someone would throw them a piece of bread. I could not hear their voices, but I saw their outstretched hands. Some stood there holding their children. They would lift them up so people could see their famished little bodies as if crying: "A crumb of bread, please! It's not for me; it's for my child!"

I suddenly reached for my sack and grabbed the rest of our loaf of bread. Ahead, I noticed a woman with two small children. They needed a miracle, I thought. I opened the window, and as the train approached them, I threw the bread in their direction. I could not see what happened to it as tears were blurring my vision.

Soon we arrived at our station. Before taking the road home, I wanted to find some kind of a stick for Mother as she thought it would be easier for her to walk with it. While looking for something suitable, I strayed behind some auxiliary buildings adjacent to the railroad station. The scene I saw there has been haunting me ever since. Now, after fifty years have passed by since that moment, I can still feel the terror that seized me when I came face to face with that ghastly view. In front of me, in open view, was a heap of frozen human corpses like some discarded woodpile. Some of the bodies were completely naked; others were half-clothed; still others were fully clothed but barefoot. Their frozen arms and legs were sticking out from under the snow like tree limbs in an intricate configuration. I stood there aghast, unable to move from fright and horror. For quite a while I stared at those human bodies, with outstretched frozen arms, as if they still were begging for food and mercy. Then I ran back to my mother, with her walking stick, trembling all over, but consoled by her company.

By the time we finally reached our house, it was dark; however, our shopping adventure had not yet ended.

On the way home, Mother seemed troubled and uneasy. When I asked her what was bothering her, she confided in me. Her anxieties centered about the form we had had to fill out when we traded the medallion at the Torgsin and I understood the danger we were in.

The decree to turn in any coins and foreign currency was ignored by the villagers, resulting in many arrests and tortures by the GPU. We had not violated the decree with the medallion as it did not fall into the category of valuables. But we had made the mistake of entering the medallion as "a coin" on the official appraisal form. This "minor" mistake could now turn out to be a "major crime" against the state.

Our apprehensions soon became a reality. One afternoon shortly after our shopping adventure, a large group of government officials made a visit to our home. It was composed of familiar members of the Hundred's Bread Procurement Commission, accompanied this time by an armed militiaman, and the chairman of the village soviet. The militiaman was a stranger, apparently especially sent to our village by the county government. This man, and the presence of so many officials, indicated to us the seriousness of our situation.

After the group entered our home, the chairman of the village soviet stepped out in front. He looked at a document in his hand, and read aloud the name of my mother for identification, even though he knew my mother very well. Then he declared that, according to "reliable sources," we possessed gold which was supposed to have been delivered to the state treasury long ago. He informed us that the militiaman was sent to us with the order to take our gold to the county center. He also added that if we handed the gold to him voluntarily, the whole case would be closed and forgotten. Our failure to cooperate would result in the arrest of the head of the household as "an enemy of the people."

Their demand to deliver our nonexistent gold seemed ridiculous to us, and the idea that my mother was to become an "enemy of the people" was absurd. Mother had gone through many such difficult situations far too often to lose her composure now. She categorically denied that we had ever had gold coins to deliver to the state. She, for one, couldn't even tell what a gold coin looked like. Our purchase of food at the Torgsin was made with a gold medallion, not a gold coin. Such an exchange of a medallion for food at the store owned by the state could not possibly be an illegal act, she insisted.

Just the same, the village chairman ordered a thorough search of our house. Every corner and nook was examined; each piece of clothing was pulled out; each lid from each pot was removed. They looked everywhere and into everything but found nothing. There was nothing to be found with the exception of the one remaining medallion which was carefully hidden in what was once our pigpen.

Finally, they departed with nothing, and afterwards, much to our surprise, they left us alone.

CHAPTER 25

In THE latter part of February, the cold became very intense. Temperatures sank below zero; violent storms raged. The roaring and whistling winds tore frozen limbs off trees and ripped roofs off some houses. But even such a severe winter could have been borne were it not for the hunger. To be cold and hungry, without food or fuel, and without hope of getting any, is a horror defying imagination.

Our village became completely isolated. High snowdrifts made roads and paths impassable. The snow deposits were so heavy that sometimes it was difficult to open the front doors of the houses. People had no intention of leaving their homes anyway; there was no place to go. Our village was snowed in, and its inhabitants were slowly dying of hunger in their houses.

We kept our house locked. We tried unsuccessfully to suppress our feelings of hunger by reading and telling stories. We prayed often. Mother would fall on her knees in front of the icons, and we would join her, repeating the words of the prayer after her. We felt more secure then believing that our prayers would be heard by God who would soon send us some relief. I often heard my Mother addressing the icons: "Oh, Almighty God: You sent upon us Your wrath and punishment at a time when Satan is also torturing us. Why do you treat us this way, Great God? Be merciful to us and help us to withstand Satan's treatment."

Then, as if feeling remorse for reproaching God, she would recite a long suppliant prayer. My brother Mykola had his own prayer. He also wanted to know the reason God sent such torture upon the people who so fervently believed in Him. He always ended with the plea to God to send us some bread. And so we spent our time in prayers, dreams, hopes, and expectations of a miracle.

There was an endless succession of days and nights with mostly raging snowstorms. But one morning, the storm broke and it was calm outside. Feeble rays of sunshine penetrated the frosty windowpanes. Mykola and I decided to go outside, but we had a hard time opening the door. We finally succeeded after repeatedly shoving and pushing it against the drifts, and stepped out to a beautiful morning of gleaming snow, azure sky, and clear fresh air.

There was silence and the monotony of snow everywhere throughout the village. The only signs of life came from the chimneys here and there, with tiny streams of smoke rising in the sky. Many houses in our neighborhood did not have any smoke coming out of their chimneys. Hadn't the people inside made any fires? How could they possibly stay alive, we wondered, in subzero temperatures, without their houses being heated?

To find out for ourselves, we ran first to Dmytro's house which showed no signs of life. Dmytro had never returned home after he had been taken to the county center. His young wife Solomia was left alone with their daughter. She had gone to work in the collective farm, taking her little child with her. As the wife of a banished man, she too was considered an "enemy of the people," and her child was refused admission to the nursery. Later, Solomia was expelled from the collective farm, and thus forced to seek a job in the city. That was impossible, however, because she could not show a certificate of release from the collective farm. She found herself trapped in the circle of the Communist death ring. She had to return to her village.

When winter came, Solomia went from house to house, willing to work for just a piece of bread. She was too proud to beg. People were sympathetic and helped her as much as they could. However, as the famine worsened, and the villagers were no longer able to help her, she was not seen on her rounds any more.

We found the front door of Solomia's house open, but the entrance was blocked with snowdrifts, and it was hard to get inside. When we finally reached the living room, we saw a pitiful sight: Solomia was hanging from the ceiling in the middle of the room. She was dressed in her Ukrainian national costume, and at her breast hung a large cross. It was obvious that she had made preparations before committing suicide. Her hair was combed neatly in two braids hanging over her shoulders.

Frightened, we ran to fetch Mother. We helped her take down Solomia's frozen body, and laid it on a bench, and covered it with a handmade blanket. It was only after we finished doing this that we noticed the dead body of her little daughter. The child was lying in a wooden tub in the corner under the icons, clean and dressed in her best clothes. Her little hands were folded across her chest.

On the table was a note:

Dear Neighbors:
    Please bury our bodies properly. I have to leave you, dear neighbors. I can bear this life no longer. There is no food in the house, and there is no sense in living without my little daughter who starved to death, or my husband. If you ever see Dmytro, tell him about us. He will understand our plight, and he will forgive me. Please tell him that I died peacefully, thinking about him and our dear daughter.
    I love you, my dear neighbors, and I wish with all my heart that you somehow recover from this disaster. Forgive me for troubling you. Thank you for everything you have done for me.

Solomia.

After reading the note, we stood there for a while, motionless and forlorn. Our mother tried to suppress the sound of her weeping, pressing the corner of her head scarf to her lips. Mykola gazed at the corpses in disbelief.

In my imagination I was recreating the agony of their dying: the child's hunger cries, and then the death convulsions of its exhausted little body.

How great must have been the sufferings of the mother. She had to listen helplessly to the pleas of her child for food, while she herself was near starvation. She must have felt great relief, I thought, when she saw her little daughter breathing for the last time. Then, in my imagination, I saw the mother attending to her lifeless child: dressing her in the best and cleanest clothing she had, praying on her knees near the body, and finally kissing her for the last time before her own suicide.

Mother interrupted my thoughts. We had to fulfill the last wishes of our dead neighbor and bury the two corpses properly. My mother always wanted to do everything correctly. But, how could we do it this time? We were too weak to dig a grave in the snow-covered frozen ground, or even to take the bodies to the cemetery.

After realizing these facts, we decided to leave them in the house. For the time being, the cold prevented their decay, so we just laid the body of the child beside her mother on the sleeping bench, covered them both with the blanket, and left.

After this sad discovery, we could not sit idly at home. There were many other houses around us that had no smoke coming out of their chimneys. We realized that similar tragedies had taken place there too. My mother was especially concerned about Boris's family and also about a widow who lived with her crippled daughter in our neighborhood. She thought they might still be alive and in need of help.

Without losing much time, we went to Boris's house. He also had not returned from the village jail, but had been transferred to the county center, and no one had seen him since. His wife, Khymka, was living alone with their two children. We frequently visited her, helping the family as much as we could. Lately, during the heavy snowstorms, we had lost all contact with them.

When we reached the front of Khymka's house, we noticed a dark object protruding from underneath the snow. It was Khymka. Her body was completely frozen and covered with snow. We rushed into the house, anticipating the worst about her children: we were right. On the sleeping bench lay the corpse of Khymka's eldest son, Trokhym. His hands were folded across his chest, his eyes were closed, and his frozen body was covered with an overcoat. At his head was a saucer with the remnants of a candle. Trokhym must have died before his mother. Then, in order to try and save the life of her other child, Khymka apparently left the house in search of help. But, too weakened by hunger, she collapsed a few steps in front of her house, and died in the snow.

We also found her youngest child, a boy of about eight years of age, in a bed. He was well-covered with several pieces of old clothing and miraculously still alive! He lay there totally exhausted by hunger and too weak to move. His body had stiffened and he was apparently half-frozen.

We had to act immediately to try to save the glimmer of life still in this young boy. There was no time for contemplation and emotions.

We brought Khymka's body back into the house and laid it alongside the body of her starved eldest son. It became clear to us that we had to take the youngest boy home with us, if we wanted to keep him alive, for his own house was freezing with not a trace of fuel for heating or food for survival. We carefully laid him on a sled and brought him home with us to revive him and care for him. Mother put him in bed, and told us that with God's help, he might recover.

She then sent us with a sled to the widow's house to bring her and her crippled daughter back with us if they were still alive. They lived close by, and it didn't take us long to reach her house.

The widow Shevchenko and her crippled daughter Lida were also victims of government policy. A few years earlier, her husband had clashed with a Party representative when the collectivization scheme was being instituted. The representative had come to our village to organize the collective farm, and during a heated argument, Shevchenko had dared to call him "a stupid parrot!" That was his end. He was accused of assailing the dignity of the Communist Party, and he was sent to the north for five years of "corrective labor." After a year or so, his wife received an anonymous letter telling her that her husband had died while digging the Baltic Sea–White Sea Canal. His widow now lived all alone with their daughter, who had been crippled from birth and needed constant attention. Widow Shevchenko had twice as difficult a task as the other villagers in providing food and other necessities for the two of them. Being tied down at home by the daily care of her handicapped daughter, she could not go to work. She could not get any official help either, since she was the wife of an arrested "enemy of the people." She became a beggar, completely dependent upon the goodwill of her fellow villagers. When the whole village was struck by the famine, her fate was sealed.

We found her house on a hill not far from ours, completely snow-bound, with the front door blocked by the snow.

We had a hard time clearing it away, and when we finally opened the door, we found the poor widow dead, just as we had feared, lying on the threshold halfway in the entrance hall. We carried her body into the living room and laid it on a bench. We found her daughter Lida, lying on a sleeping bench wrapped in many layers of rags but still alive. We carefully laid her on our sledge and rushed her back to our house.

At home, Mother was still occupied with Khymka's young son. She was rubbing his body with snow, and there was also something cooking for him on the stove.

When we brought Lida indoors, Mother began ministering to her needs, and we took over the care of the young boy. After making them as warm and comfortable as we could, we tried to feed them porridge and some homemade herb tea prepared by Mother, but our efforts to force some food and warm drink into them were all in vain. Except for their slow and spasmodic breathing, they didn't show any other signs of life, lying there completely motionless. When night fell, we witnessed their horrible death throes. At midnight, Lida died and the young boy followed shortly after.

Now we found ourselves in a peculiar situation. We had two corpses of people not related to us in our house. We could not keep them like that in our house too long, and burying them in the cemetery involved certain risks.

It was dangerous to show sympathy to starving villagers, particularly to people who, like this boy and girl, were looked upon by government officials as "enemies of the people." Trying to save the lives of these two young people came as natural to us as trying to save our own lives, but the Communist Party looked upon such an act as high treason. Nevertheless, come what may, we decided to bury their bodies properly in the cemetery.

The next morning, Mykola and I loaded the bodies on our sledge, covered them over, and started toward the village center where the cemetery was located. It was very hard for us to pull the sledge with such a heavy load; we had very little strength for such a task, especially in the deep snow and freezing cold. Moving along the main road, we saw a few more corpses; some of whom we recognized as the remains of neighbors. There were also strangers among them who had probably come from other villages in search of food. The fact that all the corpses were covered with heavy snow suggested to us that they had been lying on the road for quite some time.

As we came closer to the village center, we saw a pair of horses pulling a sleigh and galloping toward us. We knew that such a luxury was only afforded Party and government officials. The road was narrowed by the high snowdrifts, so we could not give way. The rearing horses stopped almost in front of us. At first we heard only swearing coming from the sleigh; then we were commanded to move aside. While we were trying to do this, our heavily-loaded sledge became firmly stuck in the snow. As we vainly attempted to push and pull our sledge out, we inadvertently uncovered our cargo. The attention of the officials was instantly riveted to our sledge. They dismounted and came over to us for a closer look.

There were two of them and both were strangers to us. They were warmly dressed and looked well fed and prosperous, as in olden days. One of them with a fur coat, stepped forward and demanded to know what we were pulling in our sledge.

"You see what we're pulling!" I replied, pointing to the corpses. The other stranger was eyeing us with curiosity.

"Who were they, and how did they die?" the man in the fur coat continued his interrogation.

What a superfluous and ridiculous question! I casually answered that the corpses were those of our neighbors. Then, instead of explaining to him the cause of their deaths, I pointed out that one could see many corpses on the road, and that there were many more dead and dying in their homes. He apparently must have been very displeased with my answer because he asked me angrily who we were and stepped closer to us.

"You certainly don't want to tell me that the entire population of the village died, or is about to die out, do you?" he continued, raising his voice. Then hurling more insults and curses at us, he took a notebook out of his pocket and wrote down our names.

The other man watched this whole procedure silently. After the man in the fur coat put his notebook away, they both returned to their sleigh, and passed swiftly by. It was no small effort for us to finally extricate our sledge from the deep snow.

It was quite a relief when we at last reached the cemetery, for we were very cold and utterly exhausted. Here we found ourselves among dozens of corpses. They lay scattered on both sides of the road. Some of them were piled up into heaps—probably all members of one family or of one neighborhood. Others were thrown all over in a haphazard fashion.

The cemetery was deathly quiet. No one was around. Nobody bothered to bury the remains of these miserable wretches.

A "proper" burial in the cemetery in those tragic days consisted of simply depositing the dead in one of the common graves or in graves that had been opened by looters and gold hunters. Even strong grave diggers would have had a hard time digging a grave in that frozen, snow-covered earth. For the ordinary village man, weakened by hunger, it was an impossible job. So we just lowered the bodies of our dead friends into one of the opened graves half filled with snow, and covered them with additional snow. We quickly departed for home.

On the way home, we met a man who lived close to us and was also going in our direction. It was good to have his company. He told us that he had gone to the center to inform the authorities about the great number of people who had starved in his neighborhood and whose unburied corpses remained in the houses and everywhere else. He was very upset by the fact that his story didn't make any impression on the men in the village soviet, and no one even wanted to believe him. The chairman of the village soviet even went so far as to object to the word "starved" and accused him of misinterpreting the facts. The chairman had his own interpretation. He admitted some deaths, but those could have happened only to the idle and lazy who didn't like and didn't want to work in the collective farm or to the "enemies of the people" who had to be exterminated anyway. Our companion realized he could accomplish nothing there. They had no use for further explanations and arguments, so he left the village soviet office an embittered man.

We, in turn, related to him that these same conditions prevailed in our neighborhood, and that we were just returning from the cemetery where we had buried two of our unfortunate neighbors' children. We also told our companion about our encounter with the two strangers on the way to the cemetery. From him we learned who those men were. The one in the fur coat was the new chairman of the village soviet. He had been appointed to that position by the county government and had just recently arrived in our village. The other man was a journalist sent from the capital city to our village to write an article about progress in collectivization and the meeting of grain delivery quotas. Only now it dawned on us why the man in the fur coat, our new chairman of the village soviet, became so embarrassed and furious when we talked about the corpses of the starved people. It was obvious to us now that he had been trying to hide the terrible reality of the misery of the villagers from his friend the writer.

From that day on we stayed at home, becoming more and more debilitated as the days went by. We watched with great anxiety our last hidden food reserves slowly diminishing, and the cold winter outside still in full swing.

CHAPTER 26

TOWARD the end of March, the famine struck us with full force. Life in the village had sunk to its lowest level, an almost animallike struggle for survival of the fittest.

The village ceased to exist as a coherent community. The inhabitants who still managed to stay alive shut themselves within the walls of their houses. People became too weak even to step outside their doors. Each house became an entity in itself. Visits became a rarity. All doors were bolted and barred against any possible intruders. Even between immediate neighbors, there was little, if any, communication, and people ceased caring about one another. In fact, they avoided each other. Friends and even relatives became strangers. Mothers abandoned their children, and brother turned away from brother.

Some of those who still had strength left continued to forage for food, but as unobtrusively as possible, quietly and stealthily, as if feeling guilty for still being alive.

But what could they find under the snow? On the streets, in the fields, in gardens and orchards, and on the frozen river, everywhere lay the frozen bodies of starved villagers. Their corpses became petrified monuments, perfectly preserved by the snow and frost. They became memorials to the starving children, men and women, old and young: an indictment of official Communist policy and morality.

As the snow continued to fall, the drifts became higher and more inpenetrable. There was no one to clear them from the roads and pathways. Children who used to enjoy playing in the snow, making snowmen, skating and skiing, were nowhere to be seen. Cats used to purr more loudly, and dogs used to bark more lustily in winter. But, by the end of February our village had no pets left: all of them had either starved, become meals for starving families, or been shot by Thousanders. The barns and barnyards had been empty since most of the domestic animals were confiscated by the state and transferred to the kolhosp. A few cows that still remained in the possession of the farmers were well-kept under lock and key as some kind of fabulous treasure. Indeed, even the farm buildings that used to house the domestic animals or serve as storage places, were now practically gone. They had been torn down long ago to be used as firewood. People burned everything in sight to keep warm: even fences, and furniture. In desperation, people dismantled abandoned houses or parts of living quarters.

Death had established its kingdom in our village. No human or animal voices were to be heard. The inhabitants inside their homes were either dead, or barely alive and paralyzed by starvation. Outside, everything was frozen and covered by snow and ice. The only sound that could be heard from time to time was that of the wind howling and whistling. What a contrast from the songs of our nightingales who were destroyed by the Thousanders.

There were other atrocities that no one wanted to talk about. Everyone knew that they occurred, but there seemed to be some taboo about discussing them openly. One of them was the terrible curse of cannibalism. It still is something very difficult to think or talk about.

One must consider the inexorable pressure of hunger under which a person can completely become bereft of his or her senses and sink to an absolute animallike level. That happened to many of our villagers. The more resistant ones who kept on living with minimal or no food at all for some time, felt no more of the initial hunger pangs. They either lapsed into comas, or existed in a semicomatose, lethargic stupor. But some reacted differently. They became like madmen. They lost all traces of compassion, honor, and morality. They suffered from hallucinations of food, of something to bite into and chew, to satisfy the gnawing pains of their empty stomachs. Intolerable cravings assailed them; they were ready to sink their teeth into anything, even into their own hands and arms, or into the flesh of others.

The first rumors of actual cannibalism were related to the mysterious and sudden disappearances of people in the village. Such was the case of Maria and her eleven-year old brother, children of Boris who had been deported long ago as an "enemy of the people." They disappeared without a trace. Their sick mother plodded from house to house through the deep snow searching for them. They had gone out to bring back firewood but had never returned. The neighbors had not seen the children and did not know anything about their whereabouts. No one was able to help the distraught mother. Then there was a widow who had been existing only on beggar's handouts. She too disappeared with her daughter, never to be seen again. Soon after that, two other women and a girl were reported missing.

As the cases of missing persons grew in number, an arrest was made which shook us to our souls. A woman was taken into custody, charged with killing her two children.

Another woman was found dead, her neck contorted in a crudely made noose. The neighbors who discovered the tragedy also found the reason for it. The flesh of the woman's three-year old daughter was found in the oven.

One morning, my friend Ivan, who had been living with us, left our house and did not return that day or that night. Days passed and we never heard from him nor found him. Ivan and I had been schoolmates and good friends for a long time. Shost, his father, had never returned from the village jail where I had last seen him. From there, he had been taken to the county center, and then to Siberia. Ivan's mother also was denounced and arrested only a few days later. Their farm and belongings had been turned over to the kolhosp. The children, Ivan (fifteen) and his pretty nineteen-year old sister, had been left homeless and at the mercy of their neighbors.

As often happened in such cases, the sister soon married. It was the only way for her to find a home and some measure of security for herself and her brother. Her neighbors thought that she acted wisely, and they admired her for her love and consideration of her young brother. They all moved into a house on a small hill near the forest, and for a while it seemed that her action had brought happiness commensurate with those times, to all of them.

But the marriage, unfortunately, was of brief duration. Only a few months later, she was arrested as the daughter of a kurkul, and was herself labeled a "dangerous element in the socialistic society." So great was the kolhosp organizers' fear of farmers' resistance that they tried to destroy not only stubborn farmers but also their wives and children. They did it lest some tiny spark of love of freedom remain that might be fanned into flames of revolt.

The daughter followed the trail of her parents into oblivion, and young Ivan was again on his own. He didn't wish to remain with his sister's husband, so my mother invited him to live with us. Thus he became a member of our family, and we obviously missed him after his disappearance and became very apprehensive about his fate.

As the days passed with no sign of Ivan, our anxiety grew. Mykola and I finally decided to undertake a thorough search for him.

Although Ivan had a strong dislike of his sister's husband and even for his house, there were several reasons why it was possible for him to have gone there. Before collectivization, Antin, Ivan's brother-in-law, was known in the village as an industrious and respectable young farmer. He was very good-natured and happy, and especially well liked by children, to whom he was very friendly. We had known him since early childhood, and in winter we used his hill for skiing. Antin encouraged this by keeping the hill in good skiing condition, and he even built a ski slide for us. When someone's skis broke, he would repair them, and after skiing, we would warm our frost-nipped hands and feet by his fire. Although the hillside often became noisy with the shouts and cries of children, he didn't mind it. On the contrary, he obviously enjoyed our frolicking in the snow.

But now, as the famine worsened, strange rumors began spreading about Antin's house on the hill. Someone heard a woman scream in his house. Then a second more dreadful tale went around. It was alleged that the smoke coming out of his chimney bore the odor of roasting human flesh. Thinking of these rumors now, we began to see some connection between them and Ivan's disappearance.

Could all these rumors have some truth in them? And even if true, could he have done such an unspeakable thing to his own wife's brother? We had to find out once and for all. With these terrible ideas in our minds, we slowly pushed our way towards the hill. Mykola, much younger than I, was pale with fright. He tried to persuade me to return home, but my feeling and concern for my friend Ivan were stronger than my fears. I had to find out whether Ivan was still alive and if he needed help.

I trudged on further while Mykola reluctantly followed me. We got nearer through an unbroken blanket of snow. Upon reaching the house, we thought of Mother's warnings to take certain precautions. She advised us that Mykola should stay outside, and that I should scream for help if someone inside should attack me. This would divert the attention of the attacker, and signal to Mykola to bring whatever assistance he could.

In accordance with this plan, Mykola took his place at the window clutching a club in his hand. I entered the hallway, leaving the outside door half open. Here I was met by Antin. Without answering my greeting, he gestured toward the door to the front room. As I stepped in, signs of abject poverty struck me from every direction. The walls were bare, there was no furniture, and it was very cold. As I looked at Antin closely, I saw him staring at me, as if estimating my strength.

It was a very unpleasant moment. His eyes were bloodshot and filled with tears. His nervous fingers dangled from his long arms, as if suspended and not belonging to his body at all.

It was apparent that he did not recognize me. I tried to help him remember by mentioning my name and the names of my mother and brother, but it was hopeless. Antin just kept staring at me blankly and silently with his bloodshot eyes.

The man had gone mad, I said to myself. Then the fearful realization came to me that he was twice as big as I! Again, I pictured what those still-strong, violent hands could do to me.

I slowly and cautiously began to back toward the doorway. My movements must have jolted him from his stupor and reminded him of something because he suddenly blurted out:

"You came to ask me where Ivan was?"

It was a relief to hear his voice which, though gruff and unpleasant, relieved the tension.

"Yes, Antin," I exclaimed, "but—"

He didn't let me finish the sentence.

"What do you mean by 'but'?" he interrupted me angrily.

"I mean—how could you know that I came looking for Ivan," I stammered. "Maybe he is . . ." I did not finish the sentence, realizing that I had gone too far; or said it too soon at the wrong moment.

But a surprising change came over him. He became more calm and sensible. There were no more outbursts on his part, though he remained agitated and nervous. He kept moving his hands, as if he didn't know what to do with them; his gaze kept shifting first to the window at his right, then to the one behind him, and finally it again rested on me.

My fear returned as he stood staring at me again. I didn't have any idea what to do next. In my dilemma, my heart started pounding and dizziness and weakness overcame me. I wanted to yell, cry and scram. Just at this moment, Antin turned and, going into the kitchen, remarked over his shoulder: "I will ask my mother about it."

But I didn't wait there any longer. A cold sweat broke out on my forehead and my whole body started trembling. An inner voice commanded me to run—as fast as I could, and my body automatically obeyed. I rushed out of the room and reached the hall, but it was too late. Antin quickly slipped through the kitchen door leading to the hall, and in seconds, stood in front of me. In one hand he held a shiny butcher knife, in the other a dirty rag.

Seeing these, I started shouting for help, and I continued shouting even after I tasted that dirty rag being pressed to my mouth. At that moment, there was the crash of breaking glass as Mykola shattered the window with his club. All of this was accompanied by Mykola's loud cries for help. My assailant hesitated for a moment and loosened his grip. I used his brief second of confusion to twist myself free and dashed out of the house. Mykola and I both started running as fast as we could through the deep snow, and didn't stop until we were safely inside our home. It was only then, behind locked doors, that we realized we had both had a very narrow escape.

We decided not to say anything to anyone about our trip to the house on the hill. The mystery of Ivan's disappearance remained unsolved until one day in April.

CHAPTER 27

I CANNOT find the words to describe what my eyes saw in the spring of 1933, but since those awesome memories still haunt me, I shall endeavor to convey my recollections of the sufferings and deaths of my fellow Ukrainians.

World War II was a reality, and I was a part of it. I saw the multitude of dead and mutilated bodies; I heard the cries of despair, and the moans of agony all around me. Day after day, I felt cold and hunger. I was constantly in fear of death. But all of that is now seen through the mist of time. In the haziness of those memories, I see a dim spark of light. This spark is the recognition that those sufferings were caused by war, that I and others at that time had a chance to fight for our lives, to defend ourselves no matter how slim those chances might be. Above all, I realized that while fighting in the war, I had not been completely abandoned. The military was always there with daily food rations, no matter how deficient in quantity and quality. We were also clothed (after a fashion), and barracks as such for sleep when possible were provided. The sufferings of war pale in comparison with the events in our village, all of which remain in my memory as absolute in horror.

Those of us who were still alive harbored a secret and final hope that the coming of the spring of 1933 would bring us some relief. We thought that the new vegetation would help us live through the long months of waiting for the new bread. Nourished by this hope, we were able to carry on until we saw the first signs of green. Sadly, however, many of the villagers were no longer alive by the time the long-awaited spring finally arrived. And many of those who lived long enough to see the passing of winter found their death in the very vegetables and grasses they were so hopefully and patiently awaiting.

That spring of 1933 in Ukraine was unusually cold. In our region, the spring weather usually set in around the beginning of April. The snow would melt quickly, and the green blanket of vegetation would immediately appear in its place. But in 1933, snow was still visible everywhere in mid-April. An icy-cold wind blew continually. It would often bring heavy clouds of rain or snow, or both, and the village would sink deep into mud and slush again. Then a freeze would turn all that into knobs of dirty ice.

Starvation in our village now reached a point at which death was a desirable relief. Many houses around us had already been standing for a long time with no signs of life. As the snow slowly melted away, human corpses were exposed to view everywhere: in backyards, on roads, in fields. Those dead bodies constituted a pathetic problem for the living. As the weather warmed, they started to thaw and decay. The stench which resulted plagued us, and we could do nothing about it. The villagers who survived were unable to bury the dead, and no one from the outside seemed in a hurry to do it, so the bodies were just left wherever they happened to die. Those in the fields or in the forest, fell prey to wild animals; those in their homes became the prey of countless rats.

For the third time, the village was stricken with panic. Those who were fortunate enough to remain alive were in the depths of despair. The resources they possessed had been used up long ago. They all finally had to face the shocking truth that there was nothing to eat, and no hope of getting any help: that death from starvation was their imminent fate.

Most of these desperate villagers reconciled themselves to this fact. They stayed at home, and their conditions were indescribable. They were unkempt and haggard, and so weak that they could hardly drag one foot after the other. They just sat, or lay down silently, too feeble even to talk.

The bodies of some were reduced to skeletons, with their skin hanging grayish-yellow and loose over their bones. Their faces looked like rubber masks with large, bulging, immobile eyes. Their necks seemed to have shrunk into their shoulders. The look in their eyes was glassy, heralding their approaching death.

The bodies of others were swollen, a final stage of starvation. Their faces, arms, legs and stomachs resembled the surfaces of plastic balloons. The tissues would soon crack and burst, resulting in the fast deterioration of their bodies.

The thaw brought with it a new wave of beggars. Those who still had strength enough to move left their dwellings and took off in search of food. Old and young, mostly women and children, slowly moved from house to house dragging their rag-covered feet. They pleaded for food: a potato, or a piece of bread, or at least a kernel—a single kernel! —of corn. At the onset of the famine, I remember how the emaciated would come to the doorstep, often sobbing, and would ask for some spare food. If refused, they would excuse themselves politely and go away, apologizing for bothering us.

But this spring's beggars presented an entirely different picture. These desperate people, numbed by cruelty and injustice as well as hunger, were no longer the modest, honorable small farmers they had been before. Their fear of starvation was so great that they lost all semblance of self-control, becoming more like wild, hungry beasts in their search for food. They no longer distinguished friends from enemies and were ready to commit even murder for a mere scrap. Their clothes had long ago turned to rags, and they themselves were worn out and exhausted to the point of collapse.

With protruding frightened eyes and outstretched hands, they would approach someone, but this time they did not plead: they were voiceless; they just cried. Often their heavy tears were mixed with fluid slowly oozing out of the cracks in their swollen faces. They whispered and begged for a crumb of bread.

Another sign of almost imminent death from starvation was the body lice, those small, flat, wingless, parasitic insects who were the constant companions of the wretched and impoverished. The starving villagers were no longer able to take care of their sanitary needs, nor had they strength to fetch water, let alone heat it in order to bathe themselves, or wash their clothes and their bedding. Those who still had strength could do some washing, but not properly because they had no soap. For a few years now, not a single bar of soap had been seen in the village. But, even if soap had been available, we could not buy it. First, we had no money; second, we were prohibited from buying any merchandise in the stores as our grain quotas had not been met. As a result, all of us were dirty and infected with lice.

As the limbs of a starving person turn cold with the approach of death, the lice begin to migrate to the warmer facial areas such as the eye sockets, ears, mouth corners, and nostrils. When this happened, it was an unmistakable sign that the starving person's sufferings would soon come to an end.

The plight of the children was one of the most heartbreaking experiences for me during that time, and their pathetic faces, parched or swollen, and streaked with tears, will remain in my memory forever.

They could not understand why they couldn't get a piece of bread or something else to eat. They were not able to comprehend what was going on in their own small world. Thinking of them still makes me tremble with horror. God is my witness that as I write these words, the paper is wet with my tears.

Not many children in our neighborhood had survived the terrible winter, but those who had were reduced to mere skeletons, too weak to cry. The heads on their small thin necks looked like inflated balloons. Their small bony arms and legs were like sticks protruding from their little bodies. Their stomachs were bloated to unusual proportions, and water flowed uninterruptedly from their genitals. Those childish faces looked prematurely aged and twisted. They resembled old folks: wrinkled, listless, and very, very sad. At their stage of starvation, they were in a constant stupor which is peculiar to those who suffer from extreme hunger. It seemed as if nature itself had conspired with the Communist regime to add a final touch of pathos and horror to the sufferings the children had to endure. Hair had started to grow on the faces of some, mainly on their foreheads and temples. I saw a few such children and they looked so strange to me —like creatures from another planet, and they left me with a feeling of helplessness and doom.

Often starvation would sweep away an entire family. The adult members would die first, leaving the children alone in a cold house, half-naked and hungry, to fend for themselves. One can imagine what happened to such hopeless children: these orphans, scantily clad and feet wrapped in rags, joined the rest of the beggars. Struggling in the snow, they would first go to their nearest neighbors only to find that they too were dead. Then they would go to another house and yet another farther away. Compassionate villagers who were still alive would let a child or two stay with them only to watch them slowly die.

Yet miraculously, some children managed to survive. These were mostly boys and girls between ten and fifteen years of age. With the coming of spring, they saw their chances of survival in terms of leaving home, and going to the city. A few, but *very* few, children managed to do just that and were fortunate in finding help and understanding from some of the urban dwellers. Others, less fortunate, were picked up by the militia and locked up in the Children's Detention Home. These children had a better chance of surviving the famine, although we heard that many of them also died. And then, there were those whose fate it was to join the ranks of the city's juvenile criminals. God alone knows what happened to them. Finally, there were those who neither reached the city nor were picked up by the militia. They lay dead wherever they had fallen for days or even weeks, until someone would drag them out of sight into some ditch like a dead animal.

I saw many tragic events in which children were the innocent victims, but one episode in particular emerges from my memories of that spring as a symbol of humanity gone completely mad. It was sometime at the onset of April. One early morning while we still lay in our beds, we heard a child's cry and a weak knocking on the door. I was the first to jump out of bed. As I opened the door, I saw a small girl of about four. She stood trembling from the cold and exhaustion with streams of tears flowing down her famished little cheeks. We knew her! It was Maria, the daughter of our neighbor Hana, who also had a seven-year-old son and lived about half a mile from us. Hana's husband, a young and industrious farmer, had been arrested like many others, for no apparent reason, and exiled somewhere to a concentration camp about two years before. Hana was left alone with her two children to struggle for food, like all the rest of us. However, as winter came and starvation struck us, we lost track of her.

I let the child into the house.

"My mommy won't wake up!" the child announced, wiping away the tears with the sleeve of her dirty coat.

Mother and I glanced at each other. A short while later, my brother Mykola and I were on our way to Hana's home. When we entered the house, our fears were confirmed. Hana was dead, lying on her back on the sleeping bench. Her bulging glassy eyes seemed to be looking at us. Her widely opened mouth still seemed to be gasping for air. We could see that she had met her death not too long before Maria had knocked on our front door. On Hana's cheek we could still see the traces of her tears; we could also see the lice still moving back and forth like ants, in search of a warm spot. Next to her, wrapped in some cloth, lay her dead son. The one-room house was empty and dirty. There was no furniture except for two benches, and no trace of food. The mud floor had been dug up all over, and there were holes in the walls. The chimneys of the cooking and heating stoves were totally ruined. We recognized immediately the work of the Bread Procurement Commission. There was no doubt that they had been there recently, searching for "hidden" foodstuffs.

Mykola and I stood there aghast. I felt the impulse to either run away screaming, or to sit down next to their dead bodies and hold their cold hand in mine in sorrow and sympathy, but I did neither. I just stood there petrified, and looking at the dead mother and her young son, I asked the question:

"Why? Why did they have to die?"

We left the bodies in the house hoping that soon the kolhosp burial brigade would pick them up on their daily search for bodies. This brigade was set up about two months before for the purpose of collecting and burying the corpses of the starved villagers.

Little Maria survived the famine. She stayed with us for a while until her relatives, who lived in one of the cities, took her into their family.

CHAPTER 28

ONE DAY, at the end of April 1933, I remember my mother suggesting that my brother and I make a visit to our distant relative Priska, who lived about four miles from our home. We gladly agreed. On our way we could also visit some of our acquaintances and school friends whom we had not seen since the beginning of last winter. We often wondered what had happened to them, and we were prepared for the worst.

We took the road along a strip of sand dunes that separated the woods from our neighborhood. It was here we had hidden some of our food. It was a pleasant, sunny spring day. All around us birds fluttered form bush to bush, chirping cheerfully. New greenery was visible everywhere, but not a single human being was in sight; there were no human voices to be heard. We did not see any cats or dogs. It was as if some terrible plague had passed through the village, leaving alive only the birds and the insects.

We passed by Antin's house on the hill where a few weeks before we had looked for our friend Ivan. Approaching closer, we heard to our surprise some boisterous voices. There was activity around Antin's house: some people were searching for something. We couldn't help stopping to see what was going on, and what we discovered was the Hundred's Bread Procurement Commission in action. The village Thousander, Comrade Livshits, was personally overseeing the search and seizure operation. He stood in front of the house shouting orders from time to time. Several Commission members were digging around the house with spades. Others were busy inside the house and in the shed.

Absurd as it may seem, the Bread Procurement Commission in our village continued its search for "hidden" foodstuffs, in spite of the mass starvation raging all around them. They continued going from one house to another, paying special attention to those who showed some signs of life. They also continued demanding grain quotas, or simply searched farmers' premises without even bothering to ask their permission. It was also necessary and mandatory for us to attend meetings and listen to propagandists, agitators, and other Party officials harangue us endlessly about the merits of grain delivery to the state, or what the Party and government position was on certain issues and events, or what decrees had newly been passed by the state. Naturally, only a very few individuals were seen at such meetings since many of our number had already been killed by famine. Those left alive no longer had the physical strength to leave their homes.

But thanks to those meetings, those of us able to attend learned that sometime in January the Communist Party of the Soviet Union, after accusing Ukraine of deliberately sabotaging the fulfillment of grain quotas, had sent Postyshev, a sadistically cruel Russian chauvinist, as its viceroy to Ukraine. His appointment played a crucial role in the lives of all Ukrainians.

It was Postyshev who brought along and implemented a new Soviet Russian policy in Ukraine. It was an openly proclaimed policy of deliberate and unrestricted destruction of everything that was Ukrainian. From now on, we were continually reminded that there were "bourgeois-nationalists" among us whom we must destroy. They were the ones causing our "food difficulties." Those hideous "bourgeois-nationalists" were starving us to death, and on and on went the accusations. At every meeting, we were told that the fight against the Ukrainian national movement was as important for the "construction of socialist society" as the struggle for bread. This new campaign against the Ukrainian national movement had resulted in the annihilation of the Ukrainian central government as well as all Ukrainian cultural, educational, and social institutions. There were also arrests in our village as a result of this new policy.

With the arrival of Postyshev, the grain collection campaign was changed into a Seed Collection Campaign. The fact that the farmers were starving did not bother the authorities at all. What they worried about was the lack of seed for the spring sowing. I remember one of Postyshev's speeches in which he instructed all Party organizations to collect seed with the same methods used in collecting grain. He also ordered the expropriation of grain seed which had supposedly been stolen or illegally distributed as food for the members of collective farms. It was made clear that the needed seed must be collected and delivered immediately and at all costs. But it was beyond our comprehension that the Communist authorities could so ruthlessly demand grain at a time when the bodies of starved farmers were littering the roads, fields, and backyards. As we listened to these harangues, we often thought that perhaps there was hidden sabotage at work to discredit the Communist Party. But we were naive. Devoid of all human emotions, the Party wanted grain from us; starvation was no excuse. The Party officials treated us with contempt and impatience. All this was heightened by the traditional Russian distrust and dislike of Ukrainian farmers. Thus we were forced to listen to the endless lies of these Russian officials that there was no famine; that no one was starving. Those who died were the lazy ones who refused to work at the collective farm. They deserved to die.

But, let's return to Antin's house, where the Bread Procurement Commission members were searching his premises on the hill. There were rumors that Antin and his mother, deranged by hunger, had become cannibals. But that was not the reason the commission had come there on that particular day. We learned that Comrade Thousander had once met Antin and noticed he still looked well fed and vigorous. To Comrade Thousander that only meant that Antin had some hidden food, so he arranged with the First Hundred commission to have a thorough search made of Antin's place for "hidden" foodstuffs. Imagine their surprise that instead of finding grain, they found human remains. We, at that point, noticed Antin and his mother standing at some distance from Comrade Thousander. Their hands were tied behind their backs, and they were guarded by one of the Thousanders armed with a shotgun. In front of them, was a heap of human remains, bones and skulls. It was a nauseating sight, and so is its sordid memory. There was no doubt in our minds that the remains of our friend Ivan were in that horrible pile.

We left the scene with revulsion and disgust, hurrying on to Priska's house.

Priska's fate was not much different from that of many of the unfortunate villagers' families. For refusing to join the collective farm in 1930, and then failing to meet the state taxes and delivery quotas, her husband was labeled a kurkul and banished like many others to a distant notorious concentration camp. Later on, her husband was interned in a forced labor camp from which news reached Priska that he had died while digging the Baltic Sea–White Sea Canal. Priska was left alone with her two children: a boy about seven and a five-year-old daughter.

Priska was at home when we reached her place. She was famished to such a degree that she could hardly move. She told us her sad story laboriously since it was already difficult for her to talk.

Left alone, she had to work hard to support her children. Her work consisted mainly of running around searching for food. There was not much she could find: a couple of beets, a few potatoes, a slice or two of bread. Still, it was not so bad during the summer and autumn when she was able to work at the collective farm. While working there, she received two pounds of either bread or flour. In addition, she, like the rest of the kolhosp members who were able to work, received two hot meals daily. It was usually some kind of millet or buckwheat gruel or porridge. With her food rations, she was also able to feed her children, but when winter came work stopped at the kolhosp, and her bread rations and hot meals also ceased. The small amount of food that she had received as payment in kind for her labor didn't last very long. Nevertheless, she and her children managed somehow to stay alive until March. Then came the inevitable: her son succumbed to starvation. She buried him in the orchard under a cherry tree. She also wished to be buried under a cherry tree after her death.

Now left with her little daughter, Maria, she knew that soon it would be their turn to die. She was afraid of the possibility that she would die first, leaving her young daughter all alone. That thought was unbearable to Priska; she had to do something to save little Maria from that fate. She had heard rumors about a Children's Shelter in a town about twenty miles from our village. One April morning, the two of them started their twenty-mile journey on foot. Arriving at the so-called Children's Shelter, she discovered that it was a Militia Detention Home for Children. Even though she was frightened, disappointed, and frustrated with this turn of events, she decided that even that place would be better than caring for her child alone. After thinking very carefully, she instructed little Maria what she should do and say and sent her to the entrance door. As soon as the door was opened and little Maria entered, Priska disappeared around the street corner, never to see her little daughter again.

At this point in her story, Priska became silent. Her bulging glassy eyes had a stunned look, and her lips trembled, but she did not cry. We just stood there watching her silently.

After Priska regained her composure, she completed her story. She had no peace in her heart after giving up Maria and leaving her to an unknown destiny. She was heartbroken and had feelings of great guilt and remorse. She could not stop the tears from flowing. During the long cold sleepless nights, in her hallucinations little Maria would appear before her. Sitting down on the bench in the corner under the icons, Priska could sense her staring at her. Then Maria would burst out crying, begging for bread and saying:

"Mama, why have you abandoned me? Don't you love me anymore?"

Each night her little daughter would appear, Priska said, and each time she would ask her the same question:

"Mama, why have you abandoned me? Don't you love me anymore?"

Finally, in her frenzied state, she walked those twenty miles again to where she had left Maria. Her efforts were in vain, and she never did see her again.

It was growing dark by the time Priska finished her story, and we had to leave for home. The next day, Mother sent us back to Priska's house with some food, but it was too late. We found her dead on the floor. In her despondency, she chose to die a quicker, less agonizing death. She mustered all her remaining strength to poison herself by inhaling charcoal fumes.

We remembered her desire to be buried under a cherry tree, and at nightfall we buried her close to her young son.

Such suicides became a common occurrence in our village at that time. Many people took their lives by carbon monoxide poisoning like Priska did. It was simple and painless. Those who decided on such a step were mostly women whose husbands had been arrested and sent to concentration camps, and who had lost their children in their heroic struggle with starvation. They would seal the chimneys, the doors, and windows, make a fire in the oven or in the middle of the room on the mud floor, and die from the deadly fumes. Others would set the whole house on fire.

But the most common form of suicide was by hanging. Among those who chose this way were the village functionaries, especially the leaders of the Tens and Fives. Some members of the Communist Party also committed suicide in one way or another. The authorities were aware of these mass suicides, but did nothing to stop them.

During the following days, we visited other relatives and friends about whom we were anxious. Anything could have happened to them since we last saw them.

First, we stopped at my friend Vasyl's house. His father had been arrested and banished to some northern region. He had lived with his mother and two little sisters, but we had heard nothing from him since he had dropped out of school sometime in December of last year. As we entered the house, we saw the two famished girls and their mother. All three of them looked like living mummies. They were crouched silently in the middle of the room on the mud floor. They were cooking weeds, orach and nettle, which grew abundantly in our region. The girls left our greetings unanswered. All their attention was concentrated on the bubbling liquid in the pot. They watched it greedily, with spoons in their hands. The mother started weeping upon seeing us. It took us quite a while to calm her down so she could answer our inquiries about Vasyl, and then she told us his story.

At the onset of the famine, Vasyl had joined some men experienced in traveling to distant places. He went with them to Russia to buy food. He was lucky. He returned home with several loaves of bread and about thirty pounds of flour. That was last December. In March of 1933, when the famine reached its most disastrous proportions, Vasyl decided to repeat his trip, but this time he was not so lucky. He somehow managed to catch a train to a small Russian town not far from Moscow. From there, he was able to inform his mother in some way that he was on his way home. However, he never returned. His mother later learned that he had been arrested at a border railroad station, and eventually tried as a black marketeer, convicted, and given a sentence of five years of hard labor. No one had heard from him since.

There were many cases like Vasyl's. Despite the official prohibition against travel in search of jobs and food, and in spite of our miserable living conditions and the fact that we were practically in a state of collapse from hunger, we couldn't simply give up. No one who could still stand wanted to resign himself to death without a struggle.

There was no attempt of any kind to organize some relief for the starving families in our village either by the authorities or by private individuals. On the contrary, when a local teacher tried to put some relief in motion, he was arrested and sent to dig the Baltic Sea—White Sea Canal. He was accused of "spreading false rumors that our villagers were starving." The idea of organized relief vanished together with him. We were on our own to fight the disaster individually without the benefit of social organization. The mass exodus of the villagers was not only to neighboring towns and cities. Many, like Vasyl, went to farther regions and even to Russia where there was no famine. It was not easy to do, even if one had money. As I've noted before, we were not allowed to buy train tickets, except when we had special permission from the village soviet. In 1933, the ordinance was being enforced much more strictly. The trains were guarded by soldiers of the special forces, and it was impossible to sneak onto a train without showing a ticket. Besides that, the villagers did not have the passports which had been introduced the previous December, so it was easier to check all passengers traveling north or east from Ukraine and catch the "illegal" ones. Anyone caught was forcibly returned to his village or sent to a labor camp.

This was an ideal time for the city black marketeers. With their personal passports, they could buy train tickets for travel wherever they wanted to without any difficulties. Then they in turn could resell the ticket to a villager for an exorbitant price. A ticket to Moscow on the black market, for example, would usually cost four or five times as much as its original price.

CHAPTER 29

MOST OF our attempts to find help outside the village were doomed to failure. Wherever a Ukrainian farmer turned up to seek food outside his village, he was hunted like a wild animal. We were forced to forage for our own food from nature.

The lucky and skillful might catch a fish or a bird. Others would try to satisfy their hunger with the tender juicy parts of the abundant river plants and vegetables. The forest offered the hungry its berries, mushrooms, all kinds of roots, and even the leaves and bark of bushes and trees. There was game in abundance too for those with expertise in catching or trapping. But we had no hunting weapons, since all guns had been confiscated long ago.

The fields were the favorite places for foraging. There one had the hope of finding something, mainly root vegetables from last year's crop, preserved by the winter snow and frost. Potatoes, beets, and onions were priceless for the starving people, even if frozen. "A starving man does not sniff his food," says the old adage.

As soon as the snow had melted, one could see the miserable figures of the hungry wading in the watery fields in search of something edible. The best find was potatoes. Often those who found them didn't eat them right then and there, but brought them home and made a kind of potato pancake, mixing them with leaves or even bark.

However, it wasn't an easy task for people weakened by hunger to wander around in the fields hunting for vegetables. Just to reach the faraway areas required strength and stamina, and many could not make it. Even if they succeeded, many fell dead in the fields from exhaustion before finding anything.

One afternoon, the mother of my school friend Petro came to see us. Crying, she told us that Petro was dying in the field, about two miles from our village. A neighbor who had returned from her frozen potato field trip brought her the news. She had seen Petro in his distress, but was not strong enough to help him. Petro's mother pleaded with us to help her bring him home, dead or alive.

The story of Petro's family was no different from that of many other villagers. His father had refused to join the kolhosp, as had all the farmers at first. But the government officials were persistent and used every trick and means to destroy him as an individual farmer. Two years ago, he was appointed leader of a Five. That meant that his house became a meeting place for five farmers and he was fully responsible for them before the government. As the government pressed the farmers to join the collective farm, he had to collectivize all the farmers who belonged to his Five, and, of course, he had to be the first to join the collective farm.

This trick worked well in many instances, but not in the case of Petro's father. He and the members of his Five loathed the collective farm, and wanted to stay away from it, but he paid dearly for his stubbornness. Petro's farm was overtaxed, and when he could not meet the tax quota in kind and money, he was arrested as an "enemy of the people" and disappeared somewhere into the Russian north. His farm was confiscated, and his wife and two young children had to move into her parents' home.

Misfortune followed his wife there too. During the spring of 1932, her parents and her young daughter starved to death, leaving her alone with Petro.

Now, after both of them had somehow managed to survive that famine, young Petro was dying somewhere out there alone in the field.

We could not refuse Petro's mother's pathetic please for help, although we ourselves hardly had sufficient strength to stand on our own feet. However, Petro was our friend and neighbor, and since there were no men around in our neighborhood who could help or risk the trip to the field then, we decided to do what we could to rescue Petro.

The only means of transportation we had to bring Petro home was a pushcart, since our horse and wagon had been confiscated two years ago. Taking the cart, Mykola and I headed for the potato field, followed by Petro's mother, who insisted on accompanying us. We took a field road which, at that time of the year, was very muddy and in many places covered by pools of water coated with icy slush. Our footwear, if one could call it that, was completely inadequate for such a road. Petro's mother had her feet wrapped in rags; Mykola and I had some old worn and torn shoes wrapped in pieces of tarpaulin. The heavy tarlike mud stuck to our footwear and made it difficult for us to walk. To add to our problems, crossing the mud puddles ankle deep, our footwear got soaked through by the icy, muddy water, making the trip more hazardous and extremely difficult. Petro's mother, who was trying to keep up with us, could not humanly follow our pace, but sobbing quietly insisted she had no intention of returning to the village; she still lived in the hope of seeing her son alive. Mykola and I decided to put her on the pushcart and tried desperately to pull her. However, she was too heavy for the size of the cart, and, realizing she was holding us up by her persistence, she got off, and we yielded to her wishes to leave her behind.

As we continued our way to the field, we found two dead bodies. As we reached a shallow depression between two hills, my brother spotted an object lying in a furrow, a few feet off the road. We left the cart, and went to see it. We discovered a man's body lying face down in the mud. There were no signs of a struggle. Apparently the man had fallen down and was just too weak to get up. He must have died quite a while ago and his body had lain there under the snow during the entire winter. We tried to turn the body over to see his face, but we could not. It was still frozen and stuck to the ground.

At this point Petro's mother had caught up with us, and upon seeing the corpse she let out a loud cry but avoided getting near it. She urged us to keep on going and to hurry.

Naturally, she was unable to keep up our pace which we were doubling now, so we left her as we hurried on. Evening was approaching and heavy clouds began descending from the horizon onto the fields. Far away it was pouring rain and we could watch the storm slowly moving in our direction.

Yet we were delayed again. After trudging for about half a mile, a few feet off the road we spied the body of a woman whom we recognized. Her death, however, wasn't caused by starvation. We could see instantly that she had been killed by a shotgun. She lay there on her back in a pool of blood mixed with mud, and her eyes seemed to be staring at us blankly. Apparently she had met her death quite recently. I tried to figure out what had happened to her. Her assailant could not have been an individual crazed by hunger like someone who would kill for a few frozen potatoes. No ordinary villagers had guns; only officials and guardsmen were in possession of arms. So it was most probable that the woman had been shot by a kolhosp field guard for foraging on the kolhosp potato field.

As before, we had to leave the body behind us and move on. The rain was coming nearer, and it was growing dark. We strained with all our might to get to the place where we hoped to find Petro. When we finally arrived, panting and perspiring, we found him. He was lying in the road still alive and breathing slowly. The long track behind him told us that he had crawled for quite a distance in the mud before he had passed out.

We somehow managed to put him on our cart with his feet hanging over the edge as he was too big for it. Our way back was even more difficult as it had started raining. We inched our way through the mud, pushing the cart with our heavy load.

We were expecting to meet Petro's mother and we started worrying about her when she did not show up on the road. After a while we found her. She was lying in the mud, unable to move any farther. She had apparently also lost her speech. She just stared at us with her wide eyes. We were frightened, for we could see that her death was imminent. However, she made a slight movement, signaling to us that she wanted to see her son. We lifted her to her feet. With our help, she reached the cart, but then she fell on it with all her weight. This was an impossible situation. There was no way we could have pulled or pushed the cart with both of them on it since Mykola and I were at the point of exhaustion.

As if sensing our plight, Petro's mother slowly raised her head and tried to say something, but she could not. She slid down from the cart, and slightly lifting her right hand, she pointed at Petro. We understood that she wanted us to leave her behind while we hurried with her son to the village. She still hoped we could save him.

We left her there, intending to return for her later, and hurried home with Petro as fast as we could in spite of the bad weather and our waning strength. It was pitch black when we finally reached home, and raining heavily. Mother was very relieved to see us and with her help we brought Petro inside.

Not stopping to rest, we set out to bring Petro's mother back for she could not last out there in the dark for long. Mother had decided to go back with us, so she wrapped Petro, who was still breathing slowly but evenly, in some warm clothing, gave him some broth to drink, and made him comfortable. Then we left the house, taking the cart with us again.

We found Petro's mother alive but unconscious. After placing her on the cart, we headed slowly homeward with our heavy load. It was impossible to see the road in the darkness and pouring rain, and we often had to wade through pools of water. Our cart turned over several times, throwing Petro's mother into the mud, but we never gave up. Drenched to the skin, we finally made it home where Mother, soaking wet herself, hastened to put dry clothes on Petro's mother, while Mykola and I turned our attention to Petro. We wanted to change his clothing too, but bending over him, we discovered that he had died. We all made Petro's mother as comfortable as we could, but she never regained consciousness and she died in terrible convulsions. We were sad, but also glad that at least they had not succumbed in the mud and pouring rain that dark night.

Once again we were confronted with the problem of what to do with the bodies of our friends. They could not be left in our house, but neither could they be taken to the cemetery to be buried properly, as Mother usually insisted. This time she realized that we were too weak for that, so we decided to take them to their home and let the Thousanders dispose of their bodies. This we did that very same night.

CHAPTER 30

THE FROZEN potato rush took on a new fervor toward the end of April. This was the time when the kolhosp planted a new crop. The hungry villagers thought that now it would be easy for them to get some potatoes. One could go out and simply dig them up, and some did just that. Others worked out another system: they found the first potato, and then followed it down the row.

But in reality it wasn't that simple or easy. The government soon stepped in to protect its kolhosp fields. It was announced that foraging in the fields was prohibited. Anyone caught stealing the planted potatoes or other vegetables would be executed.

Those villagers who disregarded the official warning and ignored the guardsmen were arrested and locked up in the county jail. Soon rumors spread that the jailers in the county prison fed the prisoners well, giving them bread and other food to eat. As a consequence, many villagers, instead of looking for potatoes looked for guardsmen to arrest them and put them in the county jails. People were exchanging their homes for prisons which were places of refuge from hunger. Thus the number of "criminals" rapidly increased.

But it didn't work for long. Obviously the county prisons became overcrowded. Besides, the authorities surmised the true reason for the increasing number of "enemies of the people." In order to stem the flow to the county jails, it was officially announced one day that the village "criminals" would have to stay in the *village* jails. Prisoners in the village jails received no food from the jailers, and their families had to feed them. Also, the prisoners who still could walk had to work. Usually, they dug graves in the cemetery, or worked on the roads, or in the kolhosp fields.

Throughout April it was cold and uncomfortable in our house. We had already burned everything that would burn in order to keep warm. The barn, pigpen, and the fence had all been torn down and burned. When the snow started melting away, we began collecting dry weeds in gardens, backyards, and along the roads for fuel. But in spite of all our hardships, we were still better off than many other villagers, since we still had some potatoes and a few small bags of grain hidden in a haystack.

And we still had our cow! Just having her assured us a better chance of survival. She would soon be giving us milk, as she was going to calf sometime at the beginning of May.

We treated our cow as our savior. Since the beginning of winter, we had been keeping her in the other half of our house, and we cared for her as best we could. We tried to give her plenty of suitable food.

But one April day, our hopes were shattered. A notice came that within twenty hours we had to deliver about 250 pounds of meat to the state in the form of livestock. This meant we had to give up our cow. We never cried so much as we did on that day. It was as if we were losing our very lives, which indeed was not far from the truth.

The Bread Procurement Commission arrived at our place toward evening. They had not even given us the promised twenty-four hours' notice. While a few commission members kept a watchful eye on us huddled in the house, the others quickly led our cow out and left. The whole procedure was more like a holdup than a legal, orderly process.

The next day found us in a very desperate state. We had been living in constant hunger for five months already. We had not seen normal food since December, except for some of the groceries we had bought at the Torgsin. Our only hope for some substantial food had been the one we had just lost—a steady supply of milk. That had been our constant topic of conversation; our daydream. Now, being deprived of it, we had nothing left to hope for.

Meanwhile, hunger assailed us mercilessly. The pangs in my empty stomach were unbearable. I felt constant faintness, dizziness, and I was unsteady on my feet. I thought I was going mad: I couldn't think of anything else but food, wherever I was, or whatever I was doing. I had fantasies about all kinds of food, but most of all I dreamt of bread: freshly baked, soft and warm, hot out of the oven. I smelled and inhaled the aroma; I tasted the fresh bread. I saw in front of me breads of all kinds, shapes, and colors: white and dark. If only I just had one piece! I would not want anything else in the world. I wouldn't care for anything else!

Such daydreaming was a beneficial lull, making me forget the hunger pangs. But then I would awaken from that dreamworld, just to feel those burning, sharp hunger pangs in my stomach again; a pain that was driving me mad.

But, thank God, in spite of these sporadic hallucinations, we could think lucidly most of the time. No one with a sound mind wishes to starve to death without struggling first to save his life. We had to survive somehow, even without our cow. We held a family council, at which time we decided to act immediately. Mother urged us to go to the river and try our luck at fishing.

Immediately, Mykola and I took some bags and homemade traps, and headed for the river, about two miles from our village. Each year, beginning with Easter and until winter set in, we used to swim and play in its gently flowing warm water almost daily. Above all, we liked to fish there and to hunt for bird eggs.

Those carefree days were long past. We now turned to our beloved river with the hope that it would help us in our life and death struggle. The day was foggy and rather cold as we stepped on the sandy road we had walked thousands of times before. We knew every bush and tree along the way. However, this road now offered us some surprises.

After passing a deserted windmill, we noticed an object at some distance in front of us. Approaching closer, we saw that it was the body of a woman. We recognized her at first sight. She was our neighbor, Oksana Shevchenko.

Oksana went through the same ordeal as had many of our villagers. Two years before, her father who had been labeled a kurkul, had been arrested and taken away from the village. A few months later, Oksana's mother died thus leaving the eighteen-year-old girl to care for her twelve-year-old sister and seven-year-old brother.

But Oksana's real troubles had just started. One day she received a note from the village government stating that her family, being kurkuls, had to deliver a certain quota of grain and meat to the state immediately. The demand was utterly ridiculous, for everything the family possessed had already been expropriated before the arrest of her father, and for the last two years the family had been starving. That was not a valid excuse as far as the state was concerned.

The Bread Procurement Commission appeared on their doorstep the day after the note was received. They searched everywhere for meat and grain, leaving not a stone unturned, but found nothing. One would have assumed that Oksana and her charges would now be left alone, but the government officials had a different idea. Oksana was informed that, inasmuch as she was refusing to deliver the required quotas to the state, her house was to be expropriated and declared state property. Incidentally, the house had a tin roof, which was another unmistakable sign that it belonged to a kurkul.

Oksana's tears and pleas were of no avail. Neither were the officials moved by the cries of the two small children huddled around her, holding fast to her skirt.

On the contrary, the leader of the commission tried to further terrify them with his gun. He quickly drew it, and pointing it at Oksana, warned her that he would kill her if the children didn't stop crying. After failing to impress them into silence with his gun, he ordered the members of the commission to forcibly remove the children from the house. When they hesitated, he threatened to kill the nearest member of the commission, pointing his gun at him. This had the desired effect. The children were dragged out, kicking and screaming. Oksana fainted and was dragged out also. The Bread Procurement Commission sealed the doors and windows, and left, ignoring Oksana and the children in their pitiful plight.

After surviving that horror, Oksana and the children took refuge in her aunt's house. A few months later, the little sister died of pneumonia. Her aunt soon followed, dying of starvation. Oksana was left alone with young Stepan.

All these tragedies had happened about a year ago. Now, she lay dead before our eyes on the sandy road. She too had apparently tried to reach the river or the woods as a last resort in her quest for something edible. But she was not destined to do it. The marks in the sand indicated that she had tried to crawl. She lay face down, her swollen hands stretched out, her teeth biting deeply into the sand as if she were trying to eat it.

It was a sad picture, but we had already seen so many that we only stared at her body for a while in silence, and then moved on. There was nothing we could do for her now.

Soon we took a shortcut through the woods to the river. It was quiet there. Walking through the woods, we had the feeling that the trees and the bushes were aware of our tragedy. There was no wind, yet it seemed that the branches of the tall, dark pine trees were mysteriously whispering something to each other. Now and then the silence would be disturbed by the cracking of twigs or the screeching of a magpie. The fog hung low, and the tree branches were dripping wet. My brother and I had always used to follow this shortcut path when going to the river for, besides reducing the distance, it was scenic. However, this time we took it for a different reason. We wanted to explore it for something edible. We separated, and started our search. I found nothing but a few useless poisonous mushrooms. Suddenly, Mykola called me excitedly. When I approached him, he was greedily eyeing a hedgehog.

"Why are you so excited about a hedgehog?" I asked him almost angrily.

"Don't you remember that book about Africa, and how the jungle people ate anything alive? Why couldn't we enjoy this clean little fellow?" responded Mykola, ignoring my agitation and pointing at the hedgehog sniffing some dry mushrooms.

Mykola had a point. I looked closer at the animal.

"Hey!" I shouted excitedly. "Look at his snout! It looks like a pig's!"

"I'll bet it tastes like a pig, too," Mykola remarked.

"But how are you going to skin it?" I asked.

"We'll singe him like people used to prepare pigs before Christmas in the old days."

Without hesitation, he skillfully bagged the animal. He had convinced me completely. If other people ate lizards, snails, and even rattlesnakes, why couldn't we eat hedgehogs once we had singed their shaggy coats and sharp quills?

The Communist Party had not as yet passed any law against eating hedgehogs, or any other wild creatures for that matter. Amusing myself with such thoughts, I searched eagerly under the trees and bushes for more of these animals, but was unsuccessful. Mykola, however, found another one, and I could hear him happily shouting that it was much bigger than the first one. Our day was not wasted. We had caught and bagged two hedgehogs, and there was the possibility that we would be just as successful when we reached the river.

Mother had asked us to visit Prokop's family, our distant relatives who lived on the very bank of the river. Prokop had been arrested last spring for failing to meet the grain and meat quotas. He was taken away one night to the county jail, and that was the last we had heard about him. No one ever had found out his fate. His wife continued living alone with her six-year old daughter in their little house on the river. The last time we saw them was in November, before the first snowfall.

Mother was anxious to know what had happened to them during the cold winter, so we thought a visit to Aunt's home was a good idea since she knew her way around the river quite well. She also knew much better than we how to charm fish into traps, and we could use her boat.

It was late in the afternoon when we reached Prokop's house, and we approached it with some trepidation. The past winter had been long and very severe. Many things could have happened to our relatives in their little house by the river. As far as we could tell, it stood safe and sound, but there were no signs of life around it. A small drift of dirty unmelted snow lay in front of the door. The front windows were curtained with some cloth.

We knocked at the door gently at first, and then louder, but no one answered. I grasped the latch and tried to open the door. It was locked. We ran to the windows in the back of the house, but they too were covered with cloth. We saw no other way than to force open the door with all our strength. As we did so, a nauseating stench assailed us. We ran to the windows and tore down the curtains for it was dark inside. The broad daylight streaming through the windows revealed a shocking sight to us. Aunt's headless body lay on the floor; her head was a few feet away. Apparently it had been torn off her body by some force, but there was not much blood around.

We soon solved the mystery. Looking around, we noticed a rope, ending in a noose, dangling from a beam. Aunt had hanged herself. After a while, her neck had no doubt given way as the body decomposed, which explained the absence of blood.

After overcoming our initial shock, we looked around for the little daughter. We soon found her lying on a sleeping bench. She must have died before her mother. Her eyes and mouth were closed; her tiny hands were folded on her chest. She was neatly dressed in the blue dress she used to wear when she visited us, and her hair had been combed nicely too.

Otherwise, the house was empty. All the furniture had probably been burned for fuel. There was no trace of any food. It was obvious to us that having lost her husband, and having been struck by famine which also took her little daughter, Aunt like our neighbor, Solomia, saw no more sense in living and struggling. Before taking her own life, she carefully locked the door and covered the windows. Her house became their coffin.

The gruesome sight and sickening stench of the decaying human bodies and the awesome silence almost overcame us. We stood there speechless and helpless. Even after so many previous encounters, we felt the creeping horror of death. At that point, we could not stand it any longer, and suddenly had to run outside for fresh air and to regain our composure.

The idea of foraging in the river and on its banks seemed absurd after what we had just experienced, so we suddenly lost all interest in our hunting and fishing expedition, and headed back home.

When we told mother what we had seen in Prokop's house, she at first reacted to it, as always, very calmly. But she could not completely suppress her emotions for long. After asking us a few more questions, she suddenly turned away from us and gave way to her tears.

We spent the rest of that day preparing our hedgehogs for supper. Mykola expertly dressed them, as if he had been doing it all his young life. The roasted hedgehog meat with potatoes tasted heavenly.

After we had gone to bed, I could not fall asleep for a long time. My aunt's head staring at me from the floor with her glassy, frightened eyes was still in my mind.

Mother woke us up the next morning before sunrise to go to the house at the river to bury our dead relatives. By the time we arrived there, it was already broad daylight. It had to be a burial without coffins for we had no wood, nails, nor strength to fashion them, neither could we dig a grave. Instead, we used an abandoned potato pit for their remains. We wrapped them in their own hand-woven blankets, and slid them gently into the makeshift grave. After filling it with dirt, Mother said a little prayer, and I placed a wooden cross which I had made by tying together two sticks into the earth above them.

We could no longer cry. We had lived through so much sorrow, and had suffered so many tragic losses that we were left numb.

"Why did they have to die?" Mykola suddenly asked, interrupting the dead silence.

"I wish I knew," Mother answered.

On the way home I was thinking about our own burial, and who would be left to bury us. I could think of no one.

Epilogue

BY THE beginning of May, our village had become a desolate place, horror lurking in every house and in every backyard. We felt forsaken by the entire world. The main road which had been the artery of traffic and the center of village life was empty and overgrown with weeds and grass. Humans and animals were rarely seen on it. Many houses stood dilapidated and empty, their windows and doorways gaping. The owners were dead, deported to the north, or gone from the village in search of food. Once these houses were surrounded by barns, stables, cattle enclosures, pigpens, and fences. Now only the remnants of these structures could be seen. They had been ripped apart and used as firewood.

Not even the trees were saved from the destruction. The willows, a common sight in Ukrainian villages, stood stark, stripped of branches. It had been too much for the starving villagers to cut down their heavy trunks, and so now they stood alongside the roads, monuments to the battle between the cold winter and the dying people. The fruit trees met the same fate. Half of the famous Ukrainian orchards had been destroyed and consumed as fuel. The remnants were in bloom: one could still see cherry blossoms, apricot blossoms, and blossoms of other trees. But the blooming this spring was different.

In the front yards, backyards, gardens, and all around the villagers' homes, the ground was pitted with open holes, reminders of the Bread Procurement Commissions' searches for "hidden foodstuffs."

The village looked like a ghost town. It was as if the Black Death had passed through, silencing the voices of the villagers, the sounds of the animals and birds. The deathly quiet lay like a pall. The few domestic animals that miraculously survived the famine were looked upon as exotic specimens.

At the end of May 1933 the starvation abated. The mass hunger ceased. Vegetables and fruits were plentiful for everyone who was able to go out and look for them. Also, the authorities needed farm workers, and they had no choice but to supply the working kolhosp members with sufficient food rations to sustain their existence. Thus, the villagers who still managed to stand—numb, oppressed, exhausted by starvation as they were—tried their best to reach the kolhosp and earn their food rations, a piece of bread and a scoop or two of some buckwheat or millet gruel. Those who were not able to work were left at the mercy of their relatives or friends, provided any survived.

I was lucky. In spite of my wretchedness and exhaustion from starvation, my dream to attain higher education never left me. And because of this drive for further education I managed to escape from the village for good.

Thus, starved as I was, living in absolute poverty amidst corpses of farmers and their families, I nevertheless had been doing my utmost to complete my secondary education.

At that time, our village had a nine-year school which was a combined four-year elementary and five-year secondary school. Such a school prepared the students for higher education.

In 1933 I was a senior and our graduation was supposed to take place in June. But many of the members of our graduating class never saw their diplomas. With the famine's onslaught, our number decreased precipitously. Some died of starvation. Others left the school and went foraging for food. Still others managed to migrate to other parts of the Soviet Union, mainly to Russia, where there was no famine. Many were deported together with their families to faraway places, into exile. Consequently, early in March, our school was closed and those few of us who still held on had to fend for ourselves. But, in spite of all the odds, I wouldn't give up my dreams, and my persistence was crowned with success: I was accepted at the secondary school of a neighboring village and I graduated at the end of June. This was a turning point in my life. I decided then to escape. I cannot remember the date exactly, but it remains the most important day in my life.

One night, with a piece of bread in a bag and five *karbovantsi,* or rubles (less than one dollar), in my pocket, dressed in a patched pair of pants and an oversized shirt, and barefoot, I stole out of the village toward the county seat. There, I had heard, college preparatory courses were opened for those with secondary diplomas. Luck was with me: with the help of some good people, I was admitted to the courses, and after completing them, I eventually enrolled at the Teachers' College. I was graduated from it in four years and started my career as a secondary school teacher. Then World War II broke out and I became a soldier and, eventually, I was taken prisoner of war by the Germans and interned in STALAG 3 in Germany.

After the war was over, knowing that all Soviet prisoners of war were declared deserters and traitors by Stalin's order and faced the firing squad, and because of my desire to live in the free world, I decided to stay in West Germany as a displaced person, and later on I emigrated to the United States where I found my new home.

My mother and my brother, who suffered with me, who shared with me the last morsel of food, and to whom I owe my survival, remained in the village. They had no other choice but to continue working on the collective farm. World War II separated us and what happened to them afterwards I don't know.